MY BUDDHIST WRITINGS

Tumhehi kiccamātappaṁ akkhātāro Tathāgatā

—Dhammapada : 276

Other Books by SOBTI

Nibbāna in Early Buddhism (1985)

Studies in Buddhism and Sikhism (1986)

Studies in Panjabi Fiction (1987)

Nirvāṇa in Tibetan Buddhism (1988)

Prajñāpāramitā in Tibetan Buddhism (1988)

The Sikh Psyche : A Study of Fictional Writings of Bhai Vir Singh (1990)

Vipassanā : The Buddhist Way (1992)

Theravāda Buddhism (1993)

MY BUDDHIST WRITINGS
(BASED ON PĀḶI TIPIṬAKA AND ĀDI GRANTHA)

HARCHARAN SINGH SOBTI
M.A. (Panjabi); M.A. (Philosophy);
LL.B. Ph.D. (Buddhist Studies)

Eastern Book Linkers
DELHI :: INDIA

Published by
EASTERN BOOK LINKERS
5825, New Chandrawal, Jawahar Nagar
Delhi-110007

First Published : 1994

ISBN 81-86339-01-9

Price Rs. 500-

PRINTED IN INDIA

Published by : Shamlal Malhotra for Eastern Book Linkers, 5825, New Chandrawal, Delhi-110007 and Printed at Suman Printers, Maujpur, Delhi-110053.

For

PROFESSOR MAHESH TIWARY

with reverence and gratitude

Who put me on the Path of the Buddha

CONTENTS

HARCHARAN SINGH SOBTI

PREFACE

I have known the Buddha, ever since, I learnt reading meaningful books. My interest in him got further impulse during 2500th anniversary of his *mahāparinibbāna* in the year 1956. During this period, I had an ample opportunity to appreciate the Buddha, more, while attending number of Seminars and reading some inspiring books on the subject. The greatest impact I had that of Navketan's film, *Anjali*, based on Buddhist theme. Ānanda falls victim to the sorcery of a mother, practised, to help her daughter so as to win over the love of Ānanda. The Buddha comes to his rescue. This episode, I found was full of hope and promise, in case, I could dare to belong to the Buddha. But, then, I could *see* my inclinations to discovering spiritual realm hidden within. So, I sought an aid from spiritual heritage. Since, I had my first love for literature, so, I read Tagore's work. There too, I found some Buddhist themes which kept my response to Buddhism, alive. The process once set in generated favourable circumstances that gradually brought me closer to the Buddhist lore. Now, it was a ripe time to study Buddhism earnestly and systematically. I took up regular study of Buddhism for my Doctorate, completed it and qualified for the Degree in the year 1983.

The present work is a selection of my writings, primarily devoted to Buddhist themes, covering one full decade, since 1983. During this short span of my life, when I was working on Buddhism, I came across people, mostly, belonging to my own profession, displaying peculiar reactions as to why and how a Sikh was interested in Buddhism. This act of raising eyebrows gives rise to number of questions, I shall refrain from addressing myself to. But, one thing I must state that there is, definitely, something wrong with our system of education that educates us on communal lines. Thus, fails us to inherit and imbibe the spiritual heritage that belongs to us, All.

This decade had been a period of great ordeal for me, vacillating between opting for Truth or Power. This state of affairs, also, always kept me reminding of Siddhārtha Gotama's first encounter with *Māra*, when the latter requested to dispense with an idea of realizing Truth in favour of acquiring Power, and the future Buddha refused to oblige *Māra*.

Indian wives are rarely blessings for their writer husbands, and I am one blessed with Jindi, my wife.

I shall look forward to, that Shilpi and Rishi my sons, also, become heirs to the common Indian spiritual heritage.

21st January, 1994 **Harcharan Singh Sobti**
D-13A/30 Model Town,
Delhi-110009 (India)

ACKNOWLEDGEMENTS

For romanization of Nānakbāṇī and translating it into English, I am greatly indebted to C. Shackle for his book, *A Glossary of Gurū Nānak* (1981), a classic, indeed, in the field of Sikh Studies.

I would like to express my appreciation for Dr. Intizar Mirza, my friend and colleague for his gracious interest in the subject of the book and its publication.

I am also grateful to Mr. Ravi Bansal, my grandson, for his help in preparing index.

—H.S.S.

ABBREVIATIONS

A	Aṅguttara Nikāya
Ā.G.	Ādi Granth (Holy Book of the Sikhs)
D.	Dīgha Nikāya.
Dhp.	Dhammapada.
It.	Itivuttaka.
Jā.	Jātakaṭṭhakathā.
M.	Majjhima Nikāya.
M. pūraṇi	Manoratha pūraṇi.
Mp.	Milindapañho.
Mv.	Mahāvagga.
P. Dipaṇi.	Paramatthadīpanī.
P. Jotika.	Paramattha Jotikā.
P.T.S.	Pali Text Society.
S.	Saṁyutta Nikāya.
S.B.B.	Sacred Books of the Buddhist.
S.B.E.	Sacred Books of the East.
Sum. Vil.	Sumaṅgala Vilāsinī.
Sn.	Sutta Nipāta.
Ta.	Theragāthā.
Ti.	Therīgāthā.

U.	Udāna.
Vin.	Vinaya Piṭaka.
Vm.	Visuddhi maggo.

Note : Quotations wherever referred to or given are from P.T.S. Romanized editions. Where numerals e.g. M.i. 80 separated by a dot is given, the first refers to the volume and the second to the page excepting e.g. U. 80 etc. where numerals refer to page, whereas, in the case of Dhp., Jā, Sn, Ta and Ti the reference is to the number of *gāthā* or *kathā*.

I

DUKKHA

Man has his roots in the past identified as heritage. All that is part of the heritage, at any point of time, is not necessarily conducive to achieve results favourable for the humanity, at large. Therefore, it becomes imperative to see what ought to be disinherited. The heritage finds its manifestations through various forms forming part of the contemporary living. The Buddha through his alive response to the contemporary modes of thinking and living articulated his views on living beings and their final destiny. To appreciate the Buddha's reactions and responses he had displayed towards his contemporary thinkers, is our primary concern, at the moment.

2

Ancient India contemporaneously known as *Jambūdīp*,[1] consisted of generally accepted five-fold zonal division. Rājśekhra (880-920 A.D.) in his book *Kāvyamimāṁsā*[2], a treatise on poetry, has identified these zones, *viz.* :

(i) *Madhyadeśa* (Central India).
(ii) *Udiya* (Northern India) known a *Uttarpatha*.
(iii) *Prācya* (Eastern India) also called *Pūrvadeśa*.
(iv) *Dakshināpaatha* (Deccan).
(v) *Aparānta* (Western India) also identified as *Pāścadeśa*.

Madhyadśea or in Pāli *Majjhimadeśa*, birth place of

Buddhism that covered the area of eastern *Uttara-Pradeśa* and Bihār,[3] and comprising of as many as fourteen *Mahājanapadas*[4] or republics e.g. *Kāsi, Kosala, Magadha, Kuru and Pañcāla* etc., during the 6th century B.C. compared with other areas, witnessed a phenomenal upsurge of religious fermentation and spiritual awakening. A number of teachers, both householders and recluses, kept themselves consistently engaged in enquiring into the nature of reality and continued to preach their doctrines among the people. Their only purpose, no doubt, was to bring the people close to reality as they had contemplated. We find repeated references made to Six Contemporaries of the Buddha in Pāli Canon[5] deemed to be quite formidable, and are thus grouped as 'heritical (*titthya*) teachers'. They exercised, one can gather from scriptural evidences, enormous psychic influence on the modes of living and thinking of their respective followers.

One among the six 'heretical teachers' was Pūraṇa Kassapa, who preached the doctrine of non-action.[6] He is mentioned to have stated his doctrinal standpoint to Ajātasattu, the king of Magadha, in the words that :

> To him who acts, O King or causes another to act...to him who kills a living creature, who takes what is not given, who breaks into houses, who commits dacoity,...or highway robbery or adultery or who speaks lies, to him thus acting there in no guilt. If with a discus with an edge sharp as a razor he should make all the living creature on the earth one heap one mass of flesh, there would no guilt thence resulting, no increase of guilt would ensue. Were he to go along the south bank of the Ganges, striking and slaying, mutiliating, and having men mutilated, oppressing and having men oppressed, there would be no guilt thence resulting, no increase of guilt would ensue. Were he to go along the north bank of the Ganges, giving alms, and ordering gifts to be given, offering sacrifices, or causing them to be offered, there would be no merit thence resulting, no increase of merit. In generosity, in self-mastery, in control of the senses, in speaking truth there is neither merit, nor increase of merit.[7]

Obviously, the doctrine amounts to ethical neutrality i.e. man's actions are neither moral nor immoral. Also, Pūraṇa Kassapa's doctrine of ethical neutrality was a frontal attack on *Sīla*, the moral code of Buddhism. Pūraṇa Kassapa is also interpreted to have adhered to the doctrine of *adhicca-samuppāda*[8]. "The Buddha in the *Brahmajāla Sutta*" Suggests B.M. Barua, "distinguished the logical standpoint of Pūraṇa Kassapa from his own, as a hypothesis of fortuitous origin (*adhicca-samuppāda*) from what he called the theory of causal-genesis (*paticca-samupdāda*)[9]. "Elsewhere he [the Buddha]" rightly adds Barua, "describes the former as a theory of non-causation (*ahetu-appaccyayvāda*).[10] The doctrine of *adhicca-samuppāda* only prepares us to inculcate an idea that whatever comes into being was previously non-existent. Alternatively expressed, it means that every becoming (*bhava*) is a result of chance (*saṅgati*), therefore, absolutely devoid of any link whatsoever.

Makkhali Gosāla, another contemporay of the Buddha, was no way lesser influential than Pūraṇa Kassapa. As alleged by his opponents, he commercialized his knowledge of astrology to earn his livelihood and was therefore despised having founded the sect of Ājivakas,[11] Allegations apart, one thing clearly emerges that his knowledge of astrology did influence his own mode of thinking, when he advocated the doctrine of Fate or *Niyati*. "The cardinal point of the doctrines of its founder, Makkhali Gośāla, writes A.L. Basham, while expressing his views on Ājivakism, "was a belief in the all-embracing rule of the principle of order, *Niyati*, which ultimately controlled every action and all phenomena and left no room for human volition, which was completely ineffectual."[12] Evil *kamma*, declared Gosāla, not at all, serves as a base or cause for Suffering.[13] Also, an escape from evil *kamma* needs not to have base or cause.[14] Rather, there is hardly any base of cause for anything whatsoever. Everything, according to Gosāla, is pre-determined. All beings, according to aforementioned doctrine of *niyati*, are governed for their growth, by the principle of Fate (*niyati*), chance (*Sangiti*) and Nature (*bhāva*).[15] The denial of freedom of Will, with Gosāla, takes an extreme posture. "The powerful (*balaṁ*), the vigorous (*viriyaṁ*) and those full of energy (*parakkama*)", asserts Gosāla, "like the frail (*avasā*) weak (*abalā*) and timid (*avariya*), all are governed by the one and the same principle of *niyati*, *saṅgati* and *bhāva*.[16] And, a ball of string is made to serve as a simile to convey the whole idea, thus :

> Just as when a ball of string is cast forth it will spread out just as far, and no farther, than it can unwind, just so both fools and wise alike wandering in transmigration exactly for the allotted term, shall then, and only then, make an end of pain.[17]

Makkhali Gosāl's doctrine of strict determinism, only theoretically leads to fatalism. L. D. Barnett's observation is quite convincing when he writes, that, "man is not a logical creature: he does not abstain from effort although he may believe the issue to be pre-determined..."[18] Therefore, keeping in view the practical side of man's functioning it would be erroneous to submit to the notion of denial of freedom of Will. Man is not absolutely dispossessed of freedom of Will, his Will or volition does operate, but, in no way transcending the limits of Universal Law binding over things and beings, alike.

Next is Ajīta Kesakambalī, who not only influenced his own followers so as to bring them into his fold, but, also had some impact on the mode of teaching of the Buddha, though in a negative way. The body, according to Kesakambalī consists of four elements *viz.* earth, water, fire and air. These constituents of the body, after its dissolution, merge to their respective genetic sources under the law of regression. Earth returns to earth, water to water, fire to fire and senses disappear into *ākāśa*.[19] Ajīta Kesakambalī, therefore, was though and through materialist and consequently believed and preached that there is no life after death.[20] He was an unimbiguous annihilationist (*uccheda vādinī*).

The doctrine foremost in importance, for us, and attributed to Pakudha Kaccāyāna, yet another contemporary of the Buddha is that of *Sassatavāda* or eternalism. *Kaccāyāna* in the *Sāmaññaphala Sutta* is stated to hold the view that earth, air, water, fire (these four elements), *sukkha* and *dukkha* and life-force (*jīva*), these seven,[21] are neither created nor caused to be created, hence exist eternally. Kaccāyāna is called Empedocles[22] (492-432 B.C.) of India, the latter only replaces love and hatred instead of *sukha* and *dukkha*.

Sañjaya Belatthiputta also reckoned as significant among the contemporaries of the Buddha was identified as sceptic who preached uncertainty about all matters man could be interested in. Whenever questioned, say for example, about the existence of another world,[23] he would always refrain from committing to either of the positions, generally held. Man does not relish uncertainty about things and beings, and so desires, otherwise. But, one thing is abundantly clear that the notion of uncertainty certainly destroys the premise of dogmatic thinking and renders speculations substanceless. May be that uncertainty about all matters creates conditions to bring about tranquillity of mind.

Nigaṇṭha Nātaputta, identified as no other than Mahāvira, the founder of Jainism as stated in *Sāmaññaphala Sutta* preached *Cātuyāma-Saṁvara*[24] or 'four-fold Self-restraint'. This doctrine of Mahāvira comments B. M. Barua, means that "the way to self-possession, self-command and imperturbability consists of 'a four-fold self-restraint' such as restraint in regard to all water, restraint as regard all evil, and restraints by way of the purification of sin and feeling a sense of ease on that account".[25] Further, quoting from Pāli sources, Barua adds that "in Mahāvira's view the established path to the realm of highest bliss lies through abstinence from killing, abstinence from the adultery, from lying and such austere practices (*tapo-guṇa*) as nudity, penance, confession and the rest"[26]. The second set of principles, in part, stated to have been preached by Mahāvira, is no other than *Sīla*, also popular with the Buddhists.

3

To understand, the doctrinal standpoints of 'heretical teachers,' we have, no doubt, depended on the Buddhist records. The reputation might have been "unfairly blackened" using L.D. Barnett's expression "by the *odium theologicum* of their rivals,"[27] the Buddhist monks in the present case. Our main concern, at the moment, is to ascertain the Buddhist position. Confrontation of the Buddha with his contemporary teachers and vice a versa, is helpful in the sense that it is through these discourses and discussions, we learn about the prevailing 'climate of opinion'. The contemporary milieu, so to say, helps us not only to appreciate the mode of teaching but also the message of the Buddha. The Buddha's doctrine of *paticcasamuppāda* can be better understood, referred to earlier, when juxtaposed to Pūraṇa Kassapa's hypothesis of *adhicca-samuppāda.* Again, when once a wandering ascetic Vacchagotta visited the Buddha and enquired from him as regard to the existence or non-existence of 'Self' (*attā*), the Buddha kept silent and Vacchagotta as if annoyed, left. After Vacchagotta had left, Ānanda asked the Buddha as to why did he remained silent and Buddha clarified, saying:

> If, Ānanda, when asked by the wanderer: "Is there a self," I had replied to him: "There is a self", then, Ānanda, that would be siding with the recluses and brahmins who are eternalists. But if, Ānanda when asked: "Is there not a self" I had replied that it does not exist, Ānanda, would be siding with those recluses and brāhmins who are annihilationist.[23]

The Buddha was not only refraining from associating himself with either the eternalists like Pakudha Kaccāyāna or annihilationist like Ajīta Kesakambalī, but was also silently subscribing to middle position.

The proposed doctrines of 'heretical teachers', more or less speculative, therefore, evasive in nature and thus deviating from the existential problem of human Suffering instead of guiding the people to overcome their ignorance (*avijjā*) the root cause of Suffering bewildered then, all the more. The resultant paths prescribed by them, necessarily, failed to satisfy the spiritual hunger of the multitudes of their followers and the problem of man's emancipation from ignorance continued to remain intact and alive. It was in the background of such a 'climate of opinion' that the Buddha emerged carrying a light of practical wisdom to dispel the darkness of ignorance. He was exclusively concerned with the existing problem of life and advised his followers not to alineate themselves from existing reality. He confronted the basic problem—the problem of Suffering-and searched for methods and mean for its eradication. The Buddha like a physician (and not like a philosopher) diagnosed the disease, discovered the remedy only thereafter prescribed a prescription, (forming into a Path), leading the beings, when put into practice, from the state of perpetual Suffering to the state of eternal bliss, 'to be realized by the wise in their own interior'.

4

But, there is a peculiar tendency among both the followers and scholars of religions to indulge in things and ideas discarded by the founders of the religious, as spiritually unrewarding. The Buddha, in a way, was critical of similar practices then prevailing when, besides refuting the charge of preaching 'extirpation of existing creature (*Sato Sattassaucchedaṁ*)' and reiterating his pragmatic view of things, he not only attaked misreading of his intentions, but also summed up the kernel of teaching, saying:

> Though this is what I affirm and what I preach, yet some recluses and brāhmins wrongly, erroneously and falsely——charge me in defiance of facts, with being an annihilationist and with preaching the disintegration, destruction and extirpation of existing creatures. It is just what I am not, and what I do not affiirm, that is wrongly, erroneously and falsely charged against me by these good people, who would make me out to be an annihilationist. Both in the past and to-day, I have consistently-preached Ill (Suffering) and the ending of Ill.[29]

Pāḷi Cannon is believed to constitute a coherent whole and all that consists in it, whether attributed to the Buddha himself or to *theras* or *therīs*, form an integral part of the teachings of the Buddha. The theme of the Buddha's Sermons, therefore, can be identified not only in different forms, but also through different channels contained in the Canon. For instance, Sāriputta in the *Mahāhatthipadopama Sutta*, describes one of the cardinal principles of Buddhism i.e. Four Noble Truths (*cattāri āryasaccīni*), making use of the simile of footprint of an elephant, thus:

> Just as the foot of every creature that walks the earth will go into the elephant's foot-print which is pre-eminent for size, even so, sirs, are all the right states of mind comprised witin the Four Noble Truths which are Noble Truth of Ill (Suffering) the Noble Truth Truth of origin of Ill and the Noble Truth of the Way that leads to the Cessation of Ill.[30]

Sāriputta, in a formentioned passage, without having a 'close fist' reveals what the Buddha aimed at, in other words, his total concern that concerns singular problem the problem of Suffering and its solution.

5

The Buddha, in his very First Sermon, *Dhamma-Cakka-ppavattana Sutta*, delivered at Isipatana, now called Sārnāth, near Benares, and addressed to the *Pañcavaggiyā Bhikkhu.*[31] categorically stated that:

> Birth is attended with pain (or is painful) decay is painful, death is painful. Union with the unpleasant is painful, painful is separation from the plcasant; and any craving that is unsatisfied, that too is painful. In brief, the five aggregates which spring from attachment (the conditions of individuality and their cause) are painful.[34]

And, the Buddha identified this part of his sermon as *dukkhaṁ ariyasaccaṁ*: Noble Truth of Suffering."[33]

Some of the key-expressions, found in the above passage, we propose to analyse. Better to begin, in a way, from the beginning, we call birth, and which is bracketed with Suffering (*jāti pi dukkhā*). What is, after all, meant by the expression 'birth. ? The Buddhist scriptures are certainly not silent on the question. We find the problem posed and solved in the *Saṁyutta Nikāya*, which reads as under:

> And what, brethern, is birth ? That which, of this and that being in this and that group, is birth, continuous birth, descent, reproduction, appearance of component factors, acquiring of sense-spheres. This is called birth.[33]

An expression, 'of this and that being in this and that group', deserves special attention. Normally, when we refer to birth we mean to convey the idea of birth of human beings. But in Buddhism the phenomenon of birth enfolds any living creature, inhabiting any one of the five realms of existence that constitute *Saṁsāra*.'[35] Thus, according to Buddhist tenets. LIFE IS ONE and it extends the range of limit of LIFE to as vast as *Saṁsāra*. This also explains the transit of LIFE from one realm to another. We learn from *Jātaka* stories that the Buddha passed through the various forms of life, covering a very vast range of animal and bird-life; sometime as a stag and sometime as a quail; and so on so forth. This means, that every living creature can ascend to the peak of *arahathood* or in later Buddhism to Buddhahood. Here, in the context of grades of life, Copleston's attempt to draw distinction between a Buddha and one who has only attained *Nibbāna* is quite revealing. "It is only, indeed, in the human stage". writes Copleston, "that the highest achievement, that of a Buddha, is possible; but *Nirvāṇa* is accessible to all, to the superior deities and to men directly, and ultimately to all that lives".[36] The precept of non-killing, and, compassion for animal and bird life, derives its moral sanction from this very fact of phenomenal existence.

Nothing that exists in phenomenal world exists in isolation. This, and precisely this is the spirit that pervades throughout the *Paṭiccasamuppādd*'[37] or the Doctrine of Dependent Origination. It would suffice to mention, at this stage of our enquiry into the domain of *dukkha*, that 'birth' is only one link or *nidāna* in the grand scheme of the Chain of Twelve Links, (*dvadasngapaticca-samuppāda*) worked out the in the said doctrine. The old age and death also form other links of the same Chain. The basic idea set forth in this doctrine is that everything for its origination or arising, inevitably, depends upon something else. One hardly needs any support from scriptures to conform to the self-evident fact of existence that old age and death are dependent upon birth.

Birth, old age and death, as a normal course, constitute integral parts of the continuous process of change, that, in Buddhism takes the form of Doctrine of *Aniccā* or Impermanence that in itself is only one aspect of the Doctrine of Three Marks of Existence, or *tilakkhaṇa*, *dukkha* and *anattā* being the rest of the two.[38] One of the fundamental causes of Suffering lies in the impermanent nature of things or transitoriness of their character. *Yaṁ aniccaṁ taṁ dukkhaṁ*: whatever is transitory that amounts to suffering"[39] is the dictum quite often pronounced in the Buddhist scriptures. This idea finds its expression in the *Majjhima Nikāya*, in the following form:

What do you think, Almsmen ?

> Is visible form (body) permanent or impermanent ?
> Impermanent, Sir.
> And is the impermanent, a weal or a woe ?
> A woe, Sir.[40]

Another important expression is *Pañcaupādānakkhandha pi dukkhā*:[41] Five aggregates constitute suffering'. Now, in the light of Buddha's assertion, we can well appreciate why do these five aggregates generate Suffering ? We know, that old age means decaying of organism and death is its final disolution. In other words, old age and death has reference to the bodily organism which we know from our experience the way it undergoes the gradual process of decaying: it grows weak, withers, it is exhausted, senses lose their vitality. The description speaks of the body being plagued with transitoriness. The transitory nature of body is also explained through the nature of constituents it is composed of. The matter consists of four chief elements, namely, earth, air, water and fire, which are subject to the iron law of Universal Flux, yet, another expression subscribing to the idea of transitoriness. Now, when the four chief elements can not escape from the Universal Law of Flux, it is hard to imagine that anything formed by these can. The body has to share the fate of all these things which come into existence by virtue of the combination of these elements. This also explains the nature of *Saṅkhārā* described as "*Sabbe Saṅkhārā aniccā'ti*: Transient are all conditioned things (or Productions)."[42] This idea of transitoriness is so fundamental that 'a time will come' as contemplated in the Buddhist Canon,[43] when all these elements, and, hence the entire world which is compounded of these elements, shall abide by the same law to its ultimate destruction.

So far we have described the transitory nature of things termed as *Saṅkhārā* or Production, including bodily organism with all its constituting factors. And, we have only stated that Suffering has its root-cause in transitoriness also described as *aniccā* or impermanence. This premise needs little elaboration. The bodily organism does not come into existence on its own, or it is not at all the result of accidental combination of four basic elements. What brings these elements together to bring forth a kind of production we call bodily organism? In order to meet the demands of this query the Buddhist scholars invariably identified *chanda* or will as a factor that brings these elements together and it is by virtue of an exercise of Will, we gain body. This does not happen only in the case of *Saṅkhārā*, sometimes referred to as mental productions, but the whole gamut of personality falls within its range of influence. To substantiate their views on the subject, these scholars have, time and again, fruitfully made use of these utterances, as: *Chandamūlakā āvuso sabbe dhamma:* In the Will all things are rooted."[44] Again, *Pañcaupādānakkhandhā Chandhrmūlakā*: Five Aggregates are rooted in the Will."[45] These assertions, also, though indirectly, refer to another very significant Buddhist term *taṇhā* or craving. The Will that serves as a cause for *bhava* (Becoming), seems to be identical in its meaning with the craving, in the sense, that the latter is also described as cause for rebirth. The Buddha, while pronouncing "*dukkha samuddyaṁ ariya saccnṁ*: Noble Truth of Suffering,"[46] held *taṇhā* in its threefold mode of operation—i. *kāmataṇhā*, ii. *bhava taṇhā* and iii. *Vibhava taṇhā* the sole responsible for *punnabhava* or rebirth and which, as already analysed, is bracketed with Suffering. It is, in fact, this craving that the Seeker on the path of the Buddha is instructed to annihilate.

It is the Will, pregnant with *taṇhā* (craving), that is the root-cause of Suffering. It is our common experience that we feel happy, when we find our Will fully executed. In other words, happiness stems from the satisfaction of our Will. The perpetual happiness is only possible if neither the Will nor the realm of existence in which it operates, is subject to impermanance. Whereas, the fact is that Will and the realm in which it is exercised, both are governed by the Law of Universal Flux. We find, as a consequence of pervading this Law in the phenomenal existence, the impediments in the way of satisfaction of our Will. We desire the state of affairs to exit permanently, which are conducive to yield the fruit of happiness. And, the fact is contrary to our desire. We experience change of circumstances, we do not relish. The change, irrespective of our liking or disliking, occurs. In fact, nothing is permanent, but change. It is the change that rules as Sovereign over the territory of phenomenal existance. Earlier, we have referred to a discourse, describing 'what is transitent amounts to suffering.' Under the Law of Universal Flux, both the animates and inanimates are subject to perpetual change, and, thus, the state of permanence is only illusion. The Will, intune with this illusion only, begets Suffering. When this illusion is predominent; as a result, Suffering predominates.

The existing state of Suffering can also be explained in terms of the Doctrine of *Anattā*. The doctrine, in its essence, refers to a state, combining both, physical and mental, *that one is not*, and this doctrine is beautifully summed up in *Saṁyutta Nikāya* in the following words:

> Then is it proper for one thus to regard what is impermanent, woeful, by nature, changeable :— 'This is mine, this am I, this is the self of me' ? asked the Buddha, 'Surely not, 'Lord', Ānanda replied.[47]

We know from our experience that the five aggregates e.g. *rūpa*, *vedanā*, *saññā*, *saṅkhārā* and *viññaṇakkhandha*' that constitute our personality, function, most of the time, contrary to our Will, or desire, so to say. We fall sick, grow old and die, in spite of wishing, otherwise. A stream of unpleasant ideas flows in our mind, and, quite often, we fail in our attempt, to stop it. In the *Majjhima Nikāya*,[48] while explaining the Doctrine of *Anattā* to Aggivessana, the Buddha has referred to the position and power of a ruling king and contrasted with a person who presumes that 'Body is my Self' and unlike a king possesses no power to control his body as the former does possess within his kingdom. Obviously, anything over which one has no control cannot belong to one-self. And, to identify one-self with that which does not belong to oneself, can hardly yield anything except Suffering. This is, in short, the substance of discourse, entitled the *Cūla-Saccaka-Sutta*, in which the Buddha, in a public discussion, brings round the Jain, Saccak, clarifying the existential status of *khandhās*, and we quote:

> What say you, Aggivessana ? Is material shape (*rūpa kkhandha*) permanent or impermanent ?

Impermanent.
Is that which is permanent an Ill or reverse ?
An Ill.
Is it proper to regard what is impermanent and an Ill and the creature of change, as being mine, or I, or my Self ?
No.
... ...[49]

The same argument is put forth and the conclusion drawn to the satisfaction of Aggivessana, in the case of remaining aggregates. Again, when the bodily organism, which in itself is nothing, but an organic form of the four basic elements, does not belong to one Self, it is difficult to contemplate, that anything else that exists in the phenomenal world, consisting of four elements, can be identified with Self.

This means, that entire functioning of human personality consisting of six sense organs e.g. eye, ear, nose, body, tonugue and mind, and also things other then these, and existing in the phenomenal world, are to be (identified) as *anattā*, and to identify Self with anything that is transient, yields only a bitter fruit of Suffering.

References and Notes

1. For detailed descriptions of naming of ancient India, see: Law, B. C. *Historical Geography of Ancient India*, pp. 8-11, (Introduction).
2. Dalal, C. D. and Shastry R. A. (Eds.) *Kāvyamīmāṅsā of Rājśekhara*, pp. 93-94.
   Tatra vārāṇasya parataḥ pūrvadeśaḥ
   ... ...
   Māhiṣmatyā parataḥ Dakshināpathaḥ
   ... ...
   Devasabhāyā parataḥ paśchātdesaḥ
   ... ...
   Prithadakāt parataḥ uttarāpathaḥ
   ... ...

Vinasanaprayāgayoḥ Ganga—Yamunāyosca antaraṁ Antravedi.

3. Sharma R. S., *Material Culture and Social Formations in India*, p. 89.
4. A. i, 213; iv, 252, 256, 260.
5. References made to six 'heretical teachers' in *Tipiṭaka*, detailed as under:
   (i) *Pūraṇa Kassapa*: D. i. 52, 53; S. i. 65; S. iii. 68, 69; S. iv. 398; S. v. 126; A. iii. 383; A. iv. 428.
   (ii) Makkhali Gosāla: D. i. 53; M. i. 231, 238, 483. S. i. 66, 68; S. iii. 211; S. iv. 398; A. i. 33f, 286; A. iii. 376, 384.
   (iii) Ajit Kesakambali; D. i. 55; M. i. 515; S. i. 98; S. iii. 207; S. iv. 398.
   (iv) Sañjaya Belatthiputta: D. i. 27, 58; Vin. i. 39, 42; A. i. 286.
   (v) Pakudha Kaccāyān. D. i. 56; M. i. 198, 250, 517; M. ii. 4; S. i. 66, 68; Sn. p. 91.
   (vi) *Nigaṇṭha Nātputta*: D. i. 57; D. iii. 119, M. i. 91 ff; 371, 373 ff; M. ii. 31, 214 ff; S. i. 66; S. ii, 214; S. iv. 298 ff, 398; A. i. 220; A. iv 180 ff; A. v, 150.
6. D. i. 53: *akiriyaṁbyākāsi.*
7. D. i. 52-53: *karato kho, Mahārāja kārayato...... pāṇaṁ atimapāyato, adinnaṁ ādiyato, sandhiṁ chindato, nillopaṁ harato......paripanthe tiṭṭhato, paradāraṁ gacchato, musā bhaṇato karoto na karīyaṭ pāpaṁ. Khura-pariyantena ce pi cakkena yo imissā paṭhaviyā pāṇe...... eka maṁsa..... puñjaṁ kareyya, n' atthi tato-nidānaṁ pāpaṁ, n' atthi pāpassa āgamo. Dakkhinañ ce pi Gaṅgātiraṁ āgaccheyya hananto ghātento chindanto chedāpento pācanto pācento, n'atthi tato—nidānaṁ pāpaṁ, n' atthi pāpassa āgamo. Uttarañ ce pi Gaṅgātīraṁ gaccheyya dadanto dāpento yajanto yajāpento n' atthi tatonidānaṁ puññaṁ, n' atthi puññassa āgamo. Dānena damena saṁyamena saccavajjena n'atthi puññaṁ n'atthi puññasa āgamo.*

   Rhys Davids T. W., *Dialogues of the Buddha*, Part I, pp. 69-70.
8. D. i. 28-29.

9. Barura, Benimadhab, *Histroy of Pre-Buddhistic Indian Philosophy*, p. 279.
10. Ibid. cf. S. iii. 69.
11. Rhys Davids, *op. cit.* p. 221 (Introduction to *Kassapa. Sihanāda Sutta*):
 "Those who claimed to be especially strict in their rules as to means of livelihood."
12. Basham, A. L., *History and Doctrine of the Ājivikās*, p. 3.
13. D. i. 53: *N' atthihetu...........n' atthi paccayo sattānaṁ saṁkilesāya.*"
14. D. i. 53: "*Ahetu—a 'paccāya suttā visujjhati.*"
15. D. i. 53: "*Niyati—saṅgati-bhāva-pariṇatā*"
16. D. i. 53: "*N'atthi purisakāre, n' atthi balaṁ, n' atthi viriyaṁ n'atthi purisa-thāmo n'atthi purisa-parakkamo Sabbe sattā avasā abalā aviriya niyati-saṅgatı-bhāva-pariṇatā.*;'
17. D. i. 54; "*Seyyathā pi nāma sutta-guḷe khitte nibbeṭhiya-mānam eva phaleti, evam eva bāle ca paṇḍite ca sandhā-vitvā saṁsaritvā dukkhass' antaṁ karissanti.*"
 Rhys Davids, *op. cit.* p. 73.
18. Foreword to Basham. *op. cit.* p. xii.
19. D. i. 55 : "*Cātum-mahābhūtiko ayaṁ puriso; yadā kālaṁ karoti paṭhavī pathavi—kāyaṁ anupeti anupagacchati,........ ākāsaṁ indriyāni saṁkamanti.........*"
20. D. i. 55: "*N'atthi ayaṁ loko, n'atthi parloko,........ Na honti param maraṇā.*"
21. D. i. 56: "*Katame satta ? Paṭhavi-kāyo āpo-kāyo tejo-kāyo vāyo-kāyo sukhe dukkhe jīva-sattame...... Satt'ime...... kāyā akaṭā akaṭā-vidhā animmitā animmitā vañjhākūṭaṭṭha esika ṭṭhāyiṭṭeitā......*"
22. Empodocles (492-432 B. C.) of Acragas-modern name of Acrages is Sicily in Greece-hence a pre-Socratic philosopher who is said to have written two long poems—— (i) On Nature and (ii) Purifications. The second poem is a religious-mystical poem on Personal Salvation.
23. D. i. 58: "*Atthi paro loko*" ? *ti itı ce taṁ pucchasi,* "*atthi paro loko*" *ti* '*iti ce me assa,* "*atthi paro loka*" *ti te naṁ vyākareyyam. Evaṁ pi me no, Tathā ti pi...... me no. Aññathā ti pi no. No ti pi me no. No no ti pi me no......*"
24. D. i. 57: "*......Nigaṇṭho cātu-yama-saṁvara-saṁvuto hoti.*

Kathañ ca...... Saṁvuto hoti? ......Nigaṇṭho Sabba-vāri-vārito ca hoti, Sabba-vāri-yuto ca, Sabba-vāri-dhuto ca, Sabba vāri-phuṭṭho ca...... yato......evam...... saṁvuto hoti, ayam vuccati...nigaṇṭho gatatto ca yatatto ca thitatto ca ti." *cf.* M. ii. 35-36.

25. Barua, op. cit., p. 378; Rhys Davids, op. cit., pp. 75-76.
26. Ibid. p. 379. cf. S. i. 66.
27. Foreword to Basham, op. cit., p. xii.
28. S. iv. 400: "*Ahṁ Cānanda, Vocchogottassa paribbhājakassa 'atthttā' ti puṭṭho samaṇo 'atthtta' ti byākareyyam, ye te, Ānanda, samaṇa brāhmaṇa sassatavādā tesametaṁ saddhiṁ abhvissa. Ahṁ cānanda, Vacchagoṭtassa paribbhājakassa 'natthtā' ti puṭṭho samaṇo 'natthtā' ti byākareyyam, ye te, Ānanda, samaṇabrahmaṇa ucchedavāda tesametaṁ saddhiṁ abhvissa.*"......Woodward, Part iv, p. 282.
29. M. 22: (*Alagaddūpama-Sutta*) or 'Simile of the water-snake.' In this Sutta, a monk learning the doctrine of the Buddha, contrary to its spirit, is censured and his mental act is described like catching a snake by the tail. (M.i. 133-134).

    M. i. 140:

    Evaṁ vādiṁ kho maṁ, bhikkhave, evamakkhāyiṁ e' ke samaṇabrahmaṇa asata tucchā musā abhūtena abbhāci-Kakhantivanayiko samaṇo goto, sato sattassa ucchedaṁ vināsaṁ vibhavaṁ paññāpeti. Yathā cāhaṁ na, bhikhave, yathā cāhaṁ na vadāmi, tathā maṁ te bhonto samaṇabrāhmaṇā asatā tucchā musā abhūtena abbhācikakhanti vanayiko samaṇo Gotamo, sato sattassa ucchedaṁ vināsaṁ vibhavaṁ paññāpeti'ti. Pubbe cāhaṁ bhikkhave, etarahi ca dukkhaṁ ceva paññāpemi, dukkhassa ca nirodhaṁ.

    Chalmers, Vol. I. p. 99.

    cf. M. 26: (*Ariyapariyesana-Sutta*): M. i. 161-163. In this Sutta the Buddha talks about two quests: the Ariyan and the Unariyan quest.
30. M. 28; M. i., 184-85: *Seyyathāpi, āvuso, yāni Kānici jaṅgamānaṁ pāṇānaṁ pada jātāni sabbāni tāni hotithopade Samodhānaṁ gacchanti, hatithapadaṁ tesaṁ aggamakkhayāti yadidaṁ mahantattena; evameva kho, āvuso, ye keci kuslā dhammā sabbete catūso ariya saccesu saṅigaham gacchanti.*

Katamesu catūso? dukkhe ariya sacce, dukkha smudaye ariyasacce, dukkhanirodhe ariya sacce, dukkhanirodha gāminiyā patipādaya ariyasacce.
Chalmers Vol. 1. p. 133.

31. The name of these Bhikkus are: i. *Kondañña*; ii. *Bhaddiya* iii. *Vappa*; iv. *Mahānāma*; v. *Assaji*. These fire *Bhikkhus*, at one fime, had joined with Gotama in his austeraties at Uruvelā. When Gotama, after realizing the futility of ascetic practices had abandoned the path of self-motification, quite popular with the recluses, and adhered, to the Middlepath, all the five desereted him, as if Gotama had gone astray. After Gotama attained *Sambodhi* and became the Buddha, he could find them, with his Buddha-eye, where they were. He went there and preached to them the *Dharmma* and they became his disciplies.

32. S. V. 421. (*Dhammacakkappavattana-Sutta*): *Jāti pi dukkhā, jarā pi dukkha, vyāhdi pi dukkho, maraṇaṁ pi dukkhaṁ, appiyehi sampayogo dukkho piyehe vippayogo dukkho, yaṁ picchaṁ na labaṭhi taṁ pi dukkhaṁ saṁkhittena pañcaupādānākkhandha pi dukkhā.*
Rhys Davids, T. W. Vol. XI (S. B. E.) p. 148.
For an idea of the ommnipresence of *dukkha* see the story Kisā Gotamī : Rhys Davids, Mrs. (trs.) *Psalms of the Early Buddhists-1*, pp. 106-110.

33. *Vinaya P.* (*Mahāvagga*): *Dhammacakkappavattnaṁ.*

34. S. ii. 3: Rhys Davids, C. A. F. Part II, p. 3.

35. For details see: Sobti, Harcharan Singh, *Nibbāana in Early Buddhism*, pp. 20-25.

36. Copleston, R. S., *Buddhism-Primitive and Present*, p. 103.

37. D. 15: (*Mahānidāna-Sutta*) ; D. ii. 55.

38. A. iii. 134. In this discourse the Buddha, while staying at the Veluvana, the bamboo grove at Rajagha, rather emphasized the point that whether Buddhas arise or do not arise, the existence continues to be marked with the three characteristics viz. *aniccā*, *dukkha* and *anattā*.

39. S. iv. 1.

40, M. 22: (*Alagaddūpama-Sutta*): M. i. 138: Chalmers, Vol. 1, p. 97.

41. The expression *Pañcaupādānakkhandha* consists of three

components: *pañca+upādāna+khandha*, *Pañca* means five. *Upādāna* stands for clinging and *Khandha* refers to aggregates which are five in number viz., *rūpā, vedanā, saññā, viññāṇa* and *saṅkhārā* that constitue the corporeal organism of man. The aggregates, when associated with *upādāna* cause Suffering. When *upādāna* is eliminated there remain *pañca khandhas* intact, but, now free from Suffering.

42. *Dhp.* 277, Also, for detailed analysis pertaining to the transitory nature of *saṅkhārā* see. A iv, 100-103, where reference to the appearance of Seven Suns is made and which shall result in the total disapperance of all that is produced also termed as *saṅkhārā*,

43. *Saṅkhārā* is derived from the verb *Saṅkharoti* that means to make or put together. It refers to anything produced hence synonymous with production. The terms *saṅkhārā* or Production can be used, therefore, for anything existing in the phenomenal world, since, everything is produced.

44. A. V., 107 *Chandamūlka āvuso Sabbe dhammā.*

45. M. 109. (*Mahā-Puṇṇama-Sutta*): M. iii. 16. *Ime kho bhikkhu pañcaupādāna-kkhandhā Chandamūlakā.*

46. Vinaya P. Mahāvagga (*Dhammacakkappavattana-Sutta*)

47. S. iii. 186:

"*Yaṁ panāṇiccaṁ dukkhaṁ viparināmadhammaṁ: api nu taṁ anupādāya uppajjevyuṁ saṁyojanaminivesavinibandhaj-josānā" ti?*

"*No hetaṁ, bhante.*"

Woodward, part III, p. 154.

48. M. 35 : (*Cūla-Saccaka-Sutta*): M. i. 231.

49. Ibid., M. i. 232-233. Chalmers, Vol. I, p. 166.

2

BUDDHISM: A CASE AGAINST PESSIMISM*

The Buddha's emphasis on Suffering, naturally, leads a man of ordinary intelligence, to charge Buddhism advocating pessimism, and his revolt against the creed of the Buddha is justifiable. In contrast, he visualises a picture of joys and pleasures, he experiences, during the course of his living. He recalls a very wide range of sensual pleasures. Looking at beautiful shapes and colours of things and beings; touching a smooth and soft skin; listening to melodious voices; tasting delicious dishes, inhalling agreeable smell of fragrant things; and contemplating upon pleasant ideas of whatever origin, real or illusory—all these, sometimes signular, and sometimes in association with each other, give a feeling to a person, exposed to the sensory plane of existence, that 'everything is right with the world'. No less is his experience of joy, he derives from the contacts of the persons, he loves, he admires. Who, on the earth, can deny that the loving care of mother for her child gives her immense joy and satisfaction ? The lover's surrender of Will for the well being of his beloved, is celebrated in literature, yielding a heartful contentment. The success of a student, is a great source of joy for teacher, is not mere a concept, but a fact of life. All this, when viewed from a certain level of

* Paper presented at the First International Conference on Buddhism and National Cultures, held during 10-15 October, 1984 at Vigyan Bhavan, New Delhi.

living, no doubt, puts Buddhism, advocating cult of Suffering, in questionable position. But, it would be quite misleading to assert, that, Buddhism denies the existing states of joy and pleasure. Rather, Buddhism acknowledges, that these states of agreeable nature do exist, and only, points out the momentary nature of their survival. Thus, this small rivulet of joy and pleasure, ultimately, falls head-long in the Ocean of Suffering. This insight into the fleeting nature of joy and pleasure, when acquired, proves a great asset for any one, struggling for the realization of eternal bliss, here and now, within this body.

2

After, one has gaincd an insight into the true nature of sensual joy and pleasure, one is no more a man with ordinary intelligence. His level of thinking and living, as expected, is revolutionized. He is no more superfiuous in his outlook. He is well-established in the Buddhist norms. Although, now, a man with rare intelligence, having a penetrating vision into the ultimate nature of phenomenal existence, has every possibility to fall prey to the philosophy of Schopenhauer (1788-1860), as some scholars apprehend if not guarded against, properly, and, we have an evidence of historical dimension. Once, Schopenhauer in his book, *The World as Will and Idea*, (1883) expressed his satisfaction over the result of his philosophy, that, "If I were to take the result of my philosophy as the standard of truth, I would be obliged to concede to Buddhism the pre-eminence over the rest. In any case it must be a satisfaction to me to see my teaching in such close aggreement with a religion which the majority of mankind upon the earth hold as their own."[1]

The "close agreement" has not been conceded to as a "divine revelation', and has evoked diessent in some quarters. One such dissenting voice is P. Lakshmi Narasu, who in his book, *The Essence of Buddhism*, (1907) expressed his views stating, "To Schopenhauer this avowal of a close agreement between his philosophy and Buddhism might have been a gratification, but for Buddhism it has certainly proved a misfortune".[2] Why it has proved a misfortune ? Because, "it has given rise to a serious misconception about Buddhism. The

Buddhist ideal has been misjudged to the result of of a Schopenhauerian pessimism as to the worth and promise of life."[3] This charge of misconceived notion levelled against Schopenhauer, and resulting in a misfortune for Buddhism, has not been suitably substantiated, when weighed against the charge. The charge needs to be looked into.

3

The fundamental difference between the Buddha and Schopenhauer is that one is a saint (or seer of *Nibbāna*), and other is a philosopher. Moreover, Schopenhauer is of the view that, "It is therefore just as little needful that a saint should be a philosopher as that a philosopher should be a saint"[4]. The philosopher's job is to interpret life: to add into our rational understanding of life and build up a system of thought. This is what Schopenhauer did. What precisely he did, or, what is the substance of his philosophical system ? to know this, is our need. Schopenhauer in his principal work, *The World as Will and Idea*, lays down the premise of his system with these words: "The world is my idea."[5] What he means is all that exists in the world, including, of course, human beings, exist by virtue of being perceived. In other words, things and beings have no independent reality other than perceived by some subject, and hence, are mere ideas of perception. The world as idea itself is objectification of Will, that manifests itself in perceivable form as phenomenon. And, what is Will ? It is "merely a blind incessant impulse.[6] "an endless striving"[7] "eternal becoming, endless flux, characterizes the revelation of the inner nature of Will."[8] The Will, as it strives without end can never attain permanent satisfaction, more so, because of, "that variance with itself which is essential to the Will."[9] Any satisfaction that is partial and part of the flux, as well, and only a temporary relief is, sooner or later, bound to come to an end. It is because of the very nature of Willing that, "the attainment soon begets satiety: the end was only apparent, possession takes away the charm; the wish, the need, presents itself under a new form...[10]" Therefore, it is Suffering that dominates the course of living. As regard to the freedom of Will Schopenhauer categorically denied *liberum arbitrium indifferentiate* or 'liberty of indifference'; man's course of life is necessarily predetermined as the course of a clock, therefore, man can do what he Wills to do, but he is not at liberty to determine what he Wills.[11] There is, no doubt, "close agreement" between Buddhism and Schopenhauer upto the extent that the nature of Will being transitory, its exercise in any form, in the final analysis, only begets Suffering. The matter, however, does not end, here. Schopenhauer not only explains the existing state of Suffering, but, attempts to identify the means of escape from futile striving for enduring happiness. One such escape is available through art. When one objectively, in other words, disinterestedly, contemplates upon the object of art, one enjoys, and in the words of Schopenhauer. "We keep the Sabbath of the penal servitude of Willing, the wheel of Ixion stands still.[12] And, this short duration is akin to 'an oasis in the desert". Again, it is not a path out of life, but only an occasional consolation in life.[13] Schopenhauer is not at all unware of the final escape, that the saints achieve, as a result of denial of Will. It is the assertion of denial of Will, that takes Schopenhauer, little more close to Buddhism. Before we pass final judgement over "close aggreement", we must state the position of Schopenhauer in his own words, and we quote as follows:

"......but to die willingly, to die gladly, to die joyfully, is the prerogative of the resigned, of him who surrenders and denies the Will to live. For only he Wills to die *really*, and not merely apparently, and consequently he needs and desires no continuance of his person. The existence which we know he Willingly gives up; what he gets instead of it is in our eyes *nothing*, because our existence is with reference to that nothing. The Buddhist faith calls it *Nirvāṇa* i.e. extinction."[14] "To free it from this is reserved for the denial of the Will to live, as the means by which the individual Will breaks away from the stem of species, and surrenders that existence in it we lack conceptions for that which it now is; indeed all data for such conceptions are wanting. We can only describe it as that which is free to be Will to live or not. Buddhism denotes the latter case by the word *Nirvāṇa*....[15]

"The Buddhists, however, with perfect honesty, only indicate the matter negatively, by *Nirvāṇa*, which is the negation of this world, or of *Sansāra.* If *Nirvāṇa*, is defined as nothing, this only means that the *Sansāra* contains no single element which could assist the definition or construction of *Nirvāṇa*.'[16]

If we summarise Schopenhauer's views on denial of Will, leading to final escape from Suffering, this means that in Buddhism denial of Will is identified as *Nirvāṇa* that negates *sansāra*, therefore negatively worded and also described as *nothing*. The philosopher's intellectual grasp of Buddhist *Nirvāṇa* is commendable. As already pointed out that Scropenhauer was not a saint, but, he did point to the realm he described as :

"That state which is experienced by all who have attained to complete denial of the Will, and which is denoted by the names.... illumination, union with God, and so on".[17] He could not enter this realm identified as *Nirvāṇa*, as he was not aware of the Path that straightway leads to *Nibbāna.* In short: Schopenhauer could only *know* that the denial of Will was the only way to achieve final escape from Suffering, Whereas, the Buddha has devised the path that leads a 'reasonable man' to *Nothing*, which of course is an antithesis of *Everything.* though negatively worded, but a positive state of eternnal bliss and is synonymous with *Nibbāna*, Thus, Buddhism ensures of grand escape from all or *Everything* i.e., the world of Suffering accessible through body, a sense-apparatus, to those who *walk* on the Path, diligently.[18]

References

1. Schopenhauer, Arthur *The World as Will and Idea*, Vol. II, p. 371.
2. Narasu, P. Lakshmi, *The Essence of Buddhism*, p. 154.
3. Ibid. p. 154.
4. Schopenhauer, *op. cit.*, Vol. I, p. 495.
5. Ibid, p. 3.
6. Ibid, p. 354.
7. Ibid, p. 213.

8. Ibid, p. 214.
9. Ibid, p. 191.
10. Ibid, pp. 404-05.
11. Schopenhauer, Arthur, *Parerga and Paralipomnena*, Vol. 2. p. 227.
12. Schopenhauer, Arthur, *The World as Will and Idea*, Vol. I, p. 254.
13. Ibid, p. 346.
14. Ibid, Vol. III, p, 308.
15. Ibid, p. 327
16. Ibid, p. 427.
17. Schopenhauer Arthur, *The World as Will and Representation*, Vol. 1, p. 410.
18. S. iv.: 19:
    Idaṁ kho, bhikkhave, sabbaṁ abhijānaṁ parijānaṁ virājayaṁ pajahaṁ bhabbo dukkhakkhayāyā' ti.

3

NIBBĀNA

Nibbāna is the only way out for Suffering humanity. This idea operates as a unifying principle and provides coherence to the Buddhist scriptures, otherwise amorphous in appearance. The Buddha has described the unifying feature of his doctrine and discipline, making use of a simile of an ocean and its taste—the taste of salt, as: "And even, monks, as the great ocean has one taste, the taste of salt, even so, monks, does this *dhamma* and discipline have one taste, the taste of freedom."[1] Again, *Nibbāna* as an underlying idea of the Sermons of the Buddha is expressed througe the simile of flowing of Ganga into ocean, thus: "Even as the river Ganges streams and flows to the ocean, as its bourne and finds repose only in the ocean, so does Gotama's whole congregation, laity as well pilgrims, stream and flow to *Nirvāṇa* as its bourne, finding repose only in *Nirvāṇa*"[2] So, in the Buddhist scheme of thought, the disciple is instructed to guard himself against even the slightest deviation from the Path culminating in *Nibbāna.* There is a beautiful illustration, in the Pāḷi Canon, to that effect. It is recorded in the *Saṁyutta Nikāya*, that once the Buddha was staying at Kosambi in *Siṁsapā* forest. The Buddha, took up a few *Siṁsapā* leaves scattered on the ground in his hand enquired from the *Bhikkhus,* surrounding him, whether few leaves in his hand were more or other leaves in the *Siṁsapā* wood above. The answer could not be other than this that leaves in his hand were small in number and much were in the *Siṁsapā* forest above. "Just so, monks much more in number are those things I have found out, but not revealed; very few are the things I have revealed. And why, monks have In ot revealed them? Because they are not concerned with profit, they are not rudiments of the holy life, they conduce not to revulsion, to dispassion, to cessation, to tranquillity, to full comprehension, to the perfect wisdom, to *Nibbāna*. That is why I have not revealed them".[3]

The disadvantage contemplated in the above Sermon points to the distraction of the mind from the Path. The questions leading to the disgression from the Path, the Buddha answered through silence. There is a list of ten questions, that Rhys Davids[4] calls 'Indeterminents', the Buddha refused to entertain, for the simple reason that such attempts would not help the Buddhist disciple in any way. For instance, the answer to the question whether the world is eternal or not is hardly conducive in solving the self-evident problem of human Suffering. In the *Majjhima Nikāya*, the Buddha tells Māluṅkyāputta that.

"The living of the Brahma-faring, Māluṅkāputta, could not be said to depend on the view that the world is eternal. Nor could the living of the Brahma-faring, Māluṅkāputta be said to depend on the view that the world is not eternal Whether there is the view that the world is eternal or whether there is the view that the world is not eternal, there is birth, there is ageing, there is dying, there are grief, sorrow, Suffering lamentation and despair, the suppression of which I lay down here and now."[5]

These questions do mean a lot for the scholars. The Buddha was a practical man whose main concern was to show the Path, he had discovered, to the mankind, leading to the annihilation of Suffering i.e. *Nibbāna*. The Buddha thus, does not belong to the community of scribes and scholars, whose intellectual activities end only in a blind alley of views.

2

In *Puggalapaññatti*[6] the fourth book of the *Abhidhamma Piṭaka*, there is a description of four classes of saints coinciding with the same number of stages of *Nibbāna*. The four stages are:

(i) *The Stage of Sotāpanna* : The Pāḷi expression *Sotāpanna* (Sanskrit: *Srotapanna*) consists of two component words i.e. *Sota* and *appana*. *Sotā* means stream and *apanna* means one who has entered. Thus, in Theravāda tradition, *Sotāppana* stands for one who has entered the stream—the stream that is destined to merge, finally, in the ocean of *Nibbāna*. The image of stream, though indirectly, hints at its banks inhabited by the multitudes of people and these are 'ignorant worlding' people. The *Sotāpanna* alienates himself from the 'way of the world' and puts himself on the first stage of the Path. The *conversion* is not instantaneous; it is part of the process. Sometimes, it is confined not only to a lifetime process, but, extends to a long succession of lives. He must have opened up himself to *Dhamma*, first, and then faithfully adhered to its precepts. At this stage, the *Sotāppana* gains threefold freedom, in successive order, which is celebrated in the *Dhammapada* as follows:

> Better than sovereignty over the earth, better than going to heaven, better than lordship over all worlds is the reward of *Sotapatti*, the first stage of the Path in holiness.[7]

The threefold-freedom is:

(a). *Freedom from the delusion of self*: The delusion (*Sakkayadiṭṭhi*) thought of, in this context, has direct bearing on the doctrine of *anattā*. The Buddha in his second Sermon, the *Anattālākkhaṇa Sutta*[8] addressed to the *Pañcavaggivā Bhikkhn*, has spelled out the basic postulates of this doctrine. It may be fruitful to point out that the doctrine of *anattā* was certainly not the consequence of an attempt to achieve theoretical ends. It was, in the ultimate analysis, an outcome of the Buddha's contemplative response to the existential situation, preserved in the legend of Four Sights.

Etymologically the word *anattā* consists of the negative prefix *an* and *attā*, underlying an idea of no-self or no-soul. And, again, the Buddha put forth his doctrinc of *anattā* by way of refuting different theories of soul[9] or *attā* (Sanskrit. *ātma*), deemed to be quite popular with his contemporaries with the sole purpose of liberating them from the delusion of self. In *Anattālakkhaṇa Sutta*, the *pañcakkhundha*, constituting human personality are analysed, one after the other. and concluded thus: "This does not belong to me; this is not what I am; this is *not* my self."[10] The conversation between Venerable Nāgasena and King Milinda on the subject of personality, also echoes identical views, of course, in metaphorical language, thus:

> Even as the word of "chariot" means
> That members join to frame a whole;
> So when the Groups appear in view,
> We use the phrase, "A living being.!'.[11]

Besides following the mode of analysis of *pañcakkhandha*, the ethical implications have also been looked into. Firstly, it is argued in *Anattālakkhaṇa Sutta*, in case, there happens to be some immortal entity call it soul or self, it cannot be subject to Suffering. Secondly, when all the *khandhas* are subject to Suffering, this inevitably implies they are plagued with impermanence. Now, finally, all the *khandhas* being subject to impermanence and hence root cause of Suffering, their true nature stands revealed. In the light of this discovery one develops aversion and gradually moves towards divesting oneself of passion. One who has entered the stream on his own, does not follow the course of repressing passion, he simply does not co-operate and is steadily watchful.

So, the human personality that consists of *pañcakkhandhas*, has to be kept under constant vigilance, in order to not to identify self with any one of these separately or collectively (or anything existing beyond the frontiers of personality and subject to flux). Failure shall inevitably lead to fall into the trap of delusion of self. It is precisely to guard oneself against this malady, the Buddha armed us with the doctrine of *anattā*. The entire thrust, of this doctrine is on *what one is not*.

(b) *Freedom from doubt*: The blind faith can hardly be exalted as a positive counter part of doubt (*vicikicchā*). But, at the same time, it is not possible to move a head on the Path, in case, the doubt continues to subsist with all its credibility. Lakshmi Narasu's observations in this matter, are quite revealing. "Buddhism does not underestimate the value of doubt", he writes, "during the period of investigation". Its doubt "is of that sort whose aim is to conquer itself by high aspiration and incessant toil, not of the sort which, born of flippancy and ignorance, tries to perpetuate itself as an excuse for idleness and indifference"[12]. The kind of doubt, the *Sotāpanna* casts away, concerns the truth, difficult to own, revealed through the doctrine of *anattā*. As a result, he believes in it, and, clings no more to the personality-factors i.e. *pañcakkhandhas*.

(c) *Freedom from rituals*: Buddhism is religion wherein the efficacy lies only in an individual's efforts. The Buddha never allows to be complascently disposed to the epitome of his teachings; and he exhorts the Brethern, saying "work out your salvation with diligence"[13]. The emphasis on individual's efforts was aimed at to dedivinize the human consciousness. The idea of God has no place in Buddhism, because it cannot be allowed to contradict the causal nexus operating throughout the phenomenal existence. Furthermore, belief in God helps man to shift responsibilities of his action on other/others, and also leaves him on the mercy of God, a direct reflection of his incapacity he experiences in day to day living. This way, he turns towards God, who is not there, and makes attempts to please him through the performance of religious rites and ceremonies, as if efficacious in nature. The *Sotāpanna* redeems himself from such a set of beliefs and reposes his faith in his own efforts, alone. And, practice of meditation takes the place of offering of prayers and performance of rituals etc.

Sotāpanna freed from three fetters (*Saññojana*) is compared to the sun in the background of natural setting, during autumn, as follows:

> Just so, monks, in the autumn season when the sky is clear and the clouds have fled, the sun leaping up into the firmament drives away all darkness from the heavens and shines and burns and flashes forth,—even so in the Ariyan disciple arises the flawless, taintless eye of wisdom, and along with this arising three fetters are abandoned, to wit: The view of the person-pack, dobut-and wavering and wrong handling of rite and ritual.[14]

And, he is in position to claim that:

> Hell is destroyed for me, and rebirth as an animal, or a ghost, or in any place of woe. I am converted, I am no longer liable to be reborn in a state of Suffering, and am assured of final salvation.[15]

But, the *Sotāpanna* has to take birth for seven times[16] more among men and gods, before he finally escapes the cycle of *saṁsāra*.

(ii) *The Stage of Sakadāgāmin*: At this stage, the disciple only learns to weaken the dark passions e.g. the sensual lust (*kāma*) and anger (*paṭigha*). When, in the course of satisfying sensual desires, an obstacle crops up, the mind flares up with anger. The very fact that the disciple is required, only, to weaken the passions, and a distinct stage is devised for the purpose, only shows the exent of invincible nature of these passions. After fleeing oneself from these two fetters along with the three fetters already destroyed, one becomes *Sakadāgāmin*—the Once-returner. He has only conquered the gross desires, like desire for power and status etc. but, still clings to certain subtle desires, e.g. desire to become *arahat*. The subtle desires lurking in the mind bring him back to the world for once. The result achieved at the second stage of *Sakadāgāmin* are described in *Aṅguttara Nikāya*, in the following words:

> Now, Monks, in this matter a monk keeps the law of mortality in full, he is moderately given to mental concentration, moderately given to striving for insight...... Such an one, by destroying three fetters is a stream-winner, one not doomed to the Down fall, one assured, one bound for enlightenment.[17]

(iii) *The Stage of Anagāmin*: After having successfully outgrown the first two stages, the disciple qualifies himself to enter the third stage of *Anagāmin*. Here, he redeems himself completely from the remaining foot-prints of various fetters. A small amount of clinging to body that remains with him also disappears at the time of death. He no more returns to the human world but returns to the world of pure-form. It is stated of *Anagāmin*, thus:

> Moreover, a monk keeps the laws of morality in full, he practices concentration in full, but he is moderately given to striving for insight.......... Such an one by the destruction of the five fetters bind to the lower worlds, takes birth spontaneously (in the Pure Abodes), there to pass away, destined never to return thence.[18]

(iv). *The Stage of Arahat*: The term *arahat* is derived from *ari*. *Ari* means enemy and *arahat* is one who has conquered his enemies. On the Path to *arahatship*, the disciple has to conquer the rest of five enemies or generally called fetters which are identified as follows:

6. *Rūparāga*: When attached to this desire one seeks rebirth in the world of forms that include sixteen divine kingdoms known as *Brahma-loka*. The disciple must cross the stream of existence of whatever form it may be.

7. *Arūparāga*: Across the world of forms, their exist formless worlds, four in number. The man, no more, has material forms but still he exists. This existence, by all means constitutes an integral part of *Saṁsāra*, and the Buddhist disciple must escape from this cycle of *Saṁsāra*, to attain the goal of *Nibbāna*.

8. *Spiritual Pride* (*Māno*) and 9. *Self-righteousness*. As a result of having freed oneself from several factors, it is quite normal to assume an air of pride and acclaim self-righteousness. The disciple must see to it that these fetters, no more, create problems for him.

10. *Ignorance* (*avijjā*): Ignorance may be last in the list, but it is all pervasive. It is ignorance that generates the twelve fold *Nidānas*. Actually, the disciple undergoes a discipline for the gradual elimination of ignorance, the root-cause of Suffering. The stage of *arahat* is the culmination of both the comlete annihilation of ignorance and the attainment of *Nibbāna*.

3

Nibbāna is a state of mind to be realized and not to be merely believed or intellectually grasped. All the hindrances on the way to such realization, the Buddha analysed and removed for the benefit of those alone who resolve to attain *Nibbana*. The Buddha's first attack was on the mythological character, he found as an integral part of the contemporary religious culture. He compared his *Dhamma* with a Sāl tree, free from leaves and twigs etc. thus: "It is like a giant Sāl tree on the outskirts of a village or township which, by the course of change, loses its leaves and foliage, sheds its bark and rotten stuff and poorer wood, so that in time, when all that is gone, it stands in the clean strength of its choice timber alone.... even so, in many a figure, has Gotama, made his Doctrine clear."[19] Mythologising, the Buddha considered and condemned to be an attempt at befogging what could be clearly *seen.*

Theorising is still a greater hindrance, more subtle and hence more successful in misleading the disciple from following the right Path. And the Buddha's contempt for such a mode of thinking can be well measured from the piece of advice he rendered to Bhaddiye in the *Aṅguttara Nikāya.* "Come now, Bhaddiya ! Be not misled by report or tradition or hearsay. Be not misled by proficiency in the Collections, nor by mere logic or inference, nor after considering reasons, nor after reflection on and approval of some theory nor because it fits becoming"[20]. The Buddha's instructions of detachment from oneself, and directed towards the disciple, also include the Buddha's own person and thus he adds : "Nor by the thought: The recluse is revered by us."[21] The Buddha demands from his disciple to posses a discriminating mind and further tells: "But, Bhaddiya, when you know for yourselves: These things are unprofitable, these things are blame-worthy, these things are censured by the intelligent, these things, when performed and undertaken, conduce to loss and sorrow,—then indeed, Bhaddiya, do you reject them."[22] So, the Buddha's entire thrust is 'to gain the insight' and discard all the hindrances that come on the way.

It is the insight that paves the way for the realization of *Nibbāna. Nibbāna* is to be experienced 'by the wise in his own interior'. The Buddha tells a *Brahman* that: "Brahman, one who is ablazed with lust....... depraved with malice....... bewildered with delusion....... if lust be abandoned no longer plans thus, no.... longer suffers thus. To that extent, *Brahman, Nibbāna,* is seen in this life.......it is to be realized for themselves by the wise"[23]. *Nibbāna* is to be experienced. The use of cognitive verb denoting visual perceptions is quite common. In the *Therīgāthā,* we find an expression: "I saw *Nibbnaā.*"[24] Similarly in the *Aṅguttara Nikāya*[25] the expression, we have already referred to, used for an experiential state of *Nibbāna* are: "visible here" and "inviting to come and see". A frequent use of acquisitive verbs at the time of describing *Nibbāna,* also

refers to 'escape from the born, become, made, compound' and these are the characteristic features of *Saṁsāric* existence. An indirect reference to earth, water, fire, moon and sun etc. in the passage no. (i) further adds into the picture of *saṁsāra*. Also, reference to 'craving' in passage no. (ii) and wavering in passage no. (iv) hardly refers to anything else, but the psychological impact of *saṁsāric* mode of living.

In the passage no. (i) we read : 'Thence monks, I declare is no coming to birth, thither is no going (from life)......no falling, no arising'. These expressions signifying cessation, of course, of rebirth, unimbiguously underline the state of *Nibbāna*. The concluding words : 'this indeed is the end of ill' further supports our contention. When the monk escapes from *saṁsāra* he enters into *Nibbāna nagar* described in passage no. (iii) as, 'not-born, not-become, not-made, not-compounded.' The passage no. (ii) while referring to 'Truth', attempts to add into the positive attribute of *Nibbāna*.

The transit from *saṁsāra* to *Nibbāna* is primarily worked out in passage no. (iv). The transformation is effected through renewed pattern of Causality. The non-attachment leads to non-wavering or steadiness of mind which brings forth calmness. 'When there is calm', it is stated, 'there is no bending'. The absence of bending results in 'no-coming and going', and which means cessation of rebirth. This cessation is deified as *Nibbāna*, which, in the ultimate analysis, is gained through the extinction of *taṇhā* or thirst. But, as pointed out earlier,[96] 'he retains his senses', which only wait to be destroyed, finally, by the death, he does experience pleasant and unpleasant sensations. When it is stated that there is neither earth, water, fire, air, moon and sun, nor coming and going, this simply means that an *arahat* is immune to these things or nothing that belongs to this world causes him anxiety any more.

Nibbāna means cessation of *taṇhā* or thirst. There is no *taṇhā* when there is cessation of perception and feeling, because according to the doctrine of dependent origination, "depending on feeling arises *taṇhā*."[97] Of course, there is striking similarity i.e. absence of *taṇhā*, in both the states of mind. But, these two states are not identical in nature. There is a difference and it lies in their different nature of consciousness. When we find an *arahat* exposed to pleasant and unpleasant sensation, this only means that nature of his consciousness is not devoid of differentiation. Whereas, in the case of cessation of perception and feeling, the working of sense-apparatus is altogether (although temporarily) suspended. Thus, one who has attained the state of cessation of perception and feeling, in the *Saṁyutta Nikāya*, such a state of being is compared and contrasted with a dead person, that rcads as follows :

> In a dead man, housefather, in one who has made an end, the activity of body has ceased, become calmed, So also have the activities of speech and mind,—they have ceased, become calmed. Life has run out, vital heat has ceased, the faculties are scattered. In him, housefather, who has attained the ceasing of perception and feeling, the activity of body also has ceased, becomec almed. So also have the activities of speech and mind. But his life has not run out, vital-heat has not ceased, the faculties have become clarified. That is the difference between a dead man, one who has made an and, and one who has attained the ceasing of perception and feeling.[98]

There are several instances, referred to in the Buddhist scriptures, which fairly illustrate the point under discussion. In the *Majjhima Nikāya*[99] it is stated that, reverned Sanjaya was competent enough to attain the state of cessation of perception and feeling without any hardship and he could do so while sitting any where under the foot of a tree or some solitary place. Once when he was absorbed in the said state of mind, some cow-herds, goat-herds, and wayfarers took him to be dead and these country folk gathered some grass and sticks and then offered him to the fire. After a long time Sanjaya arose from his absorption, next morning, shook his garments, got ready and went to the near by village as usual, for alms of food. It was astonishing, indeed, for those, to see him alive, who took him as dead and gave him to the fire. Thus, one who has attained the state of cessation of perception and feeling, hardly needs to exercise an effort to nullify say, the attacks of *Māra* on his sense-apparatus. On the other hand, an *arahat* remains in alive contact with the phenomenal existence. But, since, an *arahat* has gained full control over his psyche, successfully prevents the process of attachment to take place. This is why, in the description of the state of *sā-upādi-sesa-nibbāna*, reference to the cessation of perception and feeling is conspiciously absent.

Our next problem is to know about an *arahat*, when he has relinquished his psycho-physical framework, technically termed as *an-upādi-sesa-nibbāna*. Regarding this state of an *arahat*, we read in *Itivuttaka*, thus :

> Herein a monk is *arahant*...released by perfect knowledge, but in him in this very life all things that are sensed have no delight for him, they have become cool. This is called "the condition of *Nibbāna* without basis.[100]

The description of dead *arahat*, only, refers to the cooling of his feelings, which he did not relish during his life time. It is silent on the question of his survival after death. The fundamental problem, regarding *an-upādi-sesa-nibbāna*, that the Buddhist scholars have been trying to solve, is whether an *arahat* exists or does not exist after his death. Frequent reference is made to *Aggi-vaccha-gotta Sutta*, wherein, Vacchagotta, a *brahman*, once put this question to the Buddha, which the latter replied using an analogy of fire, When, Vacchagotta asserted, that after the fire is extinguished for lack of fuel to sustain it, it is not possible to locate fire, then at this juncture of time, the Buddha explains the position of an *arahat* after he is dead, thus :

> Just in the same way, Vaccha, all things material—all feelings-all perception-all plastic forces-all consciousness-every-thing by which the truth-finder might be denoted has passed away for him,—grubbed and stubbed, leaving only the bare cleared site where once a palm-tree towered,—a thing that once has been and can be no more. Profound, measuseless, unfathomable, is the truth-finder even as the mighty ocean, reborn does not apply to him nor not-reborn nor any combination of such terms; everything by which the truth-finder might be denoted, has passed away for him, utterly and for ever.[101]

The fact that the five aggregates become extinct at the time of death of an *arahat*, neither it means that he exists in some other identifiable form, nor does it imply that he is totally annihilated. The Buddha in order to avoid both the extreme positions maintained by the eternalists and annihilationists preferred to remain either silent or replied in paradoxical language.[102] But, once to the question, 'Has he (only) disappeared, or does he not exist (any longer), or is he for ever free from sickness',[103] the Buddha answered thus :

> For him who has disappeared there is no form, O Upasiva—that by which they say he is, exists for him no longer when all things (*dhamma*) have been cut off, all (kinds of) disputes are cut off.[104]

The term (*dhamma*) in this context, is used in the sense of corporeality and which is quite intune with the description of an *an-upādi-sesa-nibbāna* i.e., *nibbāna* 'without substrate left'. The very fact that a dead *arahat* is compared with deep ocean only means to suggest there is no conceptual channel to comprehend his state of 'existence'. So, the very question, that whether an *arahat* after death exists or does not exist needs to be modified, if at all possible, to avoid an error involved in the use of expression, 'exist', that belongs to the arena of phenomenal reality. 'Like can be known only by like', is a proverbial saying and in this background it may only be said :

> Just as the bourn of a blazing spark of fire
> Struck from the anvil, gradually fading,
> Cannot be known,—so in the case of those
> Who've rightly won release and crossed the flood
> Of lusts that bind, and reached the bliss unshaken,
> The bourn they've won cannot be pointed to.[105]

Notes and References

1. Cūlla vagga 238. Horner, I. B., *The Book of the Discipline*, Vol. V, p. 335.

2. M. 73 (*Mahā-vacchogotta Sutta*): M ii 493. Chalmers, Vol. I, p. 347.
3. S. V. 437. Woodward, Vol. V, p. 370.
4. D. 9. (*Potthapāda Sutta*): D. i. 186. Rhys Davids, T. W., *Early Buddhism*, p. 69.
5. M. 63. (*Cūḷa-Mālunkya Sutta*): M. ii. 430; Horner, I. B., Vol. II, p. 100.
6. Law, B. C., *Designation of Human Types*, (47-50) pp. 26-27; cf. Grimm, George, *The Doctrine of the Buddha*, pp. 307 ff.
7. Dhp. 178. Maxmuller.
8. Mv. (Vin). i. 13-14.
9. D-1. (*Brahmajāla Sutta*) : D. i. 31, 34
10. Mv. (Vin.) i. 13-14.
11. Warren Henry, Clark, *Buddhism in Translation*, p. 133.
12. Narasu, P. Lakshmi, *The Essence of Buddhism*, p. 107.
13. D. 16 (*Mahā-Parinibbānā-Sutta*) : D. ii. 162.
14. A. i. 241. Woodword, Vol. 1, p. 221.
15. D. 16 (*Mahā-Parinibbāna-Sutta*) : D. ii. 93; S. B. E., Vol. XI, p. 26.
16. S. ii 134. cf., *Points of Controversy*, book XII, Sec, 5, 9.
17. A. i. 231-232. Woodword, Vol. 1, pp. 211-212.
18. A. i. 232: Woodward, Vol. 1, p. 212.
19. M. 72 (*Aggi. Vacchagotta Sutta*) : M. i. 488-489. Chalmers, Vol. 1, p. 344.
20. A. ii. 190, Woodward, Vol. II, p. 200.
21. Idem.
22. Idem.
23. A. i. 158 Woodward, Vol. 1, p. 141.
24. Tī. 97: "*addasaṁ, nibbānaṁ*."
25. A. i, 158: "*sandiṭṭhika*'; *ehipassika*".
26. Sn. 454: "*nibbānapattiyā*".
27. Tī. 432: "*nibbānañ ca labhassu*".
28. Ta 637: "*nibbānaṁ abhiharye*".
29. A. IV, 414.
30. S. IV. 328: "*Sabbaṁ taṁ chandamūlakaṁ chandanidānaṁ. Chando hi mūlaṁ dukkhassa.*"
31. Grimm, George, op. cit., pp. 235, 262.
32. Ibid. pp. 262, 264.
33. S. V. 272: Woodward, Part V, p. 243.

'Kimthiyaṁ nu kho, bho Ānanda, Samane Gotame brahmacariyaṁ Vussti" ti ?
Chandapphanathāṁ kho brahman, bhagvati brahmacariyaṁ vussti" ti ?
"Attihi paṇa, bho Ānanda, maggo attith paṭipadā aitassa chandhassa phānāyā" ti ?
"Katmo pana, bho Ānanda, maggo katama paṭipada aitassa chandhassa phānāyā" ti ?
Also see : Grimm, George, op. cit., p. 264.

34. It 27 : *"ātāpi···nibbānāya bhabbo anuttarassa yogakkhemassa adhigamāyā".*
35. Sn. 933 : *Sāntī ti nibbutiṁ ñatvā.*
36. *Dhp.* 203 : *nibbāṇaṁ paramaṁ sukhaṁ.*
37. Poussin, *Way to Nirvāṇa*, pp. 150, 151.
38. (i) Sn. 220: S. B. E., Vol. X, part II, p. 35.
(ii) Copleston, *Buddhism Primitive and Present*, p. 205.
39. M. 71. (Tevijja-vacchagotta Sutta) : M. i. 483 : See Chalmers, Vol. 1, 341.
40. A. iii. 451.
41. Rhys Davids, T. W., *The Dialogues of the Buddha*, (S. B. B.) Vol. II, Part-I, p. 63.
42. *Kathāvatthu*, (P. T. S) p. 268.
43. *The Question of King Milinda*, S. B. E. Vol. XXVI, Part-II, pp. 56-57.
44. Ibid. Part-II, pp. 96, 97.
45. Ibid. Part-II, p. 253.
46. Heraclitus, *The Cosmic Fragments*, Fragment 12, p. 367.
47. Ross, Sir David, *Plato's Theory of Ideas*, p. 19.
48. Udāna 55 : '*evam eva kho bhikkhave bahū ce pi bhikkhū anupādisesāya nibbānaḍhātuyā pariṇibbāyanti, na tena nibbānadhātuyātinattaṁ vā pūrattaṁ vā paññāyati*'. Woodward. *The Minor Anthologies of the Pāli Canon*, pp. 66-67.
49. S. iii. 190 : *"Tanhakkhayo hi, Rādha, nibbānaṁ: I' ti.* Woodward, Part III, p. 157; cf. S. iv, 368-372.
50. Poussin, *Way to Nirvāṇa*, p. 150.
51. Oldenberg, H., *Buddha, His Life His Doctrine His Order*, p. 273.
52. Maxmuller, *Studies in Buddhism*, p. 57.

53. Dalkhe Paul, *Buddhist Essays*, pp. 47-48.
54. Maxmuller, *Studies in Buddhism*, p. 51.
55. Horner, I. B. (trs.) *Milinda's Question*, Vol. II, pp. 98, 175, 214.
56. S. iii, 190 : Woodward, Part III, p. 156.
57. S. iii. 25, Radhakrishan, Dr., *Indian Philosophy*, Vol. I, p. 386.
58. S. i. 38 : "*nibbānābhirato macco sabbadukkhā pamuccati*" *ti.*
59. M. i. 504.
60. S. iv. 370.
61. Mv. (Vin.). i. 2. Rhys Davids, T. M., *Early Buddhism*, p. 39.
62. M. 72 (*Aggi-Vacchagotta Sutta*) : M. i. 487.
63. Sn. 1075 : "*na pammāṇamatthi*" cf. *Brahmajāla Sutta*, S. B. B., Vol. II, p. 54.
64. M. 72 (*Aggi-Vacchagotta Sutta*) : M. i. 486.
65. Vm. XVI, 90. (Nyāṇamoli).
66. Dhp. 92. Maxmuller).
67. Mp. See : Dilemma 81 and 82.
68. D. 16 (*Mahā-Parinibbāna Sutta*) : D. ii. 91f.
69. S. i., 194 : "*Tesaṁ sudaṁ ayasmā Mahā-Moggallāno cetasā cittaṁ samanesati vippamuttaṁ nirupadhiṁ.*
70. S. iv. 368-372.
71. Dhp. 23, 96, 98, 99, 204, (Maxmuller).
72. A. iv. 414f. "*Sukham idaṁ, āvuso nibbānaṁ*", *ti...kiṁ pan ettha āvuso Sāriputta, sukhaṁ, yad ettha natthi vedayitaṁti ? Pañcime'...kāmāguṇā...idaṁ vuccatavuso, kāmasukhaṁ vivicc eva kāmehi...*Hare, E. M., Vol. IV, p. 279-80.
73. D. i, 71.
74. M. 76. (*Sandaka-Sutta*) : M. i. 523...*tasa carato c'eva tiṭṭhato ca suttassa ca jāgarassa ca satataṁ samitaṁ... 'khīnā me āsavā, ti apı ca kho pannaṁ paccavekkhamāno janā ti : khiṇā me āsavā ti...,*
75. Ti, 76 : Rhys Davids, C. A. F., *Psalms of the Early Buddhists*, Part-I, p. 53.
76. M. 75 (*Māgandiya Sutta*) : M. 26 (*Ariya-Pariyesana-Sutta*) : M. i. 173.

77. M. 75 (*Māgāndiya sutta*) M. i. 511 (*ārogya* : 'health').
78. S. iii, 46.
79. M. 7. (*Vatthūma-Sutta*) M. i. 38.
80. Dhp. 25, (Maxmuller)
81. Sn. 467 : *parinibbuto udakarahado va sīto.*
82. M. i, 171 : *Sītibhuto' and nibbuto.*
83. Johansson, Rune E. A., *The Psyohology of Nirvāṇa*, pp. 45-46.
84. S. iii. 110 : *Vimutti...nibbānatthā.*
85. S. i. 210 : *Nibbānam Bhagava āhu sahhaganthappamocanam* Rhys, Davids C. A. F., Part-I, p. 270.
86. U. 81.
87. *The Questions of King Milinda* S. B. E., Vol. XXXVI, p. 213.
88. Rhys, Davids, C. A. F., *Psalms of the Early Buddhists*, p. xxxviii (Introduction).
89. It. 38 : '*Saupādisesā ca nibbānadhātu anupādi-sesā ca nibbānadhātu*'.
90. Silva Lynn A de, *The Problem of the Self in Buddhism and Christanity*, p. 67.
91. It. 38 : '*...........tassa titthanteva pañe-indriyāni-yesaṁ avihātattā manāpāmanāpāṁ paccanubhati, sukhadukkham patisamvedi-yati : tassa yo rāgakkhayo dosakkhayo mohakkhayo, ayaṁ vuccati......Saupādisesa nibbānadhātu.* Woodward, *Minor Anthologies of the Pāli Canon.* Part-II, p. 143.
92. M. 86 : (*Aṅgulimāla-Sutta*) : Chalmers, Vol. II, p. 153.
93. Kalupahana, David J, *Buddhist Philosophy*, p. 73 cf. D. iii 260 *Aṭṭha loka-dhammā lābho ca alābho ca yaso ca ayaso ca nindā ca passṁsā ca sukhañ ca dukkhañ ca.*
94. Ta : 1002-1003 : Rhys Davids, C. A. F., : *Psalms of the Early Buddhists*, Part-II, p. 346.
95. U. 80-81 :

    (i) '*Atthi bhikkhave tad āyatanaṁ, yattha n'eva pathavi nā āpo na tejo na vāyo na ākāsānañcāyatanaṁ na viññānāñcāya tanaṁ na nevasaññānāsañāyatanaṁ nāyaṁ loko na paralokko ubho candi-masūriyā tad ahaṁ bhikkhave n'eva āgatiṁ vadāmi na gatiṁ na thitiṁ na cutiṁ na upapattiṁ appatitthaṁ appavattaṁ anārammaṇaṁ evataṁ, es'ev' anto dukkhassā' ti.*

(ii) *'Duddasaṁ anattaṁ nāma, na hi saccaṁ sudassanaṁ; paṭividdhā taṇhā jānato, passato n'atthi kiñcanan ti.*

(iii) *'Atthi bhikkhavetajataṁ abhūtaṁ akātaṁ asankhataṁ na ce taṁ bhikkhave abhavissa ajātaṁ abhūtaṁ akataṁ asankhataṁ, na yidha jātassa bhūtassa katassa sankhatass nissaraṇaṁ paññāyetha. Yasmā na kho bhikkhave atthi ajātaṁ abhūtaṁ akātaṁ asankhataṁ, tasmā jātossa bhūtassa katassa sankhatassa nissaraṇaṁ paññāyati'.*

(iv) *'Nissitassa ca calitaṁ, anissitassa calitaṁ n'atthi, caliteasati passaddhi, passadhiyā sati rati na hot, ratiyā asati āgatigati na hoti, agāti-gatiyā asati cutūpapāto na hoti, catupayāte asati n ev'dha na huraṁ na ubhayamantare, es' ev' anto dukkhassā'ti.* Woodward, *Minor Anthologies*, p. 97-99.

96. It. 38.

97. *'Vedanā paccayā taṇhā.*

98. S. iv. 294: Woodward, Part IV, p. 202.

99. M. 50, (*Māra-Tajjaniya Sutta*). Also see D. 16. *Mahāaprinibbāna-Sutta* wherein the states of cessation of perception and feeling of Alara Kalam and the Buddha are mentioned. Chalmers, Vol. 1, p. 240.

100. It. 38 : *'tassā idheva......sabbavedayatāni anabhinanatidāni sītabhavissanti* : Woodward. *The Minor Anthologics*, Part-II, p. 143.

101. M. 72 : (*Aggi-vacchagotta-Sutta*) : M. i. 486 f. Chalmers, Vol. 1, p. 344.

102. See Ref. 95.

103. Sn. 1074 : *'Atthaṅgato so uda vā so n'atthi udāhu ve sassatiyā arogo'.* Fousboll, S. B. E., Vol. X, Part-II, p. 198-199.

104. Sn. 1075, Ibid., p. 199.

105. U. 93. Woodward, *The Minor Anthologies*, Part II, p. 114.

4

THE MIDDLE-WAY BETWEEN WAR AND PEACE*

The Buddha's Way *is* the Middleway. And, Middleway means balancing between two extremes. War and peace—these are two extremes. Dilating on peace, one may allege, is to move from one extreme to another. Rather, it may be *defied* as deviation from the Way of the Buddha. Viewed in this perspective, can (or should) the Buddhist view adhere to and preach the practice of the Middleway between war and peace ? This is the dilemma, I propose to examine in this paper.

What are precisely the nuances of the Buddha's Middleway? The Middleway discovered by the Buddha, if one cares to appreciate, impels one in no other way than to enter upon to enquire into the anatomy of the functioning of the human mind. Mind, according to Buddhism, is the main motivating force that governs the entire gamut of man's *Saṁsāric* living. In the opening verse of the *Dhammapada*, mind is introduced as "fore-runner of all conditions. Mind is chief : and the *cetasikas* or the mental concomitants are mind-made".[1] The *modus-operandi* of mind, therefore, is to move. The mind can only move between the extremes of past and future. Movement of mind is not possible in the present. In the present there is no space, at all, required for the mind to move. Furthermore,

*Paper published in the Proceedings of the 10th International Buddhist Conference, held during 8-10 December, 1984 at Japanese Temple; Bodha-Gaya, Bihar (India).

thinking, an activity of mind exists only, when the mind can function. When the mind is brought in the middle i.e. in the present, through meditation or with an aid of any other device, the mind simply disappears, or, in other words one acquires a state of no mind. Not only the mind thus disappears, its contents such as thoughts and ego, very subtle material entities, disappear, as well. Motivations are dropped. One is neither an indulgent nor an ascetic. In the middle, one truly becomes spiritual. This is being balanced, being *Samyak*.[2]

Shakespear's play *King Lear* depicts, in some form, both an extreme and middle positions taken up by three daughters of King Lear. The king decides to divide his kingdom into three as as 'to shake all cares and business from his age, conferring them on younger strengths.' And addresses his daughters, thus :

> Tell me, my daughters
> ... ...
> which of you shall we say doth love us most?
> ... ...[3]

Goneril, the eldest-born speaks first :

> Sir, I love you more than my words
> can wield the matter.
> Dearer than eye-sight, space and liberty ;
> ... ...
> As much as child e'er loved, or father found,
> ... ...[4]

The text of the play, after this, reads as :

> Cordelia (aside) What shall Cordelia do?
> Love, and be silent.[5]

Next to speak is Regan :

> ... ...
> In my true heart
> I find she names my very deed of love;
> Only she comes too short : That I profess
> Myself an enemy of all other joys
> Which the most precious square of sense possesses.
> And find I am alone felicitate
> In your dear highness' love[6]

Now is the turn of Cordelia, 'So young and true.'

At her father's command, she expresses :

> Cordelia : Nothing my Lord.
> Lear : Nothing ?
> Cordelia : Nothing.
> Lear : Nothing will come of nothing :
> Speak again.
> Cordelia ; ... ...
> I love your majesty
> According to my bond, no more no less.
> (Cordelia continues)... ... ...
> Why have my sisters husbands, if they say
> They love you all ? Happily when I shall wed.
> That lord whose hand must take my plight shall carry
> Half my love with him, half my cares and duty
> Sure I shall never marry like my sisters,
> To love my father all.[7]

King Lear expects love from his daughters in terms of 'most'. Goneril and Regan, with an aid of clever use of the words, satisfy King Lear's ego. Later on, both of them, after manipulating their equal share of kingdom, divided into two, take the extreme positions, in conduct, in reverse order. Cordelia too, loves her father and prefers to remain silent and say 'nothing,' which, in a way, speaks of her being in the middle. Cordelia's position, when she is made to express herself, and she does, in terms of 'no more no less' is no other than of middle way. She is 'no more and no less' in the given situation, than being *Samyak*, being balanced. King Lear at a later stage, adores Cordelia, when she is no more, with these words :

> Her voice was ever soft,
> Gentle and low, an excellent thing in women.[8]

These are some of the noble qualities of a person, rooted in the Middleway.

Pāli Canon is full of such references, which, fully substantiate the view that the Buddha's way is the Middleway. The very fact that the Buddha, in his very First Sermon, identified as *Dhammacakkapavattana Sutta*, should name his Way as *Majjhima paṭipadā* or the Middleway, hardly leaves any scope for conjectures, with regard to the identity of the Way. The Buddha spelled out his Way, as below :

> These two extremes, brethren should not be followed by one who has gone forth as a wanderer :
> Devotion to the pleasures of senses—a low and pagan practice, unworthy, unprofitable, the way of the world (on the one hand) and on the other hand devotion to self-mortification, which is painful, unworthy, unprofitable.
> By avoiding these two extremes he who hath won the Truth (the Buddha) has gained knowledge of that Middlepath...[9]

Initially, of course, the Buddha, as the instant Sutta suggests, devised the Middleway only for those who had already entered the state of homelessness; but it would be erroneous to construe that the Way is meant, exclusively, for the *Bhikkhus* to practise. The Buddha, here, referred to the specific kind of extremes of self-indulgence and self-mortification to transcend, otherwise there would be hindrances in the way of spiritual progress. The realization, as such, was not the result of a rationalistic grasp of the situation, rather was based on his experiments and experiences. But, the middle between any set of extremes, if once achieved is decidedly to transform the entire outlook. The Middleway, then, never remains an isolated phenomenon, it becomes a pattern—a universal principle—and encompasses all pairs of extremes within its range of operation.

There is a beautiful illustrative reference highlighting the significance of the practising of the Middleway. Under the caption *Soṇassa pabbajja*, in the fifth chapter of *Mahāvagga*, the first book of *Vinaya Piṭaka*, it is recorded that Soṇa after his ordination at the hands of the Buddha, went to *Sitavana* to practise meditation. The manner he adopted was, "walking up and down all the while; so much so that his feet began to bleed profusely".[10] The Buddha came to know of it and went to him. The Buddha could very well see that Soṇa had failed to practise meditation, successfully. The Buddha, during the discourse, reminded Soṇa, of those days, prior to becoming *Bhikkhu*, when the latter could play upon *Vinā*, skillfully.

Thus, the Buddha helped Soṇa in restoring the balance of his psyche, while making use of the analogy of *Viṇā*. The Buddha, ultimately, made him realize that when the strings of *Viṇā* are "neither too much stretched nor loose, but fixed in even proportion", i.e. in the middle, only then it is in a "fit state to be played upon".[11] The same principle, whenever, followed must prove fruitful.

The position taken up by the Buddha with regard to metaphysical questions, demanding answers in terms of either/or, is not different and corroborates the view that the Buddha's Way is the Middleway. There is a list of ten questions that T. W. Rhys Davids calls 'indeterminates' that the Buddha refused to entertain and answered through noble silence.[12] For instance, to the question put forth by a wandering ascetic Vacchagotta, whether 'I' is existent or not existent the Buddha kept silent.[13] The Buddha refused to take either position for the simple reason that such attempts would not help, being not conducive in solving the self-evident problem of human Suffering. This indicates not only the Buddha's attitude of indifference towards futile doctrinal exercises, but, also, lays stress upon his foremost preference for contemplating on the practical side of human predicament. Besides, the Buddha's silence in the instant case is prompted by his awareness of the import of the Middleway.

The Buddha, of course, observed silence and did not take sides when metaphysical issues were involved. But, to presume that he always remained and preached indifference to whatever the situation might be, is to misconceive the Buddha's Middle. way. In *Kuṇāla Jātaka* (No. 536) the Buddha appears in the battle-field as a peacemaker. The Skāiya and Koliya, both the tribes used to avail the water of *Rohiṇi*-river for cultivating agricultural land. Then at one time, quarrel arose over the distribution of the river-water. The mighty kings of both the tribes, alongwith their armed forces had arrived at the battle-field. Both the sides were ready to attack each other, when, the Buddha reached there, on the spot.

Buddhaghosa's Jātakaṭṭhakathā records these crucial moments, as :

> The Buddha asked, "Why are ye come here, mighty kings ?"
> "Holy Sir" they answered, "We are come, neither to see this river, nor to disport ourselves, but to get up a fight."
> "What is the quarrel about, Sirs ?"
> "About the water."
> "What is the water worth ?"
> "Very little, Holy Sir."
> "What is the earth worth ?"
> "It is of priceless value,"
> "What are, worriors chief worth ?"
> "They too are of priceless value."
> "Why on account of some worthless water are you destroying chiefs of high worth. ?"[14]

The Buddha's pursuasion worked and both the mighty kings were dissuaded with success, from waging war and to settle their dispute, peacefully. Both the mighty kings after taking refuge in the Buddha, confessed, that :

> Had not the Master come, we should have slain one another and set flowing riyers of blood, It is owing to the Master that we are alive.[15]

The peaceful settlement arrived at between the two mighty kings not only timely saved the kingdoms from turning into 'the river of blood', but it also initiated the principle of peaceful co-existence to prove mutually beneficial in future too, if followed without reservations.

The Super Powers, today, are ready to wage war, presumably against each other, armed with nuclear weapons. As referred to, earlier, that in the middle when ego disappears, one truly becomes spiritual. True and enduring Compassion (not of political nature) springs up only when and where there is a spiritual balance. The Super Powers intend to cause a diversion and thus propagate that they are manufacturing nuclear weapons for the beneficial use and/or for their respective survival, whereas, the truth is that they are in competition with each other. Their prestige is involved; their ego is at stake. In short : they are caught in their own net-the spider's web.

The Buddha's main thrust, as it is amply clear from his Sermons, was to eliminate Suffering and for which he succeeded in discovering the Middleway further elaborated into eight steps reckoned as *ariyo aṭṭhaṅgiko maggo* or Noble-Eight-fold Path. The significant thing is not the number of steps but the term *sammā* preflexed to each step.[16] In *Pāli English Dictionary* the term *sammā*, and its variations are described as : 'calm, in the right way, as it ought to be, perfectly and in harmony.[17] To sum up : *sammā*, further conforms to the principle and practice of the Middlewayedness.

The need of the hour, today, is to set the turbulent world —our ancestral home—in order and to contribute to reshape it as to make it conducive for the spiritual health of mankind. Using Keats's phrase 'What ails thee oh World ?' It is extremism, manifesting in multiple forms that is causing grave anguish. The world, today, stands sharply divided into hostile ideological camps. At times, we pursue our national policies, deliberately, ignoring international interests, as if both the spheres are mutually exclusive. Zangwill seems to set the record straight when he writes that. "It takes two men to make one brother. Internationalism, far from being the antithesis of nationalism, actually requises nations to inter relate"[18] The *others* too have every right to prosper the way they Will. To subscribe to this view is to uphold the Doctrine of the Middleway. A. J. Bahm is not far from truth, when discussing the Buddha's Middleway, he observes that, "The Middleway avoids extremes yet it does not extremely avoid extremes"[19] So, the situation plays its role. The world situation, today, is such that the Middleway is the only way out from potential threats of nuclear war and must not be only advocated, but ought to be practised, even if, it is denigrated as cowardice. The precept of peaceful co-existence is the Middleway between war and peace, if practised without reservation, can go a long way to scatter dark clouds of nuclear war destined to destroy *us* and the *others*.

Notes and References

1. *Manopubbaṅgamā dhammā manoseṭṭhā manomayā*. Narad, Mahāthera, *The Dhammapada*, pp. 3, 319, 320.

2. Rajnesh, Bhagwan, *The Hidden Harmony : Discourses on the Fragments of Heraclitus*, pp. 43-44, 84, 88.
3-7. Shakespere, William, *King Lear*, Act I, Scene I.
8. Ibid., Act V, Scene 3.
9. Mv. i. 10. (*Dhammacakkapvattana Sutta*). *Dve me bhikkhave antā pabbajitena na sevītabbā. Katame dve ? Yo cāyaṁ kāmesukāmāsukhallikānuyogo hīno gammo pothujjoniko anariyo anathasaṁhito, yo cāyaṁ atthakilamatanu yogo dukkho anariyo anathasaṁhito. Aito kho, bhikkhave ubhoante anupagamma, majjhimāpaṭipadā tathāgatena...* Woodward, F. L., *Some Sayings of the Buddha*, p. 7.
10. Mv. i. 181ff. cf. *Theragāthā*, verses: 632-644; Guttila Jātaka No. 243.
    Rhys Davids, T. W. and Oldenberg, H., *Vinaya Texts*,
11. Ibid., p. 9.
12. Rhys Davids, T. W., *Early Buddhism*, p. 69, cf. S. iv. 373 ff.
13. S. iv. 400.
    Grimm, George, *The Doctrine of the Buddha*, p. 140.
    Also see, Chapter 1, *Dukkha*, p. 6.
14. (i) Fausboll. V. The *Jātakas*, Vol. V, p. 144.
    (ii) Cowell, E. B. The *Jātakas*, Vol. V, p. 220.
    cf. The Ceylonese Chronicle: *Mahāvaṁsa*, 1.12 ff.
15. Ibid. (i) p. 414.
    Ibid. (ii) p. 221.
16. Mv. i. 10 : *ayaṁ eva ariyo aṭṭhangiko maggo. sammā diṭṭhi ...sammā samādhi.*
17. Rhys Davids, T. W. and Stede, William, *The Pali-English Dictionary*, p. 695.
18. Quoted in, Narla, V. R., *Traditional Indian Culture and other Essays*, p. 124.
19. Bahm, A. J., *Philosophy of the Buddha*, p. 75.

5

ROHITASSA COMPLEX : A PSYCO-SPIRITUAL ANALYSIS*

I have coined the expression Rohitassa Complex, in the manner, similar to Freud's attempt to identify a certain state of mind and name it after Oedipus, a character in Greek tragedy, as Oedipus Complex.[1] And, who was Rohitassa ? We meet Rohitassa in the course of reading Pāḷi Canon for more than one time. The *Aṅguttara Nikāya* mentions Rohitassa, twice. First time, when Rohitassa actually visits the Buddha.[2] Thereafter, the meeting between the two is reported by the Buddha, while addressing the *Bhikkhus.*[3] The details of memorable meeting between the Buddha and Rohitassa contained in the *Aṅguttara Nikāya*, also occur in the *Saṁyutta Nikāya.*[4] What we learn from scriptural evidence is that, once, when the Buddha was staying at *Jetavana Mahāvihār*, near Savatthi, Rohitassa, a *Devaputta* visited the Buddha, paid his respect, stood at one side and addressed the Buddha enquiring, thus:

> ...*yattha nu kho, bhante, na jāyati na jīyati na miyati na cavati na upapajjati, sakkā nu kho so, bhante, gamanena lokassa anto ñatuṁ vā daṭṭhuṁ va pāpuṇituṁ vā ti* ?
>
> ...Pray, Lord, is it possible for us by going, to know, to see, to reach world's end, where there is no more being born or growing

*Paper presented and published in the Proceedings of the 9th International Buddhist Conference held during 8-10 December, 1983 at Bodhgaya, (Bihar) India.

old, no more dying, no more falling (from one existence) and rising up (in another).[5]

When the Buddha replied declaring 'that end of the world is not by going to be known, seen or reached' and to the complete satisfaction of Rohitassa, the latter told about his one hundred years futile odyssey, he had made in his previous birth, when he was a sage, Rohitassa, by name and son of Bhoja, longing to find out the end of the world. The description of futile attempt made is quite meaningful for purpose of decoding the substance of Complex, we are concerned with. Rohitassa confesses that it was his ability to walk (or fly) through the sky that provoked a longing in him to make use of the same to discover the end of the world. Telling about his speed, he compares it with a master of archery, who could easily shoot across a palmtree's shadow. And, his stride covered the distance between the eastern and the western ocean. Rohitassa further reveals that although he travelled for hundred years without even wasting his time to attend to the 'needs of nature', yet, he died on the way, before reaching the end of the warld.[6] Nevertheless, the Buddha asserted that the end of Suffering could only be accomplished by having reached the end of the world. It is here, at this juncture of discourse the Buddha unravells the mystery associated with the expression 'end of the world'. The Buddha reveals the truth not only for the benefit of Rhoitassa, but, aslo for the Man of Science of today as well, as under:

...Api cāhaṁ āvuso, imasmiṁ yeva byāmamatte kaḷevare sasaññimiha samaṇake lokaṁ ca paññapemi loka-samadayaṁ ca lokanirodhaṁ ca lokanirodhagāminiṁ ca paṭipadaṁ ti.

...In this very fathom-long body, alongwith its perceptions and thoughts, I proclaim the world to be, likewise the origin of the world and the making the world to end, likewise, the practice going to the ending of the world.[7]

The Man of Science of today is not different from Rohitassa, who had a longing to reach the end of the world, the way he thought it possible. The link-language between the two is a longing to make use of the power to fly through the sky, and, in a way, to conquer the world. The longing of Rohitassa to reach the end of the world, may appear to some, a mere fiction, and hence a fun. But, what about the similar conduct of Man of Science of today ? Who longs to reach the end of the world, which of course, can not be brushed aside as a mere fiction. Of whatever nature longing is, when viewed within the Buddhist *weltanschauung* it stems from *taṇhā* or thristing-will, which has its roots in *avijjā* or ignorance, mistaken by some as an error of intellect, when, actually, it means spiritual blindness.

The Man of Science of today suffers from a Complex, a state of mind, akin to that of Rohitassa prior to the latter's meeting with the Buddha. The Buddhist scholars, sometimes, under the influence of modern science, study *Buddhavacana* to satisfy their hunger of gaining more and more knowledge about the details and/or design of phenomenal existence. They feel satisfied when they discover certain striking similarities with that of the discoveries of modern scientific knowledge. This way they appreciate the Buddhist scriptures, but on wrong premises. To treat the Buddhist Canon as a book of science, in a very subtle way, is to destroy the source material for studying Buddhism as spiritual discipline. This tendency seems to be a *clandestine* practice that sets the process of destroying Buddhism, gradually. Because, it encourages to indulge in things and ideas, discarded by the Buddha as spiritually unrewarding. It is not only misreading Buddhism, it is also motivated to professionalize Buddhism, that needs to be disparagingly condemned as it causes deviation from the Path devised by the Buddha. The Buddha was quite aware of similar practices dominating the contemporary scene. He did not overlook the misreading of his intentions. In Alagaddūpama Sutta, the Buddha reiterated his overall practical view and summarised the substance of his teachings, saying:

> *...Pubbe cāhaṁ bhikkhave, etarahi ca dukkhaṁ eva paññapemi dukkhassa ca nirodhaṁ.*
>
> ...Both in the past and today, I have consistently preached Suffering and the end of Suffering.[8]

Furthermore, in the instant Sutta, the misreading of the

doctrine of the Buddha is described like catching a snake by the tail.[9]

The Man of Science is hardly instrumental in initiating the course of thinking and action, helpful in the Cessation of Suffering in the Buddhist sense of the term. The Man of Science is not only obsessed with curosity similar to that of Rohitassa, who had a longing 'to reach the end of the world', but is a victim of greed that keeps him always on his toes, striving to conquer the world, the way, Alexander the Great also contemplated and died on the way.

There is also the Buddhist way of conquering the world in terms of *saṁsāra*. *Saṁsāra*, according to *Mahāsīhanāda Sutta* of the *Majjhima Nikāya* consists of five realms viz. (i) *niraya* (hell-world): (ii) *pettivisaya* (world of spirits), (iii) *tiracchānayoni* (animal-world), (iv) *manussaloka* (human-world) and (v) *devaloka* (world of gods).[10] These realms, also called planes of existence, are further subdivided into thirty one. The term *saṁsāra* in Buddhism, is metaphorically described as Cycle of Existence. "Without begining or end, ye monks" says the Buddha "is this round of rebirth (*saṁsara*)."[11] The transit of LIFE from one realm to another also becomes intelligible. Buddhism is known for its precept of non-killing and Compassion for animal and bird-life and it seems that it derives its moral force from this very fact of existence. The deliverence of all living beings rather than confined to mankind alone as contemplated in religious disciplines which neither admit rebirth nor transmigration, also stands explained, and gains credibility.

It is this kind of *saṁsāra* that the Buddhism recommends us to conquer.

It is 'in this fathom-long body' that the *saṁsāra* lies in its microcosmic form. The instigating force that operates is *taṇha* or thristing-will. Thirst for existence or *bhava* is the root-cause for wandering to and fro wirhin *saṁsāra*. So, it is ultimately the extinction of this kind of *taṇhā* that causes the cessation of *saṁsāra*. And, it is the attainment of *Nibbāna* that renders *saṁsāra* inoperative. *Vāna*,[12] one of the components of the term *Nibbāna* means weaving. *Taṇhā* is interpreted as *vāna* in the sense that it weaves a conjunction of one life with another. The second, but first in order of sequence, component *Ni* is the negative particle signifying absence. *Vāna* here is no less than a metaphorical expression of *taṇhā*. Man, in the manner similar to spider weaves his own net. The Buddha helps, only those, interested to dispense with *dukkha* that permeates throughout the *saṁsāric* existence.

Not only the *saṁsāra* lies in the 'fathom-long body', 'the practice going to the ending of the world' or *saṁsāra* is also inherently present, which is to be discovered and followed diligently. What, precisely, is this 'practice'? In the Buddhist seheme of thought, this 'practice' is termed as *tividhā-sikkhā* (three-fold training), further classified into *Sila*, *Samādhi* and *Paññā*. This trinity underlines three mental states further carved into eight mental factors which, are no other than eight steps identified as *ariyo aṭṭhaṅgiko maggo*. Therefore, it is the functioning of human mind that needs to be examined in the framework of the *Dhamma*.

The *saṁsāra* in microcosmic form is contained in human mind that governs the course of living. The mind in its primordial form, in Buddhism, is characterized as pure and radiant. The mind gets defiled on account of external impurities.[13] These impurities are nothing but *nīvāraṇas* (hinderances) in the way of discovering the purity of mind. These *nīvaraṇas* are five in number viz. (i) *kāmacchanda* (lust), (ii) *vyāpāda* (malice), (iii) *thinamiddha* (sloth), (iv) *uddhaccakukkucca* (worry and flurry) and (v) *vicikicchā* (doubt and wavering). In the *Sammaññaphala* Sutta these five *nīvaranas* are beautifully explained with the help of equal number of similes. These five similes when analysed, show that freedom from debt, from disease, from prsion house, from slavery and from doubt is also aimed at.[14] Thus the freedom sought is multidimensional, helping, in its on way, the *yogāvacara* to attain the purity of mind. Had the mind been impure in its primordial form, not only, that it would have been illogical to search for the purity of mind, we would also be doomed to dwell in the state of impurity, perpetually, for no fault of ours. Transition in Buddhism, thus, is not conceived from impurity to purity. No mind is devoid of purity, altogether. Every mind is in possesion of purity, however, meagre it may be. The *conversion* of Aṅgulimāla,[15] the robber, quoting just one instance, could not have been effected, otherwise. Making use of available purity in whatever quantity, it may be, the Buddha had devised a path, promoting transition to the perfect form of purity i.e. *Nlbbāna.* A defiled mind that is fickle brings Suffering, and, a mind which is pure and hence calm, brings happiness. The purity of mind, it must be consistently kept in view, in Buddhism, is *not sanctioned* or *granted*, it is *gained*, after having undergone a strenous mental training, already referred to as *tividhā-sikkhā*, covering a long series of lives.

It is the mind that is put in the process of purification. It is *mind*, therefore, that tastes or realizes *Nibbāna*. *Nibbāna* itself uncaused, causes elimination of clinging to existence or *saṁsāra*, resulting in conquering the world. It is through this mode of conquest of the world, as a result, one 'reaches the end of the world'. It is after 'reaching the end of the world' the Buddha told Aṅgulimāla, one stops killing.[16] The Man of Science of today, in a way, is obsessed with two tendencies having close affinity with those imbibed by both Rohitassa and Aṅgulimāla, before they had met the Buddha. The Man of Science should visit *Jetavana mahāvihār*, and which is not a geographical place: it is there where *Buddhavacanas* are understood and put into practice. Thus, he should learn to conquer the world in the manner Rohitassa did. In *Dhammapada* too, the pattern of living is categorized into (i) Way of the World, and (ii) Way to *Nibbāna*.[17] It is only through Way to *Nibbāna* one redeems oneself from the 'way of the world'.

References and Notes

1. King Oedipus, according to Greek legend, killed his father Laius and married his mother Jocasta. Sophocles (496-405 B. C.) cast this legend in to dramatic form under the title *Oedipus the King*. Sigmund Freud (1856-1939), in order to identify the primordial sexual desire, latent in man's psyche, for one's mother, named it as Oedipus

Complex. Later on, Ernest Jones, in his paper, *The Oedipus Complex as an Explanation of Hamlet's Mystery : A Study in Motive*, published in *The American Journal of Psychology*, Vol. XXI (1910) at pp. 72-114, while analysing the cause of Hamlet's delay in taking revenge, discovered that Hamlet was suffering from Oedipus Complex.

cf. Jones, Ernest, *Hamlet and Oedipus*

2. A. ii. 47ff.
3. Ibid., 49.
4. S. i. 61ff.
5. A. ii. 48 : Nalanda Edition, Vol. II, p. 50.
   Woodward, F. L., *The Book of Gradual Sayings*, Vol. II, p. 56.
6. (i) Woodward, op. cit., pp. 56-57.
   (ii) Rhys Davids, C. A. F., *The book of the Kindered Sayings*, Part I, p. 86.
7. A. ii. 49: Nalanda Edition, op. cit., p. 51.
   Woodward, op. cit., p. 57.
8. M. 22 (*Alagaddūpama Sutta*) : M. i. 140.
   Chalmers, Lord, *Further Dialogues of the Buddha*, Vol. I, p. 99.
9. M. i. 133-134.
10. M. 12 (*Mahāsīhanāda Sutta*): M. i. 73ff.
11. For detailed decsriptions of *saṁsāra* with reference to the endlessness and inevitableness, see S. ii. 178ff.
    Also see, Chapter 1, *Dukkha*, 8-9.
12. Chatterjee, Heramba, *The Buddhistic Conception of Nirvāṇa*, p. 195.
13. A. i. 10. *Pabhassaramidaṁ, bhikkhave, cittaṁ, Taṁ ca kho āgantukehi upakkilesehi upakkiliṭṭhaṁ, ti.*
    Pabhassaramidaṁ, bhikkhave, cittaṁ. Taṁ ca kho āgantukehi upakkilesehi vippamuttaṁ.
14. D. 2. (*Sammaññaphala Sutta*): D. i. 71-73.
15. M. 86 (*Aṅgulimāla Sutta*): M. ii. 98ff.
16. Ibid., M. ii. 99.
17. Dhp. 75:
    Aññā hi lābhūpānisā,

aññā nibbānagāmini,
evametaṁ abhiññāya,
bhikkhu Buddhassa sāvako
sakkāraṁ nābhinandeyya,
vivekamanubrūhaye.

6

AṄGULIMĀLA

Sometimes in the sixth century B. C. and in the lifetime of the Buddha, a certain innocent lad had joined the university of Takkaśilā. After completing his course of study he returned to Kosala, his motherland. On his return, prompted by certain compulsions, he took to committing heinous crimes, thus, terrorizing the entire country. Who was this miscreant, after all ? None else, but *our own* Aṅgulimāla. It was a happy coincidence for him that the Buddha was also staying there, in the *Jetavana Mahāvihāra* for imparting training in *Vipassanā*, to the interested folk. Aṅgulimāla met the Buddha. Rather, *hiṁsā* and *kāruṇā* (Compassion) came across each other. And, I realized that antonym to *hiṁsā* is not *ahiṁsā*, it is sheer verbosity, but *karuṇā*. How did the *hiṁsā* of Aṇgulimāla give way in the face of the Buddha's Compassion, this is rarest among the rare event that is preserved in the Buddhist Canon. We need to recall, these days, such events, that would help in restoring Compassion, a practice, so dear to all the Buddhas and *Satagurūs*.

2

We know something about the Buddha. But, who was this Aṅgulimāla ? We find stray references to Aṅgulimāla in *Vinaya Piṭaka*,[1] in the commentaries of *Dīgha Nikāya*[2] and *Aṅguttara Nkiāyā*[3] and in the commentaries of some of the books of *Khuddaka Nikāya*, such as, *Sutta Nipāta*[4], *Dhamma*-

pada[5] and *Jātaka.*[6] But detailed informations are available only in the *Aṅgulimāla Sutta* of *Majjhima Nikāya*[7] and its commentary[8] and in the *Theragātha*[9] of *Khuddaka Nikāya* and its commentary.[10] What we learn from these textual sources is that a son was born to Bhaggava, a *brahmin*, who was also the Chaplin to Pasendi, the King of Kosala. On the night of his birth the armours belonging to the people of Kosala including that of the king dazzled all while radiating light. When the king noticed all this he got frightened. As he was in his bed chamber could get no sleep. The Chaplin wanted to know the cause of shining of armours. He looked into the stars, aided by his knowledge of astronomy, and came to the conclusion that his son was born under the constellation of thieves. Next morning the *brahmin* called on the king and asked about his well-being. The king told him about his restless night. The Chaplin told the reason and thus the king was satisfied. Since, the birth of the child resulted in inflicting mental injuries upon the king, so the newly born baby was named *hiṁsaka.* We are further told that since this ominous sight did not harm anyone, the name of the child, later on, was changed to *Ahiṁsaka.*

Now, *Ahiṁsaka* was a grown up boy. He was admitted to the University of Takkaśilā. During the time of the Buddha Takkaśilā was the capital of Gandhāra. Takkaśila was situated at a distance of just a few miles from modern Islamabad, the capital of Pakistan. Prior to the partition of India in to Bharat and Pakistan, it was known as *Ḍherī Shahan. Ahiṁsaka* got education from that Takkaśilā whose modern name is Islamabad. But, much more pertinent fact, we need to know, than these geographical details is, that on what account, after all, *Ahiṁsaka* turned to be *hiṁsaka,* notoriously known as Aṅgulimāla.

3

In fact, *Ahiṁsaka* during his stay at Takkaśilā, served his *gurū*-family with full dedication. As a result of that *Ahiṁsaka* became the blue-eyed-boy of his *gurū.* How could his class-fellows swallow all that. They started poisoning the ears of the *gurū.* It appears that *gurū* was one to be easily swayed by slander. He gradually became annoyed with *Ahiṁsaka.* The guru, in order to avenge oneself, very impaitently, kept waiting for the day on which the disciple was due to offer his *gurū-dakhśinā*. At last, the ceremonial occasion came. The *gurū* asked for *gurū-dakhśina* from *Ahiṁsaka*. *Ahiṁska* bowed his head before the *gurū* and enquired. "What kind of *gurū-dakhśinā* would please my Master ?" *Gurū* was already sick of *Ahiṁsaka* and he demanded one thousand human fingers of right hand. *Gurū* was of the view that it would be difficult for *Ahiṁsaka* to fulfil his obligations. On his failure *Ahiṁsaka* shall be duly punished. The *gurū* failed to gauge the strength of his disciple and, thus, under assessed him. *Ahiṁsaka* had, in fact, returned to Kosala inorder to fulfil his obligation as a disciple.

There used to be a thick forest, Jālinī by name, in Kosala. *Ahiṁsaka* would assassinate any passerby, passing through this forest, and cut off the finger of the right hand of the victim and place it on the branches of plants or trees. As a result eagles and crows would eat up the flesh leaving the bones, intact. With a view to preserve these bony fingers *Ahiṁsaka* would make a garland of it and put round his neck. This is how *Ahiṁsaka* came to be identified as Aṅgulimāla. The people, naturally, out of fear had abandoned the passage they were used to make use of. And, Aṅgulimāla as pointed out earlier, was prompted by well-defined compulsions to collect one thousand fingers. Now, Aṅgulimāla turned towards towns and villages. This perturbed the king of Kosala. He issued an order to arrest Aṅgulimāla. On hearing the order of the king, Mantānī, the mother of Aṅgulimāla, felt utterly miserable and requested her husband to dissuade Aṅgulimāla from violence. Bhaggava did not pay any heed to her request, instead, left it to the king, to decide any course of action. But, mother was after all mother, and, how could she be indifferent to the welfare of his son ? She marched towards Aṅgulimāla to dissuade him from terrorism. The Buddha with his Buddha-eye observed the departure of Mantānī, the mother and thought that if she reaches there, Aṅgulimāla, in order to complete the number of fingers required, he must cut off the hand of his mother, too. This is last birth of Aṅgulimāla, the Buddha murmured, and realized that it would be disastrous, if he fails to reach in time. Since,

Aṅgulimāla was going to assasinate none else but his mother. For the retribution of this act Aṅgulimāla shall have to undergo the torture, the resultant of number of births and deaths. While thinking on these lines, the Buddha moved towards the area wherein Aṅgulimāla was practising violence. Many people, on the way, dissuaded the Buddha and warned him not to encounter Aṅgulimāla, as the latter was a stark criminal and would not spare him. The Buddha, while treading on the path, envisaged as so dangerous, at last, arrived at in the Jālinī forest. Aṅgulimāla saw his mother and then looked at the fingers of her hand. No sooner did Aṅgulimāla moved to cut off the hand of his mother than the Buddha appeared and stood in between the son and the mother. Aṅgulimāla, by now, had already killed 999 human beings and thereby had collected 999 fingers. He needed only one finger. 'Why should I kill' he thought, 'my mother just for one finger'. 'Better', he resolved, that he should cut off the finger of this *Bhikkhu* and complete the number of fingers required'. Aṅgulimāla with sword in his hand and with a view to attack the *Bhikkhu,* moved towards him. The Buddha, with his usual grace moved away and continued with his journey. Aṅgulimāla, despite speeding up his race failed to catch up with the Buddha. Aṅgulimāla ultimately, got tired and exhausted and drenched in perspiration. Aṅgulimāla spoke with a thundering voice, thus :

> *"Tiṭha, tiṭha, O Samaṇa,' ti"*
> Stop ! stop ! O *Samaṇa* ![11]
> *Ṭhito ahaṁ Āṅgulimāla,*
> *tvañca tiṭha, 'ti."*
> I have stopped, Aṅgulimāla;
> you stop too.

Aṅgulimāla was at loss and could not understand the nuances of the statement of the Buddha and again put up a query:

> *"gacchaṁ vadesi, samaṇa, ṭhito miha.*
> *Samañca barūsi, 'ṭhitaṁ athito 'ti"*[12]
> You who profess to stop, still march ahead;
> I, who have stopped, am told by you I've not:

Again,

"Pucchami taṁ, samaṇa, thamatthaṁ—
'Katham, ṭhito tvaṁ ahaṁ aṭhito' miha."[13]

—Explain how you have stopped while. I have not.

The Buddha replies to the question of Aṅgulimāla;

"Ṭhito ahaṁ, Aṅgulimāla, sabbadā,
Sabbesu bhūtesu nidhāya dandaṁ.
tuvañca pṇaesu asaññato' ti;
tismā ṭhito' haṁ, tuvaṁ aṭhito' ti."[14]

Yes, I have stopped; for never violence do I to any;—life you still destroy.

—Thus I have stopped indeed, but you stop not!

Suddenly, the violence of Aṅgulimāla melt away in the face of the warmth of the Buddha's Compassion. Aṅgulimāla realized that this *samaṇa* was none else but the Buddha himself. Aṅgulimāla urged the Buddha to take him into his refuge. The Buddha while uttreing the pharse '*ehi Bhikkhu ti*' granted permission to Aṅgulimāla.

After taking refuge in the Buddha, Aṅgulimāla became *bhikkhu.* He took refuge in *dhamma* (Law) indeed, and certainly not in any creed or sect. While practising *ānāpāna* and *Vipassanā*,[15] that too under the personal supervision of the Buddha, Aṅgulimāla attained to *arhatahood.* When one undergoes a training of *ānāpāna* and *Vipassanā*, as devised by the Buddha, one's entire energy that is generally consumed by the dark passions (*Vāsanā*), is now transformed into Compassion. A qualitative change, thus, occurs. After becoming an *arhata* Aṅgulimāla, simultanously, becomes Compassionate. Aṅgulimāla was now an *arhata* and he had to go asking for alms in the vicinity of Śravasti, where the Buddha was staying 'for the benefit of all'. Aṅgulimāla, earlier, had killed, atleast, one of the relative of the inhabitant of that locality. When, first time, he went out for begging the people took up stones and sticks and gave him good beating. It was a great moment in the life of Aṅgulimāla. The blood was oozing from the body of Aṅgulimāla, nonetheless, Compassion was over flowing from his heart.

Aṅgulimāla came into contact with the Buddha not like the piece of iron, proverbially, coming into contact with

pārasa, the magic-stone. Aṅgulimāla learnt practising *ānāpāna* and *Vipassanā*, thereafter, attaining to *arhatahood*, thus, converting him to the Compassionate one. True Compassion is not discriminatory; it is all-inclusive. Truly religious person (one who is intune with Law a *dhamma*) is neither communal nor sectarian; he is Compassionate one.

Post-Script

We have talked about the melting away of violence of Aṅgulimāla in the face of the Buddha's Compassion. It is this aspect of Buddhism that has been pointed out, rather, out of proportion. There is another side of violence in Buddhism, as well, and which has been, generally, overlooked. I think this side of violence, also, needs to be looked into.

Once, it came into the mind of General Siha, who was devotee of Nigganthanathputta, later on, known as Vardhamana Mahāvira, to meet the Buddha, with a view to seek clarifications as regard to certain ticklish propositions. General Siha met the Buddha and asked number of questions. The question and its answer in which we are interested, at the moment, is in the form of a dialogue, between the General and the Buddha, that reads, as:

> General Siha: I am a solider. And, it is part of my duty to see that the laws, made by my king, who has appointed me are duly implemented and, also; to wage wars as desired by him. Is *Tathāgata*, whose entire corpus of teaching aims at sympathetically disposing oneself towards the Suffering lot and showering Compassion over them, permits to punish the guilty one ? Again, does *Tathāgata* not allow to fight to protect the honour and life of one's wife and children and property ? Does *Tathāgata* teach that I should surrender before that rascal, who on account of his violence robs me of my possessions. Is *Tathāgata* holds the view that even the war waged for righteousness, too, stands condemned ?"
>
> The Buddha: "Yes, *Tathāgata* is of the strict view that, that war is definately deplorable in which brother kills his brother. But, *Tathāgata* fully supports the war waged for righteousness, as a last resort."

The Buddha's views on war remind us of a verse of *Gurū*

Gobind Singh (1666—1708 A.D.) (Tenth Gurū of the Sikhs) which he wrote in a letter, *Zafar Nāmā,* addressed to Auranga-zeb (r. 1659—1707 A.D.) the Mughal monarch, that reads :

> "*Chu Kāra aza hamā hīlate daraguzashata*
> *Halāla asta burdana ba shamsheer dasta.*'[17]
>
> "When there is no option left, as a
> last resort, it is righteous to pick
> up sword in one's hands."

References and Notes

1. i. 74; Also see Chapter 3, *Nibbāna*, p. 46.
2. *Sum. Vil.* i. 240; ii. 654
3. *M. Purani.* i. 369.
4. *P. Jotikā*, ii. 440.
5. Dhp. A. i. 124; iii. 185.
6. J. A. iv. 180; v. 456.
7. M. ii. 96-105.
8. P. Sūdanī. ii. 743-747.
9. Rhys Davids, C. A. F., (Tr.) *Psalm of the Early Buddhists Brethren* (translation of *Theragāthā*) pp. 318-25.
10. *P. dipani.* ii. 57.

11-14. M. ii. 99.
Chalmers, Lord, *Further Dialogues of the Buddha*, Vol. II, p. 52.

15. Sobti, Harcharan Singh (Ed.) *Vipassanā : The Buddhist Way.*
16. Carus, Paul, *The Gospel of the Buddha*, pp. 118-119.
17. *Zafar Nāmā* (*Dasama Grantha*) Couplet, 46.

7

KĀMACCHANDA : A NĪVARAṆA

Better if we proceed from where *we are*. And, we are in the clutches of *kāmacchanda* (sensual desire), a *nīvaraṇa* (hindrance) in the way of developing *vipassanā* (Insight). *Kāmacchanda* is just one of the five *nīvaraṇas*. A good amount of energy gets wasted through this channel, alone. So, we have a case against it. We propose to examine the *modus operandi* of *Kāmacchanda* in the background of *Theravāda* Buddhism.

What is *Kāmacchanda* ? The term *kāmacchanda* consists of two word components, *Kāma+chanda*. Subjectively speaking *Kāma* means, "(a) enjoyment, pleasure on occasion of sense, (b) sense-desire,"[1] *Chanda* stands for "impulse, excitement, intention, resolution, will, desire for, wish for, delight in."[2] When both the words put together *kāmacchanda* means sensual desire and it is only enlarged term of *kāma*."[3] *Kāmacchanda*, therefore, operates through five channels of sense-organs and manifests itself in equal number of forms viz. vizible, sound, smell, taste and tangible. To add further, these forms can be classified constituting *Kāmacchanda*, only when these happen to be "agreeable, pleasant, liked, enticing, connected with sensual pleasure, alluring."[4] *kāma* not only dominates over the multifarious activities of human beings, it occupies similar position in Theravāda Buddhism, as well. It is placed number one in the scheme of the three *taṇhās*[5] (cravings): three *esanās*[6] (longings); the four *upādānas*[7] (attachment); the four *āsavās*[8] (intoxicants of mind); the four *oghas*[9] (floods of worldly turbulence); the five *nīvaraṇas*[10] (hindrances); *Satta Anusuya*[11] and the ten *sañyojanas*[12] fetters etc. And, we are concerned, at the moment, with *Kāma* (or *Kāmacchanda*) as a *nīvaraṇā* in the way of developing *vipassanā*.

When one indulges in the forms 'agreeable' and 'alluring', it does give enjoyment. The repeated performances of sensual-indulgence, in course of time, takes the form of habit and is likened to spider's web. Here, we need to remind ourselves that, "*Sabbe Kāma aniccāti*: the pleasures of senses are transient in nature."[13] The perception of *anicca* (impermanence), naturally, leads one to *anattā* (no-self) and *Dukkha*. When every thing belonging to phenomenal existence is subject to law of flux, *atta* (self) is not at all an exception to it. This realization helps one to drop ego. Again, it is through the awareness of the universal phenomenon of impermanence that one learns that the *Dukkha* is an outcome of unsuccessful attempt at manipulating things which are, infact, not things but processes. Also, in order to dispense with sensual pleasures, an indulgent one is made to visualize these pleasures, as (i) *aṭṭhikankhala* (a chain of bones); (ii) *maṇsapesi* (a peace of decaying flesh); (iii) *aṅgāra-Kāsu* (a pit of growing cinders); (iv) *asisūna* (a slaughter-house); (v) *Sappa-Sira* (a Snake's Head)."[14]

Kāmacchanda the first among the *pañca nīvaraṇa* is also described in *Sammaññaphala sutta*[15] by means of a beautiful simile. When *Kāmacchanda* preys upon a man, the latter, instantly, happens to acquire the psyche of a debtor who has failed to payback his contracted loan. Buddhaghosa (5th. A. D.) in *Sumaṅgala Vilāsini*,[16] a commentary on *Dīghanikāya* has quite convincingly explained the similarity that exists between the mode of behaviour of an undischarged debtor and the lustful being. The point of similarity, however, between them is their capacity to endure. The debtor andures all the possible forms of humiliation at the hands of his creditor. The man overpowered by *Kāmacchanda* is by no means less heroic in enduring the similar injuries inflicted upon him, in the course of seeking their gratification. The search for gratification of sensual pleasures alongwith its results is beautifully illustrated in the *Potalia Sutta*, as under:

> A butcher throws before a dog tormented by hunger, a bare and fleshless bone with which he cannot satisfy his hunger—like such a bare bone are the sensual pleasures, full of torment and Suffering, out of which only evil arise............Sensual pleasures are like a beautiful dream-vision, which vanishes when one awakes, like a borrowed treasure on account of which one is envied by those who do not know that it is only borrowing.[17]

The above illustrations make one thing amply clear that the craving for sensual pleasures is sure to lead us astray. Passions, smouldering or boiling, for sensual pleasures, are decidedly great hindrances and ought to be extinguished while looking after the spiritual aspect of the Becoming. The one emancipated from the lustful feeling is compared with the debtor who has not only paid back his debt but also earned a surplus for maintenance in future.

So far, we have tried to acquaint ourselves with *Kāmacchanda* operating as a defiling factor that pollutes the human mind. The mind in its primordial form, in Buddhism, is characterized as pure radiant. The mind gets defiled on account of external impurities.[18] These impurities are nothing but *nīvaraṇas* in the way of discovering the purity of mind. The mind overwhelmed by sensual lust is compared to a bowl of water mixed with lac or turmeric or blue or yellow dye, in the following manner:

> Suppose, *brahmin*, a bowl of water mixed with lac or turmeric or blue or yellow dye, and suppose a man with good insight should look closely for the reflection of his own face. *He would not know or see it as it really is.* Just so, *brahmin*, when one dwells with his heart possessed by sensual lust overwhelmed by sensual lust, and knows not in very truth any refuge from sensual lust that has arisen—at such time he neither knows nor sees in very truth his own profit.[19]

Vipassanā meana *'to see things as they really are'*. The sensuel lust or any *nīvaraṇa* for that matter causes blindness of insight and as a result blurs our true vision of 'things and beings' *as they are*.

Let us see how *vīpassanā is* aroused following the course formulated by the Buddha. The Buddha in *Mahāsatipaṭṭhāna*

Sutta[20] of *Dīgha Nikāya* has delineated the path of suppressing *nīvaraṇas* with the aid of *sati* (mindfulness) that straight away observes the bodily and mental phenomenon without having any recourse to the practising of *Jhāna*. The phenomenon of corporeal organism, in the instant *sutta*, is divided into fourfold foundations of mindfulness: '*Kāya* (body), *vedanā* (feeling), *citta* (state of mind) and *dhamma* (mental objects). The *pañca-nīvaraṇas* fall within the purview of *Dhammānupassanā*. Regarding *Kāmacchanda* it is stated, thus:

> "Herein, O *Bhikkhu*, a brother when within him is sensuous desire, is aware of it, reflecting: 'I have within me sensuous desire.' or again, when within him is no sensuous desire, he is aware of this. And he knows of the uprising of such desire unfelt before, knows too of his putting aside that unrisen sensuous desire, knows too of the non-arising in future of that banished sensuous desire.''[21]

As a result of regularly practising mindfulness regarding diverse mental phenomenon, one *discovers* oneself to be a *draṣṭā* (Seer) and views the rise and fall of *Kāmacchanda* from a distance, in a detached manner. There is a beautiful illustration in *Śiva-purāṇa* regarding viewing of *Kāmacchanda* in this detached manner. Let us be familiar with the details of account of '*Kāma's* destruction by *Śiva*,' relevant to our discussion.

Śiva contemplates :

> "How is it that obstacles have cropped up while I am performing the great penance ? How can be that wicked person who has made my mind highly perturbed ?
>
> With love I have described in bad taste another man's women. I have contravened rules of virtue and transgressed the bounds of the Vedas."
>
> He (Śiva) saw *kāma* stationed on His left side with his bow fully drawn and ready to discharge the arrow, *Kāma* was haughty and so was very senseless.
>
> ......Standing high up in the air, holding the arrow and the bow, *kāma* discharged his arrow, usually unerring on Śiva.
>
> The infallible weapon became futile on the Great Lord.

The furious weapon calmed down in regard to the Great Soul, Śiva.

Kāma was frightened when his weapon failed. Standing there and seeing Lord Śiva, the conquerer of death in front, he trembled.

When the gods eulogised thus, a great flame of fire sprang from the third eye of the infuriated Śiva.

That fire originating instantaneously from the eye in the middle of his forehead blazed with flames shooting up and resembling the fire of final dissolution in refulgence.

Even before the gods had the time to say; 'Let him be forgiven, let him be excused.' it reduced *Kāma* to ashes [22]

The two key-expressions that deserve special attention are 'the third-eye' and 'in the middle of his forehead'. In fact, these two underline single phenomenon. The mind of *puthujana*, using Buddhist terminology, either moves in the past or in the future and *both are not there*. When the mind is brought in the middle i.e. in the present, it simply disappears. In this state of no mind one is *draśṭā* and which is synonymous with the third-eye. The technique of *Vippassanā* when followed diligently, leads to the self-discovery of being *draśṭā*.

The perpetual practice of reviewing the phenomenon of *Kāmacchanda*, as in the instant case, results in deepening the insight or *vipassanā* to such an extent that one actually starts visualising the three phenomenal aspects of existence. The *aniccā* for him is no more a (borrowed) concept. *Aniccā* by way of corraboration helps in visualising *anattā*. Thereafter, it becomes imperative to *see dukkha* as a resultant of clinging to something *which is not there*. This way one qualifies after undergoing a practice of *vipassanā* that may be *kāyanupassanā*' *vedanānupassanā*, *cittānupasanā*, or *dhammānupassanā*, *to see things as they really are*.

When the five channels of sense-organs are plugged with *vipassanā* the leakage of energy is stopped and it is transformed into *Karuṇā* (Compassion). *Karuṇā*, in Buddhist sense, is effected through the transformation of energy, otherwise, wasted while indulging in *Kāmacchanda* or other *nīvaraṇās*.

References

1. Rhys Davids, T.W. and Stede, William, *Pāli English Dictionary*, p. 203.

2-3. *Ibid.*, p. 274.

4. *Majjhima Nikāya*, Vol. I, pp. 118-119. (Nālandā) "*Pañcme, bhikkhave, Kāmaguṇā*"........ "*Iṭṭhā Kantā manāpa pīyarūpā kāmupasaṁhitā rajaniyā, sotaviññeyyā Saddhā*........ Horner, I.B., (Tr.) *Middle Length Sayings* (translation of *Majjhima Nikāya*) Vol. I, p. 112.

5. (i) *Kāma-taṇhā*; (ii) *bhava-taṇhā*; (iii) *Vibhava-taṇhā*.

6. (i) *Kāmesanā*; (ii) *Bhavesanā*; (iii) *Brahmacariyesanā*

7. Four *upādāna—Kāma upādāna, diṭṭi-upādāna, selabbata—upādāna* and *attavāda—upādāna*.

8. Four *Āsavas—Kamāsava, Bhavāsava, Diṭṭhi-āsava* and *Avijjā-āsava*.

9. Four *Ogha—Kāma-ogha, Bhava-ogha, Diṭṭhi-ogha* and *Avijjā-ogha*.

10. (i) *Kāmacchanda*; (ii) *Vyāpāda*; (iii) *Thīnamiddha*; (iv) *Uddhacca-kukucca*; (v) *Vicckicchā*.

11. (i) *Kāmarāgai*; (ii) *Bhavarāga*; (iii) *Patigha* (iv) *Māṇa*; (v) *Ditthi*; (vi) *Viccikicahā*; (vii) *Avijja*.

12. *Ten samyojanas—Sakkāyadiṭṭhi, Vicikicchā, Selabbata-parāmāsa, Kāmarāga, Patigha, Rūparāga, Arūparāga, Māṇa, Uddhacca, Avijjā*.

13. Morris, R., (Ed.) *Aṅguttara Nikāya* Vol. II. p. 177.

14. *Pāli English Dictionary* p. 203.

15. Rhys Davids, T.W. and Carpenter, J.E. (Ed.) *Dīgha Nikāya* Vol. I. p. 71.

16. Rhys Davids, T.W. and Carpenter, J.E., (Ed.) *Sumaṅgala Vīlāsini* (commentary on *Dīgha Nikāya*) Vol. I, p. 213.

17. Treneker, V. (Ed.) *Majjhima Nikāya* Vol. I, p. 364, Winternitz, Maurice, *History of Indian Literature*, Vol. II, p. 72.

18. Morris, R., (Ed). *Anguttara Nikāya*, Vol. I, p. 10 : *Pabhassaramidaṁ, bhikkhave, cittaṁ. Taṁ ca Kho āgantukehi upakkilesehi upakkiliṭṭhaṁ, ti pabhassaramidaṁ, bhikk-*

have, cittaṁ. Taṁ ca Kto āgantūkehi upakkileshei vippamutaṁ.

19. *Saṁyutta Nikāya*, Vol. V, p. 107. (Nālandā) Woodward, F.L., (Tr.) *The Kindered Sayings* (translation of *Saṁyutta Nikāya*) p. 103.
20. Rhys Davids, T.W. and Carpenter, J.E. (Ed). *Dīgha Nikāya* Vol. II, pp. 290-315.
    Rhys Davids, C.A.F., T.W. (Tr.) *Dialogues of the Buddha* (translation of *Dīgha Nikāya*). part-II, pp. 322-346.
21. *Dīgha Nikāya*, Vol. II, p. 300.
    Dialogues of the Buddha, Part II, pp. 334-335.
22. Shastri, J.L., (Ed.) *Ancient Indian Tradition and Mythology, Siva-purāṇa* : *Satarudra Saṁhita*, Vol. II. Part II, pp. 544-545.

8

BUDDHISM : A RESPONSE TO SECULARIZATION*

Secularization, or, in other words, 'de-divinization of human consciousness', an historical process, *has* created a crisis of conscience for a reasonable modern man. This paper, aims at identifying this process and to suggest the Buddha's Way, a way out of the crisis.

The seventeenth century of modern Europe, which brought into being, the geniuses like Kepler, Galileo and Newton goes into the annals of human history, as a century of scientific revolution. These scientists, interestingly enough, were deeply religious persons. Johannes Kepler (1571-1630), German astronomer and mathematician, (who was Protestant, and later on, took refuge with Jesuits), while recognising 'a divine ravishment in investigating the works of God' states, that :

> There is God in us, and our warmth comes from His movements,
> This spirit has descended from the heavenly seats.[1]

Kepler is aptly identified as an epitome of Copernican astronomy, when, with an absolute certainity, the former conforms to the view that, "all the planets revolve around the Sun, with the exception of the moon, which alone has the earth as

*Paper presented and published in the proceedings of the International Symposium on India and World Literature held during 25th February to 1st March, 1985, at Vigyan Bhawan, New Delhi.

its centre".[2] Kepler's most revolutionary discovery was "that the orbit of the planet is not a perfect circle", on the contrary it is elliptic.[3] Thus, Kepler substituted ellipses for circles and established that each planet moves on an ellipse, which resulted in undermining awe associated with circles, considered as perfect figures, since the times of ancient Greeks.

Later on, Galilei Galileo (1564-1642), an Italian practical scientist, subscribing to empirical method, in his book *Dialogue on the Great World Systems* (1632) only, avowed the system of Copernicus. Nicholaus Copernicus (1473-1543), Polish astronomer, dedicated his book, *On the Revolutions of the Heavenly Spheres* (1543), to Pope Paul III. He refrained from publishing his book, that he might be charged with calling in question the authority of Catholic Church. Because, Copernicus's observations proved directly opposed to the system of Claudius Ptolemy (2nd Century A. D.), Greek astronomer of Alexandria, and has concluded that :

> ...You see, therefore that for all these reasons it is more probable that the earth moves than that it is at rest.[4]

To add, Copernicus observed two separate motions of the earth : the earth oscillates round the Sun once in a year, and simultaneously, the earth turns on its axis once every day. The system of Copernicus was not only diametrically opposed to that of Ptolemy, it was also not in accord with the Holy Bible.

Galileo in his 'hand writing on the margin of his own copy of the *Dialogue*', comments :

> And who can doubt that it will lead to the worst disorders when minds created free by God are compelled to submit slavishly to an outside Will ?[5]

Again, in his letter written in the year 1615 and addressed to the Grand Duches Christina of Tuscany, *Concerning the Use of Biblical Quotations in Matters of Science*, Galileo wrote:

> Methinks that in the discussion of natural problems, we ought not to begin at the authority of places of scriptures, but at sensible experiments and necessary demonstrations. For, from the Divine Word, the sacred scripture and nature did both alike

> proceed...Nature, being inexorable and immutable, and never passing the bounds of the laws assigned her,...I conceive that concerning natural effects, that which either sensible experience sets before our eyes, or necessary demonstrations do prove unto us, ought not, upon any account, to be called into question, much less condemned upon the testimony of tests of scripture, which may under their words, couch senses seemingly contrary there to...Nor does God less admirably discover himself to us in Nature's actions, than in the Scripture's sacred dictions.[6]

The book of Nature and the books of the Bible, in Galileo's view, as 'proceed alike from the Divine Word' are therefore to be adorned equally.

Of the three characters in the *Dialogue*, Simplicious holds the system of Ptolemy, unassailable, and is depicted not in acceptable form. Salviatus, another character, obviously, fashioned to advocate the system of Copernicus, asserts authoritatively, that:

> —It is most certain that it is not the Earth but the Sun, rather that is fixed in the centre of the world...[7]

Notwithstanding the warning of Cardinal Robert Bellarmine, neither to adhere to nor to defend the theory of Copernicus, being contrary to Scripture, Galileo followiag the dictate of his conscience did otherwise. Consequently, Galileo suffered at the hands of Inquisition.[8]

Sir Isaac Newton's (1642-1727) faith in the existence of Almighty God is well expressed in the third book of his classic *Philasophiae Naturalis Principia Mathematica* (1686), and under the caption General Scholium, Newton writes:

> This most beautifully system of the sun, planets and comets, could only proceed from the counsel and domination of an intelligent and powerful Being.[9]

But, these scientists, at the same time, were true to their respective discoveries, and would have been horrified if they had imagined, even for a moment, that their discoveries would result in destroying the religious faith of the people, finally, leading to the Death of God. The historical process is objective to the extent that it does not conceed to the demands of certain individuals. The historical process of secularization did commence notwithstanding, desiring contrarily. The process of secularization, as Loen E. Arnold, defines in his book, *Secularization: Science Without God* (1967), needs to be looked in to. Arnold writes:

> ...that secularization is the historical process by which the world is de-divinized. Of course, we do not mean really de-divinized as though God was at first actually present in the world and later withdrew from it, we mean divinized as far as human consciousness is concerned. Formerly, man was conscious of living in a world whose order pointed to God and in which God acted directly, to day, that is no longer true, we are neither conscious of God in the cosmic order nor of his direct activity.[10]

This process of 'de-divinization of human consciousness' that was set in continued throughout the eighteenth and nineteenth century. Pierre Simon Laplace (1749-1827), French scientist, who flourished during the eighteenth century, in his book *Celestial Mechanics*, published in the year 1802, designed to proceed further in the direction of Newton's *Principia*, with regard to the irregularities observed in the motions of Jupiter and Saturn, thus appearing inconsistent with the theory of Gravity comes forward with the novel hypothesis in his book *Celestial Mechanics*, and he observes, that:

> We developed the secular variations of the elements of the planetary system, which do not return to the same state till after the lapse of many centuries.[11]

Thus, Laplace established that the irregularities in the movements of planets were not cumulative, as Newton had contemplated, but, were self-correcting and to bring in God to correct them was nothing short of fiction.

Charles Darwin (1809-1882), the Britisher, (again a religious person who used the expression Creator in the last para of his book) delayed the publication of his book, *The Origin of Species*[12] for fear of outraging religious tradition (as Copernicus did three centuries earlier), for many years. Darwin's book, at last, published in the year 1859, was still another unintended attack on the sanctity of the Holy Bible. In the first book of Bible, called Genesis, we find that:

And God said, Let us make
man in our image, after
our likeness-......
So God created in his
own image, in the image of God
created he them.[13]

Darwin's book was an attempt to establish the theory of evolution, and thus, happened to repudiate this very notion of man as God's special creation. The theory of evolution, as propounded by Darwin, could hardly escape the wrath of fundamentalists. The controversy touched its peak in 1925, in America and gained global significance, when John Thomas Scopes, a teacher in the local high school, in Dayton, Tennessee was found guilty in the court of Law, having taught the theory of evolution.[14]

All these discoveries of science, and reactions that followed, in one form or the other, did adversely effect the religious faith of modern European. The cracks in the faith and utter disbelief in the existence of God fairly reflect in the modern European literature. Matthew Arnold's (1822-1888) poem, *Dover Beach*, composed in the year 1851, originates from the feeling of crack, occured in the orthodox faith of the poet and the people. The poet expresses his agony, thus:

... ...

The Sea of Faith
Was once, too, at the full, and round
earth's shore.
Lay like the folds of a bright
girdle unfurled.
But now I only hear
Its melancholy, lone, withdrawing roar,
Retreating to the breath
Of the night-wind, down the vast
edges drear
And naked shingles of the world.[15]

With regard to utter disbelief in God, we quote just one reference from Albert Camus' (1913-1960) novel, *The Plague* (1947). It is a dialogue between Dr. Bernard Rieux and Jean Tarrou, which reveals, as follows:

> 'It comes to this' Tarrou said almost casually,
> 'What interests me is learning how to become Saint'
> 'But you don't believe in God (exclaimed Rieux)
> 'Exactly ! can one be a Saint without God ? that's
> the problem, in fact the only problem, I'am up against
> today'. (reiterated Tarrou [16]

Jean Tarrou, and others, with similar crisis of conscience, can fruitfully seek guidance from Gotama the Buddha, an Asian from an ancient India, who discovered the Path to solve the 'only problem' which not only modern Europe is seized with, but, is also arresting the rest of the civilized world. The Buddha delineated the Path which can lead a 'reasonable man' to discover the state of *Nibbāna*, and, thus, become a Saint, an *arahat*, in Buddhist terminology, however, without professing faith in Personal God.

The Path, delineated, by the Buddha is nothing else, but a definite course for the guidance of the human mind. Significant to add, that, unlike, Jesus Christ[17] and Muhammad[18] neither the Buddha is adorned as a Son of God or an Apostle of God in the *Theravāda* Canon, nor did he like Moses[19] and Nānak,[20] in his discourses, ever maintain that, either he conversed with God, now and then, or his teachings were divinely inspired. Lest, there crops up a suspicion with regard to the authenticity of this observation, better it is to elaborate it, little more. We learn from *Brahmā Sutta*[21], that, initially, the Buddha was reluctant to preach the Way, he had discovered, and it was at the intervention of *Brahmā-Sahampati* that the Buddha conceded to the former's demand. Clarifying the status of *Brahmā* within the hierarchical set-up conceived in Buddhism, K. N. Jayatilleke has worked out the characteristics that differentiates him from the Personal God. "Although there is no Personal God" writes Jayatilleke "with the characteristics of omniscience, omnipotence and infinite goodness, there is the concept of a *Mahā-Brahmā* (Mighty God) who is morally perfect and has very great knowledge and power but is not omniscient and omnipotent".[22] Not only the distinction between Personal God and *Brahmā* is made available, the *Buddhahood* in the *Brahmaṇimantanika Sutta* is identified as "a state far exceeding the knowledge and power of any *Brahmā*.[23] There is no Personal

God in Buddhism is also self-evident from the fact that the Buddha denounced theism of Makkhali Gosāl, his close contemporary. In *Tevijja Sutta* the Buddha ridiculed the idea of God and compared the worshipper of God with that lover who loves a beautiful woman without having seen or knowing nothing about her whereabouts.[24] Besides that the Buddha categorically denies God as a Creator in *Pāṭika Sutta*.[25] Rather, the Buddha described his *Dhamma* a discovery of an ancient Path traversed by others in former times, in the following words:

> This, brethern, is the ancient path, that ancient road, traversed by the rightly enlightened ones of former times...........
> This that I have fully came to know I have declared to the brethern, to the sisters, to lay-men and lay-women.........[26]

Also, only after the attainment of *Sambodhi*, Gotama the *Bodhisatta*, became the Buddha. *Sambodhi* has been correctly characterized as *Svabodhanaṁ*, signifying the fact that one can accomplish it only through one's own efforts and without an exrtaneous aid from any divine agency.

The Buddha's last counsel (according to the legends) to the Venerable Ānanda, thus: "Be yea lamp [Sic] unto yourselves. Be yea a refuge to yourselves. Be take yourselves to no external refuge",[27] rather, delimits, even the extent of assistance sought for from the human quarters. Moreover, the Buddha, when in his First Sermon (*Dhammacakkappavattana Sutta*), preached an avoidance of two extremes: self-indulgence (*Kamasukhalikanuyoga*) and self-mortification (*attakilamathanuyoga*), thereby propounding the Middle Path (*Majjhima paṭipadā*),[28] instantly, epitomized human endeavours *he*[29] had made, during the course of his struggle prior to the attainment of *Nibbāna*.

The Middle Way of the Buddha if practised diligently can lead a reasonable modern man to become a Saint (or an *arahat*) thus, simultaneously resolve the crisis and solve the 'only problem',

References and Notes

1. Kepler, Johannes, *The Harmonies of the World*, p. 849.
2. Ibid. p. 1015.
3. Ibid. p. 892.
4. Copernicus, Nicholaus, *On the Revolutions of the Heavenly Spheres*, p. 520.
5. Galileo, Galilei, *Dialague on the Great World Systems*, p. X (Preface).
6. Burt, Edwin, Arthur, *The Metaphysical Foundation of Modern Physical Science*, pp. 72-73.
7. *Galileo, op.* cit. p. 335.
8. Santillana, Giorgio de. *The Crime of Galileo.*
   This is the most exhaustive account of an episode of trial of Galileo.
   cf. Brecht, Bertolt, *Plays* (*The Crime of Galileo*), Vol. I.
   This play is the dramatized from of trial of Galileo.
9. Newton, Sir Isaac, *Philosophiae Naturalis Principia Mathematical*, p. 544.
   cf. Ibid. pp. 543-547.
10. Arnold, Loen, E., *Secularizatian: Science Without God*, p. 7.
11. Laplace, Pierre Simmon, *Celestial Mechanics*, Vol. III, p. X (Preface).
12. Darwin, Charles, *The Origin of Species.*
    At page 560 of this book Drawin writes :
    "There is grandeur in this view of life, with its several powers, having been originally breathed by the Creator into a few forms or in to one; and that, whilst this planet has gone cycling on according to the fixed law of gravity, from so simple a beginning unless forms most beautiful and most wonderful have been, and are being evolved."
13. Genesis, 1 : 26-27.
14. Ray, Ginger, *Six days or Forever ? Tennesse vs. John Thomas Scopes.*
    cf. Lawrence, Jerome, *Inherit the Wind.* This play is the dramatized form of Scope Trial.

15. Arnold, Matthew, *The Poems of Matthew Arnold*, pp. 256-257.
16. Camus, Albert, *The Plague*, p. 237.
17. St. Matthew : 3 : 17; 16 : 16; St. Mark : 1 : 1 ; 15 : 39; St. Luke : 1 : 35.
18. Qurān : 3 : 144; 3 : 164; 4 : 170; 7 : 158.
19. Oxodus (The Second Book of Old Testament) : 3 : 13; 3 : 14.
20. Ādi Granth, p. 150 & 722.
21. S.v. 167.
22. Jayatilleke, K.N., *The Message of the Buddha*, p. 114.
23. Ibid., p. 115.
    cf. M. 49. (*Brahamaṇimantanika Sutta*) : M.i.326 ff.
24. D. 13. (*Tevijja Sutta*).
    Rhys Davids, T.W., *The Dialogues of the Buddha.* Vol. II, p. 307.
25. D. 24. (*Pāṭika Sutta*) : D. iii. 28-30.
26. S. ii. 105-106.
    Rhys Davids, C.A.F., *The Book of Kindered Sayings*, Part II, pp. 74-75.
    cf. A. iii. 134.
27. D. 16. (*Mahāparinibhāna Sutta*): D. ii. 100.
28. S.v. 420-21.
29. (i) Self Indulgence :
    A. i. 145.
    M. i. 504.
    (ii) Self Mortification :
    M. i. 81.

9

AN IMAGE OF WOMAN AS REFLECTED IN *JĀTAKAS**

There are number of stories contained in the *Jātakaṭṭhakathāvaṇṇaṇā*, which are weaved in one single pattern, aimed at to denigrate woman, and thus painted licentious, in order to 'keep wide awake' the *Bhikkhus* as regard to woman. A very peculiar thing in the Buddhist tradition, in this context, is that at the same time it eulogizes women as *therīs*, whose life-sketches in the form of the *Therīgāthā* form an integral part of the Buddhist Canon. This means, that 'woman *is* capable' to attain *Nibbāna*. Two contrary views about woman, certainly, involve a contradiction. I propose to examine this very contradiction, in this paper.

The *Jātakas* in Pāḷi language form a very vast literature containing the teachings of the Buddha. They are in the form of *555* main stories of the previous births of the Buddha (but the number of *Jātakas* available so far is *547*) and a number of interlinking stories of the *Bodhisatta* striving for the fulfilment of ten perfections (*Pārmīs*),[1] for the attainment of Buddhahood. The *Jātakas* in their original form were in verses (*gāthās*) and the number of verses contained in the available *547 Jātakas* is *2440*. The theme of teaching has been

*Paper presented at International Symposium on the Topic "Folklore in Slavonic Finno-ugrian and Indian Literature" (FOLSFULL), Department of Slavic Studies, University of Delhi, from 27th to 31st March, 1989.

interwoven through these verses. The details about them were surviving in oral tradition in the society. Since the Buddhist tradition was alive in India for centuries together, the people had no difficulty in understanding these verses and the ideas contained therein in the background of the introductory material already available in oral tradition. In course of time there was the chance of disappearence of the oral tradition. Therefore, Buddhaghosa (5th century A. D.) an eminent commentator of the words of the Buddha, understood the psychological trends of the society and put all snch materials into writing rightly adjusting them with the theme of the verses. Thus, each *Jātaka* appeared in the form of one complete story of the deeds of *Bodhisatta*. Of course, in many cases the story is further interwoven with a number of other stories connected with the theme. Every single *Jātaka* story consists of five component parts *viz.* (i) *Paccuppannavathu*, (ii) *Atitavathu*, (iii) *Gāthā*, (iv) *Veyyākaraṇa* and (v) *Samodhāna* or in other words it passes through these five successive stages. Right in the beginning, one is made familiar with the context (*paccuppaṇnavathu*) which prompts the Buddha to narrate a *Jātaka* story; then a story of the previous birth of the Buddha (*atitavathu*) when, actually he was *Bodhisatta*, is narrated; thereafter *gāthā* supported by *abhisambuddhagāthā* is recited followed by a word for word commentory of the *gāthā* (*veyyākarṇa*). The fifth and the last component part of the *Jātaka* story is *Samodhāna*. Here the characters of the 'story of the present', are identified with those of the 'story of the past' alongwith it the psychological effect of the discourse on the minds of the hearers is described.[2] Our main concern, at present, is with *atitavathu* and psychological effect on the minds of the hearers.

The *Jātaka* stories we have selected for an appraisal, in the background of the Buddhist tradition, are contained in the *Itthivagga* of *Jātakaṭṭhakathāvaṇṇaṇā*. These stories depict woman as "lustful, profligate, vile and degraded"[3] and are symbolized as "a sex composed of wickedness and guile, unknowable, uncertain as the path of fishes in the water",[4] "given opportunity all women work iniquity"[5] and last but not the least are compared to "highways, rivers, courtyards, hostelties or taverns, which to all alike extend universal hospitality".[6] The psychological effect of these stories on the minds of hearers is invariably that of renunciation of the household life in favour of entering into state of homelessness. Rati Lal N. Mehta, while writing on 'Position of Woman' in his book *Pre-Buddhist India* (1939), based on *Jātaka* stories, is quite nearer to the truth when he opines that 'these utterances are from, and for the ascetics—those who, perhaps, tired of their own weakness, and diespaired of their failures want to run away from the world".[7] But, this tutored psychological effect involves wider issues connected with the Buddhist tradition and therefore, calls for an analysis as regard to the position of woman as contemplated in the said tradition.

II

The Buddha was critical about women. This unhappy conclusion is readily derived, mainly, from three Canonical evidences. These evidences are : (i) the Buddha's reluctance to admit women into *Saṅgha*, (ii) an institution of *aṭṭhagurū-dhammā* exclusively meant for *Bhikkhunis* and (iii) the Buddha's advice to Ānanda 'to keep wide awake' as regard to woman. It seems to be a case of misreading of Canon. A misreading of Canon, whether intentional or otherwise, history of religions tells us, creates problems. At times, a misreading stems from an outlook not rooted in the soil of the land. It needs to look into an alleged hostility of the Buddha against woman, in the background of an indigenous cultural heritage.

The Buddha's reluctance, in the instant case, is rather revealing. Let us look into the circumstances in which the Buddha allowed an admission of women into *Saṅgha*. While going through the text of *Cūllavagga*,[8] (which is second sub-part of the *Khanddhaka*, second book of *Vinaya Piṭaka*), we learn, that, when the Buddha was staying at Kapilavatthu, in the Nigrodha Park, Mahāpajapati the Gotami, Gotama's aunt and later on his foster-mother, visited the Buddha and asked for his permission thrice 'to enter the homeless state under the doctrine and discipline proclaimed by the *Tathāgata*'. But to her utter dismay the Buddha continued to remain adamant in not allowing women 'to enter the homeless state.'

If Gotama the Buddha was adamant Gotamī too was determined.

The story continues. But, now we find the Buddha staying in Mahāvana at Vesālī. Imagine for a while Gotamī alongwith number of ladies of Sākya clan, having her shaven head, wearing orange coloured robes, with swollen feet and covered with dust, sad and sorrowful, weeping and in tears, arrives at Vesālī and is standing outside under the entrance porch of Mahāvana. The scene, so to say, is pathetic. Ānand, the chief disciple of the Buddha, happens to be there. He is moved and enquires about their plight and consequently intervenes in the matter. Ānand arequests the Buddha for admitting Mahāpajapati—the Goṭamī and other ladies of Sākya clan into *Saṅgha*. Ānanda, repeats the request thrice, but, in vain. At the same time Ānanda refuses to accept his defeat and changes his strategy. Now, Ānanda does not request but asks:

> "Are women, Lord, capable when they have gone forth from the household life and entered discipline proclaimed by the Blessed one—are they capable of realising the fruit of conversion, or of the second path, or of the third path, or of Arhantship ?
>
> "They are capable, Ānanda",[9] Buddha replies

Hence, at this juncture, Ānanda reminds the Buddha of Gotamī's great service rendered to him, when as aunt and nurse she nourished him and gave him milk, and on the death of his mother suckled the Blessed One at her own breast. Ānanda seems to have sentimentalized the whole situation. When Gotami, at one time, 'Suckled the Blessed One at her own breast', the Blessed One is not short of milk of human kindness. The Buddha's acceptance of 'capability' of women, and Gotamī's service rendered, prepared a ground for an admission of women into *Saṅgha*. The Buddha grants the permission, but, with condition, thus:

> "If then Ānanda, Mahapajapati the Gotami take upon herself the Eight Chief Rules (*aṭṭhagurudhamma*), let that be reckoned to her as her initiation".[10]

Woman's 'capability' and the Buddha's reluctance to initiate woman *is* disturbing. Our primary concern, at the moment, of course, is to decode the meanings of the Buddha's reluctance.

Every human being is bisexual in the sense that it combines both the masculine and feminine characteristics irrespective of being man or woman. This psychological truth was discovered in India, long ago, and projected in the myth of *ardhanāriśvra* preserved in *Śivapurāṇa*.[11] The myth of *ardhanāriśvara* takes the form of masculinity and femininity, ingrained in human psyche. *Sakhisampradāya* of Swami Haridas that advocates the view that 'there is only one male and all others are females' has its roots in this very human psyche. The male adherents of this *sampradāya* dress themselves like woman and identify themselves with Rādhā and conduct themselves likewise. Those who are attracted towards this kind of devotion to God in the form of Krishna, certainly imbibe disproportionate quantity of feminine traits in their psychic beings. It is a case of projecting femininity rooted in the male biological organism.

The fact of human beings imbibing composite psychic nature, is also acknowledged by Gurū Nānak (1469-1539). The Founder—Gurū of Sikhism, when he says, that:

> "There is a woman in man
> and man in woman
> only the wise can discern it."[12]

Bisexuality as a psychic phenomenon is a subject of study in modren psychology, too. "Every individual", discovered Sigmund Freud (1856-1939) "displays a mixture of the character-traits belonging to his own and the opposite sex; and he shows a combination of activity and passivity whether or not these last character-traits tally with his biological ones."[13] He identifies activity in woman as a masculine trait and passivity in man as feminine one. Therefore, psychologically speaking every individual is to be viewed in this background.

The Buddha on the one hand was reluctant to admit woman into *Saṅgha* and on the other hand he endorsed the query of Ānanda as regard to the capability of woman for realising 'the fruit of conversion' when 'entered the homeless state under the doctrine and discipline proclaimed by the Blessed One'. '*Woman is capable*', here, woman is viewed as a psychological being that imbibes both the masculine and feminine character-traits. The capability of woman as a psychological being is directly linked up with 'the doctrine and discipline of the Buddha'. What is there in woman and doctrine and discipline, that goes well with each other ? The basic thing in the doctrine of the Buddha is that it is meditative in nature. In order to draw any benefit from the doctrine of the Buddha it is imperative that it suits the temperament of the person concerned. In *Theravāda* Buddhism even an object of meditation needs to be selected, with the guidance of *Kalyān-mitta*, according to one's temperament.[14] So it is a temperament of the person pursuing religious discipline that works as a deciding factor.

As already stated that the Buddhist discipline *is* meditative (and not devotional) in its approach. Now, whether it suits masculine or feminine temperament, it is yet to be seen. Masculinity in its contents is through and through assertive, active and hence egoistic. It is difficult for a person having a *overall* masculine temperament to accept 'the other'. It is prerogative of feminine temperament alone to accept 'the other' and melt *oneself* therein. There is 'no other' in *Theravāda* Buddhism conducive as an object of devotion that feeds the feminine-self. Therefore, we can safely conclude that the Way of the Buddha suits the person imbibing masculine temperament, alone.

The Buddha's acceptance of 'capability of woman' to become *arahata*, refers to the masculinity inherent in her being. Mrs. C. A. F. Rhys Davids in the introduction to *Psalms of the Sisters* (translation of *Therigāthā*) has made certain observations useful for our present discussion. While drawing a distinction between 'Indian Marys and their Christian sister's she states, that:

> But herein we note a sharp contrast between these Indian Mary's and their Christian sisters. Where, he, the Central figure, intervenes, and gratitude is blent with adoration, the little poem (*Theri-gatha*) reveals no word of quasiamorous self-surrender to the person or image of the Beloved, such as characterizes not a

> little of that Christian literature for which the Song of Soloman—"I am my beloved's and my beloved is mine'—was a sacred archetype".[15]

Again, Mrs. Rhys Davids comments that:

> The utmost length a *theri* presumes to go in relating herself to her Teacher, is to claim spiritual fatherhood in Him....[16]

To add further, Mrs. Rhys Davids holds the view "that of the four notorious Magdalens who found peace and purity in the order of *Bhikkhunis*—Aḍḍhākasī, Vimlā, Abhay's mother and Ambapāli—not one expresses any deep 'feeling of personal attachment to the teacher".[17] The possibilities of imbibing feminine traits, such as, 'self-surrender', and deep personal attachment' by the *theris* numbering 101, whose, life-sketches and verses certifying the fact of having attained *arahathood*, we find in *Therīgāthā*, are ruled out. These *therīs*, therefore, are exceptional woman being dominantly masculine in their mental disposition. This is also borne by the fact that "life under the Vinaya was one of both active and contemplative discipline".[18]

III

Normally woman is more feminine and consequently less masculine. The feminitity inclines for to love that needs a partner. This resulted in the involvement between the *Bhikkhus* and *Bhikkhunīs*. After allowing woman's admission to *Saṅgha* the Buddha told Ānanda, that:

> "If, Ānanda, woman had not receive permission to go out from the household life and enter the homeless state, under the doctrine and discipline proclaimed by the (*Tathāgatā*), then would the pure religion, Ānanda, have last long, the good law would have stood fast for a thousand years. But, since Ānanda, women have now recited that permission, the pure religion, Ānanda, will not now last so long, the good law will stand fast for only five hundred years".[19]

The Buddha anticipated the decline of 'good law' and 'pure religion' on account of expressive femininity of woman.

The 'good' and 'pure' refers to the basic Buddhist doctrine and discipilne that envisages meditation demanding fullest expression of masculinity inherent in human psyche. We know that the 'good' and 'pure' declined in due course of time because of intermixing 'love' in it. Love made meditation 'bad' and 'impure'.

The Buddha's permission to woman was conditional demanding strictly observing *aṭṭhagurūdharmmā*. It is, in fact, the First Rule that caused much agitation in the minds of women for a just cause, in a way, and also for men only interested in painting the Buddha as anti-woman. The First Rule reads:

> A *Bhikkhuni*, even if of a hundred years standing, shall make salutation, to, shall rise up in the presence of, shall bow down before and shall perform all proper duties towards a *Bhikkhu*, if only just initiated....[20]

It appears that the Rule commands subservience of *Bhikkhunis* to *Bhikkhus* irrespective of the former's seniority. But, the matter is not that simple. The Rule ought to be looked into in the background of indigenous cultural heritage. We know as Indians the value of reverence shown by man and woman for each other, in day to day living. When woman, in general, (except wife, of course) shows reverence for man, due to any reason, the latter, is handicapped to forge any sexual relation with that woman. Since, when a man gets reverence from a woman it feeds his ego. Inflow of sex leading to a relation costs man an ego and which he would rarely like to forego. The First Rule was simply to guard against an inflow of sexual feeilng.[21] 'salutation', 'rising up' 'bowing down'—all these amount to show reverence for the *Bhikkhus*.

How ironic it seems to be that Ānanda who once pleaded the case of woman's admission into *Saṅgha* should ask the Buddha as to how to conduct themselves with regard to woman. The queries and its replies need to be examined in the background of Buddhist discipline. The dialogue between the Buddha and Ānanda dilating on the subject reads, thus:

"How are we to conduct ourselves
Lord with regard to women-kind ?"
"As not seeing them, Ānanda"
"But, if we should see them, what are we to do?"
"No talking Ānanda"
"But, if they should speak to us,
Lord, what are we to do ?
"Keep wide awake, Ānanda"[22]

The reference to womankind in this dialogue is generally construed to mean to denigrate woman. If we emphasize upon the expression 'seeing' and 'talking' the conclusion can not be otherwise. But, when viewed in the background of Buddhist doctrice and discipline, the emphasis should be on "*Sati Ānanda, upaṭṭhāpetabbaṁ*" or 'keep wide awake'. The *Bhikkhu* is 'to keep wide awake' at all times and in all circumstances. The reference to women is incidental.

Thus, we come across three dimensions of woman in Buddhist Canonical literature, such as, *therī*—who is exceptionally masculine and therefore has attained *Nibbāna*; *Bhikkhuni*; one who is on the path and an average woman who is painted licentious. The *Bhikkhu* is warned, if at all, as regard to licentious waman, one of the very popular theme in folk literature. He is also guarded against his own inflow of sexual feelings by means of the First Rule binding on *Bhikkhunis*. Buddhism is not prejudiced against woman as such, rather, it presents a balanced view about woman.

References and Notes

1. These ten *pārmīs* are : almsgiving (*dāna*), goodness (*sīla*), renunciation (*neśkamma*), wisdom (*prajñā*), energy (*vīrya*), patience, (*khsānti*), truth (*Satta*), resolution (*Sankapoo*), friendliness (*mettya*) and equanimity (*uppekhā*). These *pārmīs* are beautifully illustrated in *Jātaka* No. 35.

2. Mehta, Rati Lal N., *Pre-Buddhist India*, p. xix.
3. Cowell E.B. (Gen. Ed.) *Jātaka Stories*, (Vol. I+II), Vol. I, p. 147.
4. *Ibid.* p. 155.
5. *Ibid.* p. 151.
6. *Ibid.* p. 161.
7. Mehta, Rati Lal N., *op. cit.*, p. 289.
8. *Cūllavagga* x.1.2 to x.1.4
   Rhys Davids, T.W. and Oldenberg, Herman (Tr.) *Vinaya-Texts*, pp. 320-322.
9. *Ibid.* x. 1.4. p. 322.
10. *Ibid.* x. 1.5. p. 324.
11. *Śiva-purāna* : *Śatarudrassaṁhitā* chapter III cf.
    Rao, Gopinath T.A., *Elements of Hindu Iconography*, Vol. II Part I, pp. 321-331. For statutes of *ardhanāriśvara*, see plates No. 95-98.
12. *Ādigranth*, p. 879.
13. Strachey, James (Gen. Ed.) *The Complete Psychological Works of Sigmund Freud*, Vol. III, p. 220.
14. Nyanmoli, Bhikkhu (Tr.) *The Path of Purification* (translation of *Visuddhi magga)*, pp. 102 ff.
15. Rhys Davids, C.A.F., *Psalms of The Sisters-1* translation of *Therīgāthā)*, p. xxxii.
16. *Idem.*
17. *Ibid.* p. xxxiii.
18. *Ibid.* p. xxxiv.
19. *Cūllavagga* p. 256.
20. *Vinaya Texts Cullavagga*, op. cit. x.1.4.
21. Rajneesh, *Essa Dhammo Sanantano*, Vol. I, p. 77.
22. *Dīgha Nikāya*, Part II, p. 141.

10

ON BUDDHA AND NĀNAK GOING TO SCHOOL*

Harmony *is* inward. It is an inner harmony, alone, when manifested through the mental, vocal and physical activities of being/becoming brings about social harmony. Talking about social harmony without reference to inner harmony is pleading for ignorance. And, an elimination of ignorance is the sole objective of education. Legends unfold that when Gautama and Nānak were sent to school (or teacher) to study, their respective teachers confessed that they were ignorant of Truth. This did cast a reflection upon the prevailing system of education. But, one thing is considerably significant that the teachers were truthful. Notwithstanding an interval of about two thousand years, there seems to be a close affinity and there is much to learn from these two episodes, which, when analysed reveal the secret of inner harmony. An attempt is made, in this paper, to look into the genesis of social harmony and ascertain its relevance for us, today.

Our account of 'Gautama going to school' is based on *Lalitavistara.*[1] *Lalitavistara* is one of the nine[2] considerably important Mahāyānist texts, also called *Vaipulya Sūtrās*, belonging to *Vettullvaādinas* (or *Vaipulyakas*) that aims at deifying Gautama as the Great Being, believed to have appeared on earth for the good of gods and men. It is categorized *avadāna*

*Paper published in the March 1986 issue of *Buddhist Studies*, Journal of University of Delhi.

literature, composed both in prose and verse, consisting of twenty-seven chapters called *parivartas,* and written in mixed Sanskrit language. The date of its composition is tentatively believed to be first century A. D., and the fact of its authorship continues to remain a mystery.

Gautama the Prince, when grew up, as set down in writing in the 10th chapter of *Lalitavistara* entitled *Lipiśālasandarśana*[3] was escorted to the writing school, in the form and style of a procession, consisting of ten thousand boys alongwith ten thousand carts and carriages loaded with varieties of food and gold coins to be given in alms. Eight hundred thousand trumpets breathed into a musical note, whenever the procession halted on the way, say, on squares, highways or market roads of Kapilvastu. Showering of flowers, as if raining, further added into the splendure of the procession. The maidens, hundreds and thousands in number, adorned with jewellery and putting on beautiful costumes and excited, watched the glory of the procession, standing on the doors and gateways, and from the tops of the towers of balconies and palaces. Some of the maidens were carrying vessels, studded with jewels, meant to clean the way, passed on towards the *Bodhisattva.* Celestial maidens, eight thousand in number, while showering flowers, also joined in having a look of the *Bodhisattva. Devās, Nagās* and *Ghandarvās* etc. were also witness to the grand show on earth. The *7odhisattva* was received by king Śuddhodana leading the Śākyas. In this fashion the *Bodhisattva* went to school.

Viśuamitra, the school-master fell flat on the ground, as if awestricken with the grandeur and gracious presence of the *Badhisattva.* On seeing Viśuamitra in such a helpless state, Subhāṅg a *devaputta,* belonging to *Tushitsakāyika,* lifted him up and latter recited five *gāthās.*[4] *Devaputta* tells that all the *Śāstras* known in the worlds of *devās* and entire system of mathematical calculations and that of writings, all roots, all arts, known on the earth, the (*Bodhisattva*) had already learnt since the time immemorial. The second *gāthā* reveals that in order to follow the customary ways of the world and put it in to practice all his learnings besides training numerous children in these learnings and to bring others on the path of Truth, the (*Bodhisattva*) came to school. Further in the third *gāthā* we are told that the mere art of writing is of no use for him who is aware of the course of the future and has full comprehension of the cycle of creation and the way it is rendered inoperative, and is blessed with sharp memory. The fourth *gāthā* further highlights the achievements of the (*Bodhisattva*). It is stated that there is no equal to him in conduct, he is the supermost among gods and men and even the names of writing he has learnt, are not known to us. In the fifth and the last *gāthā* the (*Bodhisattva*) is described as a pure being knowing all the wonders of the world and the movements pertaining to all that is invisible. So what significance the letters have for him, which are quite visible in shape and form. After the *devaputta* finished with the recitation of the *gāthās*, he expressed his reverence for the *Bodhisattva*, while placing celestial flowers before him, and there after suddenly disappeared from the scene. Śuddhodana along with śākyas too departed. The nurses and maids present kept surrounding the *Bodhisattva*.

Ready to receive instructions from his school-master, Gautama the Prince takes the writing—tablet made of *Uragara* sandal-wood and also golden pen studded with jewels and asks the school-master as to which alphabet his master wishes him to learn ? Then, without waiting for the reply of the master, the *Bodhisattva*, one by one, enumerates sixty-four[5] kinds of alphabets viz. *Brahmilipi*, *Kharosti lipi*, *Magadha lipi*, *Ugara lipi*, *Daradlīpi*, *Cīnālipi*, *Huṇa lipi*, *Nāga lipi*. etc. On learning the *Bodhisattva* talking in this way, Viśuamitra felt as if disarmed as teacher and rather recited five *gāthās*[6] in praise of the *Lodhisattva*. In the first *gāthā*, Viśuamitra expressed his pleasant surprise over the *Jadhisattva's* knowledge of *Śāstras*, in the second over his knowledge of alphabets which even the master was not aware of. In the third *gāthā* the school-master expressed his inability to look at the face and hand of the *Bodhisattva*, thus unable to impart instructions to him and one who had already learnt every kind of alphabet. The following adorns the *Bodhisattva* as god of gods, 'the omnipresent', 'unrivalled', 'unequalled' in the worlds, known to us. The fifth and the last *gāthā* is very significant in the sense that it is in this *gāthā*, Viśuamitra, the school master *surrenders* to learn from his pupil and, only there after to teach others, thus:

> Through his grace I shall thoroughly teach the means of that knowledge which is worthy of all to even those who have already been taught.[7]

Now, Viśuamitra the school-master started teaching the *Bodhisattva* and *Bhikshus* alongwith ten thousand boys who accompanied the *Bodhisattva*, while coming to the school. Viśuamitra started pronouncing *nāgri* alphabets from *a* to *kṣa*. When the boys repeated the *nāgri* alphabets, at each letter, moral truth resounded which began with or contained that letter. When the boys pronounced syllable *a*, the following words resounded, underlying doctrine of *anitya* (Pāḷi: anicca) or impermanence:

Anityaḥ Sarvasaṁskārāḥ[8]
All aggregates are impermanent.
Similarly as regard to :

e : *eṣaṇā santthanadośa.*[9]
Desire is the cause of pain.

ai : *ariyāpathaḥ shrevān.*[10]
Virtues of *aryā* path.

o : *Oghottara*[11]
Escape from *Saṁsāra.*

ga : *gambhīra dharma pratītva samutpādavartana.*[12]
Awareness of profoundity of dependent origination.

Ca : *Caturoya satyapatha.*[13]
Path of the Four Noble Truths.

Cha : *Chandaragaordhana.*[14]
Abandoning of desire and passion.

ba : *bandhane mokṣa.*[15]
Deliverence from attachment.

bha : *bhavavibhava.*[16]
Existence and Non-existence.

Likewise all the letters upto *kṣa* were pronounced in a regular sequence resounding one or the other moral truth as conceived in Buddhism. This way, through alphabets the boys were taught *dharma* and as a consequence upon that thirty two thousand boys gained insight to perfect knowledge.

We propose to divide the entire legendary account of 'Gautama Going to School' into four parts, for analysis, viz. (i) The procession, (ii) *Devaputta*, (iii) Viśuamitra the school master and (iv) The Doctrines. Description of the procession, specially, speaks of the material richness, men and women and gods and celestial maidens. All these constitute the glamour of the *Bodhisattva* on earth and glory in heaven. The material richness of Gautama the Prince, later on, provided him an opportunity to look into its worth and, ultimately, discarding *an indulgence* as futile and fatal. Before we discard a thing we need to possess it. Otherwise, talking against *an indulgence* would only mean borrowing a concept. And, we very well know that we can only talk about it. The quantum of *an indulgence* that was available to Gautama the Prince can not be accessible to all or many. In the total absence of *an indulgence* in one's life one shall never be in a position to realize its worthlessness and as an hindrance in the pursuit of spiritual progress. Then, what to do ? Or, is it not possible for us, to follow the path shown by the Buddha, without first having become as rich as Gautama the Prince and then tasting and testing *an indulgence* ? No, this is *not* the suggestion. An indulgence, in fact, means indulging (of mind) in the extremes. An attachment of mind to self-mortification also amounts to *an indulgence*. The mind, actually, suffers from moving in to extremes. The movement of mind into extremes, in fact, makes it an indulgent. The mind needs to be cured of this disease. The Buddha's way, if followed, helps.

There is nothing peculiar about reference to men and women. Both of them constitute human society. They are there to make the description a bit lively and complete. But, reference to gods is comparatively more significant. The Buddha's teachings are not confined to for the good of men or women, alone. The gods too can drive benefits from the teachings of the Buddha. The gods are little higher than the human beings, relatively, more pure in consciousness. The gods, for that matter, are nearer to goal, but, they have yet to arrive at.

Next is the *devaputta*. He recites five *gāthās* in praise of Gautama the *Bodhisattva*. *Devās* also praise the *Bodhisattva*. He is at a higher level of consciousness than that of *devās*. The five *gāthās* recited in praise of the *Bodhisattva*, when, summed up, come to this that the *Bodhisattva*, the pure being, knows all and goes to school to teach others and to bring them on the path of Truth.

Viśuamitra the school master like *devputta*, also recited five *gāthās* in honour of the *Bodhisattva*. Viśuamitra surrendered, so to say, before the *Bodhisattva* and resolved 'to teach the means of that knowledge which is worthy of all to even those who have already been taught'. This means, that the knowledge which he now resolves to impart to others and 'through his (*Bodhisattva*) grace' is of different kind and constitutes the Buddhist doctrines.

Some of the doctrines referred to above e.g. *anityah sarvasaṁkārāh*, *esaṇasamtthanadośa*, *airvāpathaḥ* and *chandaragprahāna* etc., when understood and practised must result in creating harmony within. But why ? for the simple reason that the Buddhist doctrines do not mean, at all, to feed the mind or to add into one's *knowing*. The Buddha initiated us into an inward journey. The Buddhist doctrines, aim at the purification of the mind to the fullest extent, called *nirvāṇa*. In other words, the entire thrust of the Buddha was not on *knowing*, it was, rather, on the mode of existence of being/becoming.

... ...

There are number of biographies of Gurū Nañak (1469-1539 A. D.) known as *Janama Sākhīs* in Sikh tradition. A good few such as *Purātana Janama Sākhī*,[17] *Meharbāna Wāli Janama Sākhī*[18] and *Bhai Mani Singh Walī Janama Sākhi*[19] all these describe an episode of Nānak going to a teacher amost in an identical manner. We are concerned with those details alone which tell us about Nānak's response towards prevailing norms of learning and the manner in which Nānak *converted* his teacher.

Janama Sākhīs teli us that when Nānak was five (or seven) years old his father Kālū sent him to *pāṅdā* or teacher for receiving instructions. *Pāṅdā* wrote *akhra paitis ki ṁuhārni*[20] or the thirty-five letters of (*Gurumukhi*) alphabet on wooden-slate for Nānak to learn. Nānak started reciting *paṭṭi* in *Rāga Āsā*. This composition of (*Gurū*) Nānak we also find included Ādi Granth,[21] the Holy Book of the Sikhs. It contains the letters of (*Gurumukhi*) alphabet beginning from *sassā* and ending up to *aiṛā*. Thus, in all it contains thirty-five stanzas coniciding with number of letters of (*Gurumukhi*) alphabet and each stanza beginning with the letter is saturated with the sublime teachings of (Gurū) Nānak. Let us examine a few:

> **Uṛai upmā tā ki kije jā kā aṅtu na pāiyā,*
> *Sevā kare Sai phala pāvhi jini saca kamāiyā.*[22]
>
> *Praise only (thy) Lord who is infinite.
> Those who have realized Truth (can) only serve Him
> And, thus gather the Fruit of Life.
>
> **Ghaghe ghāla sevaka jai ghāle sabadi gurū kai lāgi rahē,*
> *Burā bhalā jai sama kara jāṇē ina bidha sāhibu ramata rahē.*[32]
>
> *If the servant makes efforts to remain alive to the words of Gurū
> And remains equanimous towards good and evil.
> Surely, in this way, dwells while in tune with Lord.
>
> **Dadai dosu na daiū kisai dosa karmā āpaṇiā,*
> *Jo maiṁ kiā so maiṁ pāiyā dosa na dījē avara janā.*[24]
>
> *Don't blame others, hold your own deeds responsible
> I have reaped the (fruit) of my own deeds,
> Let me not blame others.
>
> **Yaje janama na hovi kada hi jai kara saca pachāṇe,*
> *Guramukhi ākhē guramukha bṁhjai gurumuka eko jāṇe.*[25]
>
> *There is no transmigration after the realization of Truth.
> Thus, one, by the grace of *gurū* adorns the Lord omnipresent.

Thus, Gurū Nānak's view on Truth, when summarised amount to:

(i) Truth is to be earned (*kamāiyā*) and realised (*pachāṇe*).

(ii) Truth is to be realized through one' efforts combined with the grace of *gurū*.

(iii) There is no escape from the Truth of *karmaphala*,

(i) Cultivation of an attitude of equanimity towards good and evil is conducive for the realization of Truth.

Nānak, *Purātana Jānama Sākhī* tells us, remained silent on the following day. The dialogue between Nānak and his teacher, at this juncture, is revealing and that reads:

> "Why don't you study Nānak ?" asked *Pāṅdhā*.
>
> "Do you know anything that you wish to teach me." retorted Nānak.
>
> "I have learnt every thing. I have studied *Vedās* and *Śāstrās*. I know about income and expenditure and revenue." answered *Pāṅdhā*.
>
> "All this is futile and such learning only results in putting one's neck into the noose." Nānak told *Pāṅdhā*.[26]

Thereafter Nānak sang a '*Sabada* in Sri Rāga using writing as an analogy to communicate an idea of the *true art of writing thus*:

> "Burn thy *moha*, grind it and render it into ink, let thy awareness be a paper suitable for purpose. Let love be thy pen and (thy) consciousness the scribe, learn from the Gurū and write accordingly. Write *nāma*, His Praise, write abont infinitude. (1) Bābā learn to write like that; so that when you are asked to account (for your deeds) your accounts are settled and approved. (1 pause)[27]

Again, Nānak rciterated his stand and condemned all other learning as futile and thus recommended learning about *nāma* of *parameśvara*. Then, *Pāṅdhā* enquired as to what kind of learning could liberate a man. Nānak's response to the query is recorded in these words:

> "Listen *Swāmi* ! the manner in which ignorant worldling—scribes is of this kind :
>
> He scribes with an ink prepared from Soot, and writes on the paper made of hemp, and with pen made out of reed. Moreovcr, mind is the scribe and what (the hell) it can write except involving in the web of *Māyā*. This kind of writing generate only dark passion.
>
> And, the manner in which Truth manifests itself is of this kind :
>
> One who after burning the *moha* of *Māyā*, prepares an ink out of it and makes usc of *tapasyā* as a piece of paper.
>
> Thus makes consciousness as a scribe to write with the pen made

> of inner love, writes truly – writes *nāma* of *parameśvara*, His Praise. This kind of writing, alone, emancipates one from the dark passions. (Let him) write about the infinite glory. This (kind of) writing shall evoke tranquility and which is infinite."[28]

After Nānak has spelled out his notions of *true art of writing* he asks *Pāṅdha* if he has learnt that only then, he should teach him, otherwise not. Then, *Pāṅdhā* enquired from Nānak as to where from he had learnt all that.[29] This only implies that the *Pāṅdhā* stands disarmed. The conversation continues only the tables are turned. *Pāṅdhā* is onxious to learn from Nānak and the latter is only too willing to share his wisdom with his newly converted disciple. Nānak the Teacher, in the course of conversion tells *Pāṅdhā* about the transitory nature of *saṁsāra* and bitter fruits which are inevitable results of evil deeds. The *Paṅdita* (or *Pāṅdhā*) is stated to have expressed his surprise over Nānak's wisdom, bowed before him like showing reverence to a Perfect Being and left him to live the way of his own choice.[30]

Thus, the Child-prince Gautama and the Child-Nānak. both, went to school (or teacher) to teach.

... ...

The details described in the above two episodes might not be historically true; these are legendary in nature, partly based on teachings (or compositions) of the concerned legendary hero. While going through the life-stories of great men like the Buddha and Gurū Nānak, it is hardly of any use to look into the historicity of details contained therein. Legends are not meant to record facts of life. Focus on facts and the their interpretations is an obligation of historian. History by and large operates at surface level. It can at best tell you about the dates, names of persons and places and at times about some details of certain events. All this is on extraneous to the nature of human beings. Legends reveal human motivations. The perspective of legends, therefore, is much wider and deeper than that of history. The latter is interested in what is temporal, while the the former is devoted to what is everlasting in life. Legends are, in no way, historical records; these are literary in their mode of functioning. And, Aristotle (384—322 B.C.) in his *Poetics* rightly views literature (or poetry) as a "more philosophical and a higher thing than history."[31]

What emerges from the legendary accounts of the lives of the Buddha and Gurū Nānak is that learning devoid of spiritual contents, only, leads to an enslavement of dark passions. The treatment of this malady and hence its remedy varies a little in the legends that also reflects an attitude towards *Vedās* and *Śāstras* etc. During the period *Lalitavistara*, (whatever it may be) was written the writer shows his due reverence to *Vedās* and *Śāstrās*. This is why he mentions that the Buddha had learnt all about them. The Buddha only after learning about these scriptures is stated to have transcended them and for him it is something else that is more important. But, in the case of Gurū Nānak he is categorically stated to have condemned these because 'All this is futile and such learning only results in neck in the noose'. This attitudes of the Buddha and Gurū Nānak, as recorded, only appear to be slightly different when basically both of them denounce the significance of learning of *Vedās* and *Śāstrās*. This needs little elaboration. These holy writings are always an outcome of experience. They record experience of *riśis* (seers) and are primarily meant to lead to intended (*spiritual*) experience. What happens that in due course of time such holy writings in the hands of *lesser beings* become commodities and they commercialize them and the main purpose for which these were recorded for the spiritual wellbeings of the humanity for posterity is defeated. Then a stage comes when we talk about them in the name of academics and scholarship and we create illusions for ourselves and transmit them to others. The *Brāhmins* during the period when the Buddha and Gurū Nānak lived and taught, were in no way different from the academicians or scholars of today. The Buddha and Nānak by way of derivation do disapprove the modern concept of education.

Our educational system is, mainly, concerned with an outward journey of mind. Naturally, its emphasis is more on *knowing*. Mind wants to know more and more. The structure of mind is *logical*. Therefore, the mind wants to know reality in terms of logic. Whercas, reality, is not logical, it is a logos[32] that imbibes contradictions. In the vast realm of reality we find pair of opposites such as, good and bad, masculine and feminine, high and low, peak and valley and many more. These contradictions hold testimony to the fact that reality is paradoxical. The structure of mind being logical it inevitably fails to grasp the reality which is otherwise, in its very mode of existence. When we talk of reality being paradoxical, we do not mean to suggest that it is a chaos. There exists a unity behind the opposites. So, we call it a cosmos. It is a search of unity behind opposites that helps in *discovering* harmony within, which is in no way different from the reflection of cosmos in its microcosmic form. One who discovers unity within acquires a different mode of *being/becoming*—different from one who is busy in *knowing* more and more. Our system of education should aim at discovering unity within. This unity results in inner harmony and creates men with different quality of *being/becoming*. The Buddhist and the Sikh doctrines aim at discovering inner harmony which in the long run can help in creating social harmony.

If the Buddha and Gurū Nānak happen to go to school today they are not going to have different reactions towards the prevailing system of education in our country. But, who is going to respond the manner in which Viśuamitra and *Pāṅḍā* did ? This *is* the fundamental question !

References

1. For Original text see :
   Vaidya, P.L. (Ed.) *Lalitavistara*. 1958, pp. 87-89.
   For translation in English, see :
   i. Mitra, Rajindra Lal (Tr.) *Lalita-vistara*, pp. 181-189.
   ii. Bays, Gwenolyn (Tr.) *The Voice of the Buddha : The Beauty of Compassion*, translation of *Lalita-Vistara* from French into English, pp. 189-194 (1st volume).

2. The remaining eight texts are :
   i. *Aṣtasāhasrikā—prajñāpāramitā.*
   ii. *Sadharma-pundarīka.*
   iii. *Laṅkāvatāra,*
   iv. *Suvaraṇa-prabhāsa,*
   v. *Gaṇḍaryuha,*
   vi. *Tathāgata-guhyaka,*
   vii *Samādhīraja and*
   viii. *Daśabhumiśvara.*
3. i. Vaidya op. cit. p. 87.
   ii. Mitra, op. cit., pp. 87-88.
4. Vaidya, op. cit., pp. 87-88.
   i. *Śastrāṇi yāni pracalanti manuṣya loke,*
   Saṅkhyā lipicasia gaṇanāpica dhātu tantraṁ,
   ye shilpayoga pṛthu laukika aprameyā
   Teṣvesu shiksith purā bahukalpa koṭyaḥ.
   ii. *Kintū janasya anuvartanatāṁ karoti,*
   lipishālamagatu sushikṣitu shiṣyanārthaṁ,
   paripācanarth bahudāraka agrayāne,
   iii. *Lakuttar u catusatya pathe vidhijno,*
   hetupratitya kushalo yatha sambhavanti,
   yatha canirodhaksayu sansthitu shītibhavah,
   tasminvidhijna kimatho lipishastramātre.
   iv *Netasya ācariya uttari vā triloke,*
   Sarveṣu devamanjhṣu jyasṭḥah,
   nāmapi teṣa lipinaṁ na hi kitha yuyaṁ,
   yatresu shakshitu purā bahukalpakoṭyaḥ.
   v. *So cittadhāra jagataṁ Vividha vicitrā*
   ekaskanena ayu jnāti shuddhasatvaḥ,
   adrishya rūparahitasya gatinca vetti,
   kimvā punotha lipinoshkaradrishyarūpaṁ.
   cf. Mitra op. cit. p. 182.
5. For sixty four kinds of alphabets see :
   i. Vaidya op. cit. p. 88.
   ii. Mitra op. cit. pp. 182-183.
6. Vaidya, op. cit. pp. 88-89.
   cf. Mitra op. cit. p. 184.
7. Vaidya op. cit. p. 89.
   cf. Mitra op. cit. p. 184.

8-16. Vaidya, op. cit., p. 89.
cf. Mitra, op. cit, pp. 184-185.

17. Singh, Kirpal, (Ed.) *Janama Sakhi* ***Pramprā.*** *Purātana Janama Sākhī*, pp. 3-4.

18. *Ibid. Meharbāna Wāli Janama Sākhī*, pp. 59-60.

19. *Ibid., Bhai Mani Singh Wūlī Janama Sākhī*, pp. 331-332.

20. *Purātan Janama Sākhī*, p. 3.

21. *Āhi Granth*, pp. 432-434 cf. *Purātana Janama Sākhī*, p. 3.

22-25. *Ibid.*, cf. Singh, Gopal, (Tr.) *Sri Gurū Granthī Sāhib* (translation of *Ādi Granth* into English) pp. 428-431.

26. *Purātan Janama Sākhi*, p. 3. cf. Mcleod, W.H., *The B-40 Janama Sākhī*, pp. 5-6.

27. *Ibid.* cf. Mcleod, op. cit., p. 6.

28. Singh, Bhai Vir (Ed.) *Purātan Janama Sākhī*, p. 4.
cf. Macleod, op. cit., pp. 6-7.

29. *Ibid.* p. 4.
cf. Mcleod, op. cit., p. 7.

30. *Ibid.* p. 5.

31. Butcher, S.H., (Trs.) *Poeties*, 1968, p. 35.

32. Rajneesh, Shree Bhagwan, *The Hidden Harmony—Discourses on the Fragments of Heraclitus*, 1976, pp. 7-8.

II

THE PARABLE OF PLOUGHING

Birth is an end in itself only for ignorant worlding. And, for the wise it is an opportunity to lead a life of higher order and, thus, to achieve higher ends, *here and now*. Both, the Buddha and Nānak had abandoned the way of the world. So, they were told by their *well-wishers* that, they passed time away in idleness. Therefore, better, if they could do ploughing and, in this way, work for their living. It is in this background that they shared their respective views on ideals of life. We propose to analyse their views for the benefit of those interested in higher order of life.

While reading Pāli Canon, we find reference to the meeting between the Buddha and Kasī Bhāradvāja, twice. First time, we come across the said reference in the *Saṁyutta Nikāya*.[1] Later on, we find almost an identical descriptive refence made to the meeting in the fourth *Sutta* of the *Uragga Vagga* of the *Sutta Nipāta*,[2] the fifth book of *Khuddaka Nikāya*, only with an added information regarding Kasī Bhāradvāja having become an *arahata*. What we gather from the scriptural source is that at one time (in the eleventh year after attaining *Sambodhi*), when the Buddha was staying at *Dakkhiṇāgiri Vihāra*, near *Rajagaha* in *Magadha*, and loeated in *brāhmaṇa* village called Ekanāḷa, in one morning, in his usual dress, taking bowl and robe, went to meet Kasī Bhāradvāja—Bhāradvāja the Peasant on the occasion of ploughing festival (*maṅgala vappa*). Kasī Bhāradvāja was a *brāhmaṇa* and was so called as he had adopted agriculture as profession. When the Buddha arrived there, it was the time for the distribution of food. The Buddha, naturally, stood at one side, little away from the gathering. Kasī Bhāradvāja, the Master of show, saw the Buddha for alms and told him, that :

> Now I, recluse, plough and sow, and when I have ploughed and sown I eat. Do thou also rcluse, plough and snow, and when though hast ploughed and sown, eat?[3]

Buddha responded in affirmation.[4] Kasī Bhāradvāja got a bit perplexed and expressed his surprise saying that there was hardly any sign substantiating Master Gotama's claim to that effect when, Kasī Bhāradvāja confessing his inability to see the plaughing down by the Buddha, requests him to unravel the mystery as to 'how to know the ploughing done' by the Buddha. In response to the request the Buddha reveals the manner in which he ploughs and sows the seed, while reciting the following verses :

> *Faith (*Saddhā*) the seed, austerity (*tapo*) the rain,
> *Wisdom (*paññā*) my, yoke and plough;
> *My pole is modesty (*hīra*), mind is the strap,
> *And I have mindfulness (*Sati*)
> *For share and goad. Warded in act and word,
> *In eating, temperate (*āhāre udare yato*)
> *With truth (*saccaṁ*) and full of bliss,
> *Is my deliverance.
> *To a security (*khema*) for moil doth draw
> *Vigour (*vīrīyam*), my team in yoke :
> *And on it goes, nor turns it back; it goes
> *Where is no suffering (*socati*).
> *And thuswlse is the ploughing ploughed; and thence
> *There comes the deathless fruit (*amatapphalā*);
> *And who so hath this ploughing ploughed, set free
> *Is he from every ill. (*Sabbadukkhāpamuccatī*).[5]

In brief, the Buddha tries to make Kasī Bhāradvāja understand that his art of ploughing, too, imbibes all that the ingredients found in the normal practice of ploughing and sowing, such as seed, rain, yoke, plough share goad etc. Only, these ingredients are of different quality and yield different kind of crops.

There is a beautiful sequence, henceforth. Kasī Bhāradvāja, who earlier, not only refused to give alms to the Buddha, rather, advised him to do farming, now, after listening the verses and thereby convinced of the claim of the Buddha, offers food which latter declines to accept on the ground that it would amount to wages earned as a consequent upon reciting the verses. And, this is contrary to the norms practised by Buddhas.[6] Professor P.V. Bapat in one of his paper, *Vedic Sources of some Buddhist Bliefs* (1984) has dilated upon this very issue of declinto accept offer, made to the Buhdha by Kasī Bhāradvāja. Professor Bapat is of the opinion that no explanation is put forth by the commentator but, the same is certainly available in *Kāṭhaka Saṁhitā*, which reads :

> If a man makes some offerings after listening to some laudatory verses, then these offerings should not be accepted. For, the man is beside himself (on account of the laudatory verses) and so he cannot, (at that time), be truthful to him. When he regains his former self, then, that action of his—that giving—hurts him.[7]

The Buddha's refusal to accept offer as wages for reciting holy verses, being contrary to the norms of Buddhas, not only finds its explanation in the literature of the past, the same injunction continues to persist in the Sikh tradition, as well. Gurū Nānak the Founder-Gurū of Sikh tradition, at one place, disparagingly condemned those who deal in Divine Name in the words; that :

Damned are those who deal in (Divine) name.[8]

... ...

The parable of ploughing finds place in number of biographics of Gurū Nānak, known as *Janam Sākhīs* in the Sikh tradition. But the details are available only at one place, namely, in '*Purātan Janam Sākhī*',[9] (1635 c.). When we go through the pages of *Purātan Janam Sākhī*, we learn that Gurū Nānak became fond of *faqīr* (saints) and was found, for most of the time, in their company. Virtually, he had isolated himself from others. All the members of his family were grieved of his (unwordly) conduct. The ignorant worldling, naturally, thought, that Nānak had gone crazy. Gurū Nānak's mother talked to him and expressed her anguish over his indifference towards worldly affairs. His wife, too, expressed her deep concern over his behaviour, unbecoming of a normal person. Now, when, Gurū Nānak's father, Kālū, came to know about Nānak's state of mind, —as if gone mad— told him, that :

> "We don't interfere with your affairs. What we want is that you should do some job. It behoves the sons of *Khatri* (merchant) class), in case they have some capital, to engage themselves in some business. It is (always) to do some business. My son ! our crops st· nds ready for cutting. You (should) take it in your hand, lest, it undergoes (a waste) and destroyed. People, too, shall have a word of praise for you. (Moreover), My son ! Noneelse but the owner shall harvest it (*Khetī khasamā setī*).[10]

After listening the sermons of his father on worldly success, Gurū Nānak put forth his *own* claim of success, saying that :

> "My father ! I have cultiveted a field havin gunique characteristics and which is productive too. I have ploughed it, sown a seed, and put a fence round it. I keep vigil over it day and night. My father ! I am (not at all) complascent to look after my own field, but, I can hardly look after other's one."[11]

On hearing this, Kālū, the father, was stunned and said :

> "Look ! what does he say ?"

When, Kālū asked Gurū Nānak, that :

> "(Tell me) when did you cultivate (that) unique field ? Stop these foolish talks. If you wish I shall hand over a field to you, in future, to do independent cultivation of your choice and shall look forward for the fruitful results."[12]

And, Gurū Nānak responded politely, saying :

> "My father ! I have already cultivated and it has yielded good crop, gives a good look."[13]

Now, Kālū expresses "his inability to see the rippened field and enquires as to what does (Nānak) meant to say,"[14] Gurū Nānak, addresses his father and tells him about his art of plaughing, reciting :

> "My mind is ploughman and

(moral) deeds the ploughing.
And, with *Saram* I water the field—my body,
*I sow the seed of (divine) Name and level
it with the harrow of contentment.
*And I pursue the course of modest living
*My deeds are saturated with
*(The seed of Name shall sprout) and my home
will see, a place blessed with fortune
*Bābā *māyā* won't stand by you (hereafter),
*And, it is this very *māyā* that deludes
the minds of the people.
*(Again), only a few can comprehend (its true nature)"[15]

Gurū Nānak, while identifying two modes—of living, namely, that of Name and *Māyā*, advocates for the former.

... ...

Let us, firstly, examine the details of the parable of spiritual ploughing, delineating the Buddhist path. The foremost important thing in the course of ploughing, of course, is the kind and quality of the seed, but the nature of harvest depends upon several other factors. The seed in the case of the Buddhist parable is *Saddhā* (faith) and an expected harvest is positively identified as *amataphalā* (fruit of ambrosia) synonymous with *Nibbāna* and negatively described as *Sabba-dukkhā pamuccati* (freedom from all Suffering). The fruit of ambrosia is not the result of divine grace, rather it is an outcome of strenuous efforts which are fruitfully worked out in the said parable.

The value-terms such as *Saddhā*, *tapa*, *paññā*, *hiri*, *sati*, *sacca*, *khema*, *viriya*, *amattapphalā* etc. used in the parable are peculiar to Buddhist discipline and can be properly appreciated only, if viewed within the framework of the tradition these belong to. The foremost significant thing in the course of ploughing, as pointed out earlier, is the seed and it is *Saddhā* (faith) that is identified as seed in the parable (*Saddhā bījaṁ*). Now, what does *Saddhā* mean when viewed in the background of *Theravāda* Buddhism ? *Saddhā* is a state of mind that promotes purification of consciousness (*citta-visuddhi*) and, at the same time, it must ward off the factors which can generate impurities. In this way the process of purification of *citta* is analogous to washing the seed with water prior to sowing. The seed may be of best quality, but, it requires an aid of different kinds so as to become crop, e.g. rain. The role of rain is very briefly described as : *tapa vuṭṭhi*, which means austerity is likened to rain. Here, austerity hardly means anything else, but, discipline (*vinaya*)—Buddhist discipline. *Vinaya*, in short, means refraining from *rāga*, *dosa* and *moha*. Only seed and rain are not that sufficient to yield a crop. We need a yoke and plough, as well. It is *paññā* (wisdom) that plays the role of yoke and plough. *Paññā* is the third stage of Noble Eightfold Path (*ariyo aṭṭhangiko maggo*)[16] of the Buddha, the rest of the two being, successively, *Sīla* (morality) and *Samādhi*. The two constituents of *Sammā Sati* and *Sammā Diṭṭhi*, enlisted in the Noble Eightfold Path, come under *Paññā*. Not only these two constituents of *Sammā Sati* and *Sammā Diṭṭhi*, but, the remaining six, that come under *Sīla* and *Samādhi* are characterized as *Sammā*, too. The word *Sammā*, in a way, is keyword of the Buddhist discipline. *Sammā* denotes an action or process that results in the overall purification of corporeal organism usually classified as physical, vocal and mental. Antonym to the word *Sammā* is *micchā* that denotes an action or process which generates impurities. *Dhamma*, in Buddhist tradition, therefore, means practising, *Sīla*, *Samādhi* and *Paññā*.

The woid *Sati*, used in the expression *Sammā Sati*, stands for awareness, and one can be aware to present only and under no circustances to past or future. To bring mind in the *present* means to put it on the path of purification (*visuddhi magga*). *Sammā Diṭṭhi* springs from *Sammā Sati*. It is in this way that *Sammā Sati* and *Sammā Diṭṭhi* are described as analogous to the functioning of yoke and plough.

Next value-term used is *hīri* (humility). *Hīri* is of two kinds : *ātama-lajjā* and *loka-lajjā*. It springs in the heart and mind, when an evil (*akusala*) idea prevails upon. One looks towards one's grace and grandeur and consequent upon that confronts sense of shame that drives him away from doing anything evil. An evil deed (*akusala kamma*) in Buddhism, has singular and definite connotation, i.e., any act, physical, vocal and mental that generates impurities is *akusala kamma*. *Hīri* is described akin to pole. *Akusala kamma* are product of *akusala citta*. Getting away from *akusala kamma* needs concentrated efforts and these efforts bear fruits as a result of an aid availed of from *vīriya* (energy). The required energy is gathered not from *pamāda* (lethargy) but from *vyāma* (efforts). Another fruit that one gathers from efforts is *khema* (security). An achievement of *khema*, in fact, suggests searching for an island, within. There are some catch-expressions, such as, '*appa dīpo bhava*' in Buddhism. Here the word *dīpo* is not used in the sense of earthen lamp, as is commonly understood, but, is phonetic variation of the word *dvipa* that means an island. So, the expression '*appa dīpa bhava*' should construe meaning thereby 'to be an island unto oneself'. Dwelling on such island, alone, guarantees security to oneself.[17]

What comes to ones hand when one adopts the method and style of ploughing as devised by the Buddha ? What one gets is *amataphala*, negatively described as *Sabba dukkhābamuccati* or set free from every ill. In order to arrive at this stage one has not only to commence one's pilgrimage while imbibing purity of heart and mind, but, has also to keep in one's mind the lesson of purity, through out of the course. The Buddha constantly keeps on reminding as to the nature of the path, discovered[18] by him, saying : *essa maggo visuddhiyā*[19]—this is the path of purification. The total purification of mind, is, *via negativa*, characterized as *Nibhāna* (*Skt*. *Nirvāṇa*).

Saddhā is likened to seed for the Buddha, whereas, for Nānak it is *ñama*. *Nāma* is a term and its meaning needs to be ascertained in the context of *Nānakbāṇi*. One way can be to note down the changes that take place in the being who has entered the Realm of *Nāma*. *Nānakbāṇi*, with reference to *nāma*, contemplates two kinds of persons, such as, *gurmukhu* and *manmukhu*. One who has entered the said Realm is called *gurmukhu*. *Manmukhu* dwells outside the Realm. What is outside this Realm ? It is the state ruled over by *haūmaiṁ* (ego) as a sovereign. Not only *gurmukhu* and *manmukhu* represent two diametrically apposed style of living, these are, in fact, *nāma* and *haṉmaiṁ*, respectively that deterimine their different modes of functioning. Gurū Nānak, while distinguishing one from the other, states :

"A self-willed person (*manmukhi*) filled with pride be robbed. (Whereas), one guided by the Gurū (*gurumnkhi*) (shall) possess.[20]

The same idea is conveyed in different style as under :

"A self-willed person (*when*) forgets divine name (*nāma*) is burnt (*daddhā*) like a reed with fire of the forest (*ḍavi*).[21]

Therefore, one is *manmuku* since he imbibes *haūmaiṁ*. Or in other words, he has cut himself away from *nāma*. *Gurmuku* is also described in similar fashion, that reads :

"(When) one guided by Gurū praises divive name (then) the fire (*bhāhi*) of pride is extinguished (*nivāri*).[22]

Here, in said couplet, *gurmuku* is not only described having entered the 'Realm of Nāma', but, his abandoning of *haūmaiṁ* is also underlined. We find number of references in *Nānakbāṇi*, where *nāma* and *hhūmaiṁ* are categorically placed contrary to each other. Some of these references, we quote :

*The body in which divine name (does not form) part of it. That body is like a quarrelsome place (*vādu*) of pride.[23]

*Meditate on name of Rāma which is pure. (And) abandon all other that is pride, bitter (in taste).[24]

*While dyed in divine name results in dis-appearing of pride. While dyed in divine name results in being absorbed in Truth.[25]

What are the characteristics of *nāma* ? *Nānakbaṇi* is quite vocal in answering this query. *Nāma*, *bāṇi* states, is :

"Divine name, Oh, Nānak, is highly delightful
That one acquires (by the grace of) True Gurū.[26]

After entering the Realm of *Nāma* one's vision is qualitatively transformed. He gains, so to say, equanimity (*Samadarasi*) towards *harkhu* (rejoining) and *sogu* (sorrow) :

(He) becomes in different to rejoining and sorrow (one who) has tasted nectar and is aborbed in name of Hari.[27]

Gurū Nānak has also given an overall picture of the state of affairs, bereft of *nāma*, as :

The (whole) world is sick being devoid of divine name. (And) is sinking on account of dualism (wavering between God and the world).[28]

By way of conclusion it can be stated, that :

> None without (having tuned oneself with) True name has been able to satisfy one's hunger.[29]

This is why *Bābā* has advised that :

> Look after the divine name, Oh Nānak
> Do not sow any other kind of seed.[30]

The second value—term, that Bābā Nānak has used in the parable of ploughing is, *Saṁtokhu* (contentment). *Saṁtokhu* is akin to *Suhāgā* (harrow). What is this *Suhāgā* ? *Suhāga*, in fact, is a (harrow) made of wood. While ploughing the field the soil gets topsy-turvey and *Suhāgā* is used to level the soil. To know, exactly, to what kind of state of mind does *Saṁtokhu* refer to, we must have recourse to *Nānakbāṇi*. At one place, in *japu*, Gurū Nānak, while describing the substance of *Saṁtoku*, states :

> The Bull (*dhaulu*) akin to universal low (*dharsmu*) is a son of compassion.
>
> Which established contentment in the arrangement of the world. [31]

A forestated reference is to *purāṇic* belief, according to which the Bull is carrying earth on his horns. Gurū Nānak has used this belief with new connotations. The Bull who is carrying earth on his horns is skin to *dharamu* (Universal Law). In other words, it is the *dharamu* that is supporting earth. At the some time *dharamu* is a son of *daīā* (compassion). An inner discipline of this son of *daīā*, i.e. *dharamu* is on account of *Saṁtokhu*. In this way the state of *Saṁtokhu* is described with reference to *dharamu* and *daīā*. *Dharamu* in this context, stands for the Law of Nature and which is universal in nature. The mind derives *Saṁtokhu* while rooted in *dharamu* or Universal Law. This way *Saṁtokhu* manifests in the form of *daīā* in day to day living. *Daīā* is born, only, when there is contentment, within. This happens, when, one takes refuge in universal law,[32] that results in the transformation of energy being consumed by dark passions e.g. *Kāmu*, *Krodhu*, *Lobhu* etc. into noble passion called compassion (*daīā*). One can be compassionate only when there is contentment (or inner poise), within. And the man of compassion alone is *dharamavāna*. As we need a harrow of wood to level the uneven soil, the same way we can hardy level our uneven mind without an aid of *Saṁtokhu*. This is why it is categorically stated : *Saṁtokhu Suhāgā*.

We have not only to cultivate the soil, but, are required to look after it, also. This is accomplished through fence. Any kind of achievement *necessarily* must breed ego (*ahaṁkāra*). We have to be vigilent so as to protect ourselves from the onslaught of *ahaṁkāra*. The way that Gurū Nānak has suggested is that of *garībī vesu*. In other words to adopt the life-style of humility. This style of life shall act as a fence and guard of *ahaṁkāra* from polluting the pure state of mind.

The basic thing is mind and the suggestion to make mind *hālī* (ploughman) is laudable. Let mind be *hālī*, body as soil, water as *Saramu* (toil) and *nāma* as a seed, alongwith *Saṁtokhu* as *Suhāgā*. This combination is sure to yield rich crop. When seed of *nāma* is sowed in the soil of mind, only then *Saṁtokhu* is the fruit. It is this very *Saṁtokhu* that takes the form of *daīā*. To be compassionate alone is to be truly religious.

Gotama Buddha *discovered* the path and to Gurū Nānak it was *revealed*[33], that resulted in their emancipation from the clutches of dark passions or (*vikāru*) and both shared it with others, as well. What one gets after such an emancipation ? One is rich with purity and is identified as vibrant being. There is constant increase of peace, within. To achieve this Goal, the Buddha *discovered* the path of *Jhāna* (*Skt. dhyāna*) and Gurū Nānak that of *Nāma*. *Jhāna* and *Nāma* both stand to transform an energy into Compassion. When the Buddha went on *Cārikāvān*[34] and Gurū Nānak undertook *udāsis*;[35] both were, in fact, prompted by the noble passion of Compassion for the benefit of all. To talk of being (truly) religious without being compassionate in one's disposition, is all hoax.

Kasī Bhardvāja listened to the Sermons of the Buddha and learnt the 'way of *Dhamma*' which bore fruit and he attained to the state of *Nibbāna*, thus became an *arahata*. Whether Kālu paid any heed to what (Gurū) Nānak said or not *Janama Sākhīs* are silent on this subject. Still, the 'Path of Nāma' is open for those desiring an emancipation from the dark passions and consequent upon that dwelling in higher order of life.

References and Notes

1. S. i. 172-173.
   Rhys Davids, C.A.F., (Tr.) *The Kindered Sayings* (translation of *Saṁyutta Nikāya*) Part I, pp. 216-219.
2. *Sutta Nipāta* verses 75-82.
   Fausbōll, V. (Tr) *Sutta Nipāta*, Volume X, Part II, pp. 11-15.
3. S. i. 173 : "*Ahaṁ kho, Samaṇa, kasāmi ca vapāmi ca, kasitvā ca vapitvā bhuñiāmi, tvaṁ pi, samaṇa, kassasu ca vapassu ca, kasitvā ca vapitva ca bhuñjassu*" ti.
   Rhys Davids, C.A.F., *op. cit.*, p. 217.
4. S. i. 172 : "*Ahaṁ pi kho, brahamaṇa, kasāmi ca vapāmi ca, kasitvā ca vapitvā ca bhuñjami*" ti.
5. S. i. 172-173 :
   **Saddhā bījaṁ tapo vuṭṭhi, paññā me yugaṅanglaṁ.*
   **hīréīsā mano yottaṁ, sati, me phālapacānaṁ.*
   **Kayagutto vacigutto āhāre udare yato.*
   **Saccaṁ Karomi niddhanaṁ, so raccaṁ me pamocanopi.*
   **Vīriyaṁ me dhuradhorayhaṁ yogakhemadhi vāhanaṁ.*
   **Gacchati, anivattantaṁ, yatha gatva na socati.*
   **Evamesā kasi kaṭṭhā, sa hoti amatapphalā.*
   **Etaṁ kīsaṁ kasitvāna, sabbadukkhā pamuccati*". *ti.*
   Coomaraswamy, Anand K. and Horner, I.B., *The Living Thoughts of Gotama the Buddha*, p. 56.
6. S. i. 173:
   "*Gathābhīgītaṁ me abhojaneyyaṁ,*
   Sampassataṁ brāhamaṇa nesa dhammo.
   Gathābhīgītaṁ panu danita buddhā.
   Dhamme sati brahamaṇa vuttiresaā."
   Rhys Davids, C.A.F., *op. cit.*, p. 218.
7. Tiwary, Mahesh (Ed.) *Bodhi—raśmi*, p. 3:
   "*Yo gāthānarā śaṁsibhyām sanoti, tasya na pratigrahayaṁ.*

Anrtaṁ hi matto, yada so'matto bhavati, atha taṁ tat tupati."

8. *Ādi Granth*, p. 1245.
9. Singh, Bhai Vir, (Ed.) *Purātana Janama Sākhī*, pp. 8-11.
10. *Ibid.*, p. 8.
11-14. *Idem.*
15. *Ibid.*, p. 9; *Ādi Granth*, p. 595.
Also see: Singh, Gopal (Tr.) *Sri Gurū Granth Sāhib*, p. 577.
16. S. iv. 252: *ariyo aṭṭhangiko maggo etassa nibbānass Saccikiriyāya.*
17. The expressions such as '*nijagharu*' (one's inner self) and '*thiru sohāgo*' (permanent married bliss) found in *Nānak-bānī*, have identical connotations compared with '*dīpa*' in Buddhism.
(i) *Nijagharu*:
Bāṇi biralau bīcārsī jai ko guramukhi hoieha/bāṇi mahāpurakha kī nijagahari vāsu hoi. Only few shall meditate upon *bāṇi*, that too a *guramukhi*.
These are the words of Great Being (God) shall lead to dwell in inner self,
—*Rāgu Rāmakali Mahalā I, Ā.G.*, p. 935.
(ii) *Thiru Sohāgo*:
Nānak ahinisi ravei prītamu
Harivaru thiru sohāgo.
Nanak takes delight in beloved, day and night. (Only) God (*Hari*) is permanent abode of married bliss.
—*Rāgu Tukhāri Mahalā I, A.G.*, p. 1110.
18. S. ii. 106-107: *Ayaṁ kho so, bhikkhave purāṇa maggo purāṇañjasso pubbakehi sammā sambuddhehi anuyāto, tamanugacchiṁ—tadabbiññāya ācikkhiṁ bhikkhunaṁ bhikkhunīnaṁ upāsakānaṁ—upāsikānaṁ.*
"This brothern, is the ancient path, that ancient road, traversed by the rightly enlightened ones of former times. This that I have fully come to know I have declared to the brethern, to the sisters, to laymen, to lay-women—".
Rhys Davids, C.A.F. (Tr.) *The Kindered Sayings* (Translation of *Saṁyutta Nikāya*), Part-II, pp. 74-75.
Besides, the twenty four Buddhas whose lives are descri-

bed in *Buddhavaṁsa* (*Khuddaka Nikāya*) do confirm the fact of *discovery of* Truth.

19. Verse: 277
Sabbe saṅkhārā aniccā'ti
Yadā paññāya passati,
atha nibbindati dukkhe;
essa maggo visuddhiyā.
"Transient are all conditioned things"—
When this with wisdom one discerns,
Disgusted then is one with ill,—
This is the Path to Purity."
—Narada, Mahāthera (Tr.) *Dhammapada*, p. 207.
Cf. verse, 278, 279.

20. *Manamukhi haumaiṁ kari mussī guramukhi pallai pāī.*
—*Siri Rāgu Mahalā I, Ā.G.*, p. 63.

21. *Manmukhi nāmu visāriā jiuṁ ḍavi daddhā kānu.*
—*Siri Rāgu Mahalā I, Ā.G.*, p. 63.

22. *Guramukhi nāmu salāhi haumaiṁ nivari bhāhi.*
—*Siri Rāgu Mahalā I, Ā.G.*, p. 20.

23. *Jitu tani nāmu na bhāvai titu tani haumaiṁ vādu.*
—*Siri Rāgu Mahalā I, Ā.G.*, p. 61.

24. *Simarahu rāma nāmu atī nirmalu avaru tiāgahu haumaiṁ kauṛā.*
—*Rāgu Āsā Mahalā I, Ā.G.*, p. 415.

25. *Nāme rāte haumaiṁ jāi nāmi rate sacci rahai samāi.*
—*Rāgu Rama Kali Mahalā I, Siddha Gosati, Ā.G.*, p. 941.

26. *Nānak nāmu mahārasu mīṭhā guri pūrai saccu pāiā.*
—*Rāgu Gaurī Pūrabī Chanta Mahala I, Ā.G.*, p. 243.

27. *Harakhu soga te rahahi nirāsā ammritu cākhī hari nāmī nivāsā.*
—*Rāgu Basantu Mahalā I, Ā.G.*, p. 1189.

28. *Nāmu binā jagu rogi biāpiā bubidhā ḍubi ḍubi marīai.*
—*Rāgu Bhairau Mahalā I, Ā.G.*, p. 1125.

29. *Nānak sacai nāma bina kisai na latthī bhukkha.*
—*Rāgu Mārū Vāra Mahalā III, (Saloku Mahalā I) Ā.G.*, p. 1091.

30. *Nānak nama samhalī tū bījau avaru na koi.*
—*Rāgu Mārū Vāra Mahalā I, (Saloku Mahalā I, Ā.G.* p. 1091.

31. *Dhaulu dharamu daiā kā pūta samtoklu thāpi rakhiā jinī sūta.*
—*Japu, Ā.G.*, p. 3.
See: Shackle, C., *A Gurū Nanak Glossary*, p. 56.
32. When the disciple of the Buddha takes refuge, saying:
Dhammaṁ Sarnaṁ Gacchāmī,
(I go and take refuse in *Dhamma*).
he is not at all taking refuge in *Dhamma* as worked out in Buddhist scriptures, rather he is taking refuge in Universal Law.
33. Gurū Nānak has claimed that his *bāṇi* is a result of 'revelation'.
Jaisī maiṁ āvai khasami kī bāṇī taisṛā kari giānu ve Lālo!
—*Rāgu Tilaṅga Mahalā I, Ā.G.*, p. 722
'As the *bāṇī* (the Word) is revealed to me by my Master.
So, I communicate knowledge, Oh Lalo!'
34. Gotama Buddha not only himself went on *Cārikāvan*, but also instructed his *Bhikkhūs* to preach *dhamma* for the benefit of all, as under:
"*Caratha, bhikkhave, cārikiṁ bahujana hitāye, bahujana sukhāye, lokanukampāye, atthāye, hitāye, sukhāye, devsamanussaaaṁ*".
"Wander, O Monks, for the gain of the many, for the welfare of the many, for showering forth compassion on the world; for the good, for the gain, for the welfare of gods and men".
—*Vinayapiṭaka I*, 23.
35. Travels of Gurū Nānak are deified as *udāsis*. These *udāsis* of Gurū Nānak were prompted by his Compassion for the benefit of All.

12

BHAGAT TRILOCHAN : A STUDY OF THE LAST WISH OF MAN*

Man, inwardly, *knows* death to be inevitable. Nevertheless, he *behaves* as if *he* is immortal and death must knock at the doors of *others*. Man needs to be cured of such a disease —a disease of false notion—and made to accept death as a fact of life, so as to get closer to the scriptures concerned with analysing the last wish of man. In this paper we wish to enquire into the anatomy of last wish of man, enshrined in the holy verses of Bhagat Trilochan, forming an integral part of the teachings of Ādi Granth. We find four holy verses of Bhagat Trilochan in Ādi Granth : one in Sri Rāgu; two in Rāgu Gūjri and one in Dhanāsri Rāgu.[1] Both, the Sikh scholars and scholars of Sikh religion, have very little information about the bigoraphic details of Bhagat Trilochān. Max Arthur Macauliffe, in his monumental work *The Sikh Religion*, published in the year 1909, at one place, describes him as "Saint of the Vaiṣya caste", born in the year 1267 A.D. "He either lived at or visited Pandharpur in the Sholapur district of the Bombay Presidency", writes Macauliffe, "and was a contemporary of Nām Deva.........."[2] Only in one vesre or *Śabada*, Bhagat Trilochan has expressed his concern about the five varities of

* Paper presented and published in the Seminar organized by the Department of Buddhist Studies, University of Delhi, held in May, 1983.

last wishes of man, dilating upon equal number of consequences ensuing from them. The text we are concerned with is as follows :

Gujri Śri Trilochan jio ke Pade Ghar I.

Ant kāl jo lachmi Simray aisi cintā meain jay mare,
Sarap jone val val ohtaray ||1||
Ari bāi Gobind nām mat (i) bisray ||Rhāo||
Ant kāl jo istri simray aisi cintā meain jay mare,
Baisvā jone val val ohtaray ||2||
Ant kāl jo laḍkay simray aisi cintā meain jay mare,
Sūkar jone val val ohtaray ||3||
Ant kāl jo mandir simray aisi cintā meain jay mare,
Preta jone val val ohtaray ||4||
Ant kāl Narāyān simray aisi cintā meain jay mare,
Badit Trilochan te nar muktā Pitāmber vākey ridhey bassy ||5||2||[3]

Rāg Gujri Verses of Trilocan

Whosoever, when dying, contemplates upon godess
of wealth and dies brooding so,
He shall be born and reborn as a serpent (1)
Oh my friend ! Let me not abandon
the Name of *Gobind* (God). (Pause)
Whosoever, when dying, contemplates upon women,
and dies brooding so,
He shall be born and reborn as a prostitute (2)
Whosoever, when dying, contemplates upon sons,
and dies brooding so,
He shall be born and reborn as swine. (3)
Whosoever, when dying, contemplates upon mansions,
and dies b ooding so,
He shall be born and reborn as ghost (4)
Whosoever, when dying meditates upon *Nāyāyana* (God)
and dies meditating on Him.
'He', Sayeth Trilochan, is Released :
within him dwelleth the *Pitāmbar* (the Lord, (5) ||2||

Obviously, this *Śabada* deals with the last wish of man and provides a definite clue to the transit from one world to another, besides, pointing to the mode of meditation resulting in the cessation of *Saṁsara* or Cycle of Existence, thus, finally attaining *mukti.* The idea of rebirth in Theravāda tradition, too, is intimately connected with the last wish of man. Rebirth[4] and transmigration, in Buddhism, are *not* interchangeable expressions. There *is* difference between the two and the same is very vital. One way to specify the existing difference is to make use of the simile of a poem. After a poet has read/recited his poem to the audience, the poem, as usual, continues to be with the poet and it only takes rebirth in the minds of the audience. Therefore, the poem neither abandons the poet nor it migrates to the audience. Moreover, the poem in its new forms is neither totally different from nor absolutely identical with the actual poem. Thus, the poem is said to take rebirth. Rebirth as a doctrine in Buddhism is explained as a process identified as *palingenesis,* a compound expression consisting of Greek word *palin* that means again and genesis in English language underlines an idea of birth. George Grimm in his book. *The Doctrine of the Buddha* (1958), has very appropriately defined the term *palingenesis* and which is as under :

> For *Palingenesis* means decomposition and renewal of the entire individual, thus that the dying creature perishes entirely together with its consciousness but that there remains a germ from which a new individual arises together with new consciousness.[5]

One can ask to identify the operative force of this process. The Pāli Canon, categorically, name *Taṇhā* or thirsting-well as a main factor responsible for the renewal of the process. In Mahāvagga the Buddha conveys the same idea to the monks in the following unimbiguous manner :

> And this, monks is the aryan truth of the uprising of ill, that which is craving (*Taṇhā*) connected with again becoming, accompained by delight and passion, finding delight in this and that, that is to say : craving for sense-pleasures, craving for becoming, craving for de-becoming.[6]

Now, *taṇhā* or craving, bereft of any specific direction can not be said to acquire any recognizable form. And, it is always certain law that provides coherence to any number of occurrences, apparently, looking otherwise. The law of affinity is believed to affect the process of *palingenesis*, transforming it into some recognizable identity. This also explains the transit from one realm of existence ro another, besides, it reveals the secret of movement in specific direction and coinciding with the specific realm.[7]

The above stated hypothesis of rebirth is beautifully illustrated in *Kukkur-vatika sutta*[8] of the *Majjhima Nikāya*. This Sutta tells the story of Puṇṇa and Seniya, the two ascetics. Both of them undergo ascetic practices with a view to procure rebirth in felicitous set of circumstances. Seniya adopts the style of a dog and Puṇṇa that of a cow. Puṇṇa, a cow ascetic and Seniya a dog-ascetic, so to say, once visited the Buddha and curiously enquired from him about their fate in the future course of existence. The Buddha made them to understand that if they succeed in their respective vows, i.e. a cow-vow and dog-vow there is no escape from rebirth corresponding to their vows. This shows that the dying person when burdened with *taṇhā* for becoming or *bhava-taṇhā* is sure to be reborn under the dictates of law of affinity that provides tone and tenor to *taṇhā*. Again any one, obsessed with the tendency to killing humanbeing or beasts breathes his last, as contemplated in Buddhist scriptures, reborns in hell-world. If at all, such a person finds his way into human-world, survives for a short period of time. The law of affinity, here too, renders the case intelligible. The tendency to kill is a tendency to shorten life. Such a person, naturally, finds affinity with the germ that is destined to survive for a short period. Consequently, at the dying moment, he grasps only that germ which itself has a short span of life and, thus determines his future course of existence, accordingly. Likewise, there are persons who are sadist by temperament and, thus, relish ill-treating and, at times, deforming others. These persons are stated to have affinity with those germs alone who are by nature gifted with power to transform themselves into deformed bodies. Similarly, if we make use of mirror it testifies that anger results in disfiguring the face. An angry man, true to its inner most psyche is bound to grasp the germ that ultimately unfold its ugly from.[9]

There is a positive aspect also. One practising the precept

of non-killing "bring that person at the body's dissolution after death to bliss in heaven ; or, if his rebirth is again among mankind, then length of days in his portion in whatever station he is born into—such merciful courses tend to length of days here."[10]

Furthermore, the Buddha continuing his discourse on the subject of rebirth in *Cūla* and *Mahākamma Vibhanga Sutta*, teaches us, "how the cruel, the angry, the envious, the miserly, the haughty, one living without any interest in his future well-being, if they do not fall into hell, but reach humanity again, will be reborn, the first sickly the second ugly, the third powerless the fourth poor, the fifth in a low position and the sixth a fool. Whereas, man who have cultivated the contrary qualities, rise up to divine worlds rebon as men become respectively healthy, beautiful, well to-do of high rank or wise."[11] Thus the course of future existence, as formulated in Buddhism, is determined by the direction of *taṇhā*, taken during the course of our present life uptill the moment of death. This idea finds beautiful expression in *Dhammapada*, as :

> The craving of the man addicted to careless living grows like a creeper. He jumps from life to life like a fruit-loving monkey in the forest.[12]

To conclude : It is *taṇhā* that compels the creatures to wander to and fro within *Saṁsārā*.

Now, let us turn to the *śabada* and analyse it in the Buddhist perspective. Bhagat Trilochan is of the firm belief that whosoever, at the moment of death, is obsessed with the image of Lachmi is sure to be reborn as serpent. Similarly, if obsessed with the idea of woman, sons and mansion, one can not escape from being reborn as prostitute, swine and preta respectively.

Before we analyse the significance of corresponding consequences of various obsessions or last wishes of man; it would be useful, at this stage of our enquiry, to decode the meanings of expressions such as '*Simray*' and '*aisi cīṅtā meain jay mare*'. *Simray* signifies the sum total of psyche that thas come to existence as a result of one's entire course of life. One is by and large, bound to wish at the moment of death, in accordance with one's personal psychology. At the moment of death, senses almost cease to function, consciousness disappears, the *tanhā*, not yet dead in dying person, operates entirely devoid of cognition and intune with its innermost structure. But, this is not alway and in all cases imperative. One may at decisive moment deviate from one's personal psychology and contemplate upon certain thing or being, entirely inconsistent with the inner structure of being. This means that rebirth is conditioned by the last wish of man. The emphasis in the expression, *aisi cintā meain jay mare*' on '*jay*' or 'if' is quite significant because it testifies the notion of conditionality, further supporting our contention of possible deviation at the decisive moment. Not that the concerned person escapes the bitter fruits of his evil deeds forever, these consequences are only postponed and evil deeds are rendered ineffective for the time being. One has to take birth/births corresponding to one's *taṇhā* manifested in various forms and suffer the results till these are exhausted.

What kind of affinity is contemplated in the scheme put forth By Bhagat Trilochan, betwen the object of last wish and its corresponding consequences in the form of rebirth in some realm of existence or other ? The first object of obsession is *Lachmi* or *Lakṣamī* that results in rebirth as serpent. The problem here is to discover the probable affinity between *Lachmi* and serpent, when one is a mythical being and another factual one. The word *Lakṣamī* is derived from the word '*lakṣya*' or '*lakṣama*' which means goal.[13] Therefore, viewed in the semantic context, *Lakṣamī* is goddess of superme goal. There are various aspects of *Lakṣamī* for the various kinds of devotees. *Lakṣamī*, when adorned as consort of Lord Viṣṇu symbolizes all that is conducive in the maintenance of life. *Lakṣamī* is also worshiped as '*Shrī*' which combines grace, competence and confidence. In Viṣṇu Purāṇa, we come across, an expression. *yataḥ satyam tathā Lakṣamī*, when translated its means, 'where there is truth; there is *Lakṣami*'. One can safely conclude that when Bhagat Trilochan disparagingly refers to *Lakṣamī* or *Lachmī* as an object of last wish resulting in rebirth as serpent, has certainly some other dimensions of *Lakṣamī* in view. Yes, there is that aspect of *Lakṣamī* bracketed with worldly wealth. Needless to say that worldly people worship *Lakṣamī* in return asking for worldly gains. Whereas those with saintly bent of mind, seeking nothing but truth, adorn *Lakaṣmī* as the goddess of Supreme Goal. By way of conclusion we can say that reference to *Lachmī* or *Lakṣamī* in the *Śabada* under discussion, denotes only worldly aspect of her which the worldly people relish the most.

The second part of the first unit is serpent. What the serpent has to do with the worldly weath ? If we look at the symbolic representation of *Lakṣamī*, we find the owl sitting quietly on the left hand side of her where gold coins are falling from one hand of *Lakṣamī*. An owl, we know can not see clearly in the day-light; it is a night-bird. Darkness symbolizes ignorance. Clinging to weatlh not only testifies the ignorance of the concerned person, this also results in imbalancing the economy of society. An owl in place of serpent would have been quite close to the details of the symbolic representation of *Lakṣamī*. It appears that when Bhagat Trilochan considers serpent having a close affinity with the lust for wealth, he is making use of folk-beliefs. In our folk-tradition it is believed that serpent guards the hidden treasures and whereever dwells a serpent of quite old age there must be hidden treasure. In the Poṭhohāra (District Rawal Pindi) it is common belief among the folk-people that during the night the serpents shift hidden treasure from one place to another. More so, wherever one hears tinkling sound, this means that serpent is draging the treasure to a certain place and one can trace out the treasure by following the track of tinkling sound. Thus, serpent, according to the folk-beliefs, has affinity with wealth.[14]

Next constitutent of the scheme of *Śabada* is women. The obsession of women, continuing till the last moment of man's life results in rebirth as a prostitute. We can not say what would be the fate of a women obsessed with the idea of man in similar fashion. The whole scheme seems to be conceived from man's angle. The position of woman as a prostitute is decidedly most despicable when viewed in the context of normal mode of social living. Here the composition consisting of woman as one part and prostitute as the second half of the unit, in the form of inversion i.e. man being reborn as a prostitute, only registers the retributory consequences of lustful mental disposition. The Buddhist precept of refraining from sexual misdeeds, all the more, in its own way, supports the contention of Bhagat Trilochan.

Next in order of sequence is obsession with the idea of sons that leads to the animal world, and where one is reborn as a swine. To call a person swine is to express one's utmost contempt for that person, as it is considered to be a very strong term of abuse. The sons stand to inherit the property, and in this way help in providing immortality to the institution of private property. An illegitimate child, when condemned as a bastard, also, speaks to serve the interest of this institution. There is no denying the fact that such a child is an out come of sexual misdeed. But, it is the dominance of wealth that manifests itself in the form of dominant idea. This scheme of thought, in the *Śabada*, speaks more of wealth than anything else. This stream of thought continues and find its expression in the last worth condemning affinity between mansion and *preta*. *Preta* is a Sanskrit form of the Pāli *Peta* which according to Childers means, "the departed spirit of a dead person."[15] The distinction amongst the dead persons is quitc relevent, when viewed in the background of our present pursuit of discovering the latent meanings existing between the idea of mansion and *preta*. In the preface to *The Buddhist Conception of Spirit*, the book based on *Petavatthu*, the seventh book of *Khuddaka Nikāya*, Dr. Bimal Churn Law, while explaining the term *preta* educates us about the distinction in the following words :

> In the general sense, *pretas* are those who are dead and gone and pass either as happy dead or as unhappy dead. The stories of the first are to be found in the *Vimānvatthu* with certain exceptions to the rule.[16]

Bhagat Trilochan when refers to *preta* in the context it means the 'unhappy dead' "who suffer in the nether world on account of their misdeeds in the previous existence."[17] There are fifty one stories of *pretas* or *petas* in *Pettavatthu*. These stories hardly gives us any clue, to solve the problem of existing affinity between the obsession of mansion leading to rebirth as *preta*. Agreed, that the Buddhism was not innovator of preta-belief and these beliefs did exist prior to the advent of Buddhism. Our main concern, here, is not to trace the origin and development of preta-belief, we are only interested, at the moment, to unravel the mystery forming a link between mansion and *preta*. Here, again, the folk tradition comes to our rescue. It is a folk-belief that the 'unhappy dead' haunt houses. Unhappiness, in the instant illustration, speaks of clinging to property. As Buddhists or students of Buddhism, we know it is clinging that is the root-cause of *dukkha*. Being obsessed with the idea of mansion, at the decisive moment, is nothing but clinging to it, and which out of inumerable manifestations of *taṇhā* or thirsting-will, is just one. In short, the link between mansion and *preta* is clinging to property and clinging of whatsoever nature, in the final analysis, morally speaking, is a misdeed.

Bhagat Trilochan has not only worked out the results of clinging to wealth aad women, conceived as misdeeds, this scheme of misdeeds is further highlighted by contrasting it with an act of goodness. What is this goodness ? This goodness means meditating upon Nārāyaṇa at the time of death. Goodness as contemplated in the *Śabada*, is neither an isolated act nor a policy, it means mode of life that leads a man to attain *mukti*. *Mukti* from what ? *Mukti* when viewed within the framework of the *Śabada*, from clinging to wealth and women. So, to meditate upon *Nārāyaṇa* at the deeisive moment demands that one should have acquired the qualities akin to *Nārāyaṇa*. One can not intune oneself with *Nārāyaṇa* at any moment during the course of life or for that matter at the moment of death, without an aid of *Nārāyaṇa-guṇa*. Similar view is also depicted in *Tevijja Sutta* of *Dīgha Nikāya*. Any one, inorder to dwell in the world of *Brahmā*, after one's departure from this world, ought to acquire the qualities of *Brahmā*, that may prompt him at the decisive moment. *Brahmā-loka,* according to Theravāda is different from *Nibbāna-nagar*. *Brahmā-loka* is one of the five realms of existence that constitute *Saṁsāra*. Whereas *Nibbāna-nagar* falls out of the purview of *Saṁsāra*. One can enter into *Nibbāna-nagar*, only, after one has extinguished *taṇhā*.

It would be wrong to conclude that Bhagat Trilochan

looks down upon wealth and women. There is nothing wrong with wealth and women as such, it is clinging to wealth and craviag for women, structurally ensuring from the former, that needs to be censured. But, why to warn against clinging to wealth alone ? Clinging is to be dsspised in whatever form it is, clinging is after all clinging.

May be, that clinging to these two in its various forms is most commoh and deserves to be taken special cognisance. The Buddha, in *Dhammapada* has pointed to two roads : "One is the road that leads to wealth; another road is that leads to *Nibbāna*."[18] For Bhagat Trilochan another road is that leads to *Pītāmbara* and '*Pītāmbra vākay ridhay bassay*', dwelling of *Pītāmbara* within is an alternate expression for having become *mukta*. *Mukti* and *Nibbāna*, these two although achieved, following two different ways, are identical in nature, in the sense that both demand doing away with clinging and leads a *Bhagat* or *Arahat* to an identical end i.e. cessation of *Saṁṣāra*.

References and Notes

1. *Ā.G.*, pp. 92, 525-526 and 625 respectively.
2. Macauliffe, M.A., *The Sikh Religion*, Vol. VI, pp. 76-77.
3. *Ā.G.*, p. 526.
4. cf. Rhys Davids, T.W., *The Question of King Milinda*, Part I, Vol. 35 pp. 71ff.
5. Grimm, George, *The Doctrine of the Buddha*, p. 106.
6. Horner, I.B., *The Book of Discipline*, Vol. IV, p. 14.
7. Buddhism recognizes five realms that constitute *Saṁsāra*. These realms viz. i. *niraya*; ii. *pettivisaya*; iii. *tiracchānayoni*; iv. *manusā*; v. *devaloka* in Mahāsīhanāda Sutta (M. 12 : M. i. 74-77) are characterized proportionate to the degree of pain one undergoes during one's stay in these five realms. In *Abhidhammattha Saṅgaha* these five realms are further divided into thirtyone.
   cf. (i) Ta. 258-259.

(ii) Sobti, H.S., *Nibbāna in Early Buddhism*, p. 21; pp. 34-35f.

8. M. 57 ; M. i. 388-389.
9. M. 135 (*Cūla-kamma-Vibhanga-Sutta*) : M. iii. 203-204. Chalmers, Vol. II, p. 269. cf. Grimm, George, *op. cit.*, p. 191.
10. M. iii. 203 Chalmers, *op. cit.*, p. 269.
11. M. 135 and 136. Grimm, George, *op. cit.*, p. 191.
12. Dhp. 334 : *Manujassa pamatta cārino*
    taṇhā vaḍḍhati māluvā viya,
    So plavati hurāhuraṁ
    phaiaṁ icchaṁ'va vanasmiṁ vānaro.

    'Narad, Mahāthera' *Dhammapada*, p. 253.
13. Regarding detailed study of symbol of *Lakṣmī* see, Indu, Indergit, *Science of Symbols—Deeper View of Indian Deities*, especially pages 85-86.
14. Bedi, Sohinder Singh, *Panjābi Lokadhārā Vishava Kośa*, Vol. II, pp. 533-534. cf. JA. 73 (*Saccaṁkira-Jātaka*).
    In the *Jātaka* rich merchant is mentioned to have reborn as a Snake at the spot where he had kept his treasure.
15. Childers, R.C., *Dictionary of Pāli Language*, p. 378.
16. Law, Bimal Churn. *The Buddhist Conception of Spirits*, p. ix, (Preface to the second edition).
17. *Ibid.*, p. ix.
18. Dhp. 75 : *Aññā he lābhūpanisā*
    añña nibbānagāmini

    Maxmuller, *Dhammapada*, p. 22.

13

PANJABI LITERATURE : A RESPONSE TO BUDDHISM*

Panjabi litterateurs have displayed lively interest both in translating Buddhist classics and seeking inspiration from Buddhist themes for their original compositions. Buddhist themes, in Panjabi literature, have found expressions through a number of litetary genres, such as poetry, short stories, biographies of the Buddha, both in prose and verse and radio play etc.[1] To study the literary nuances and thus passing judgements over literary excellence and/or failure of these writings is necessarily, kept out of purview of this paper. The august audience, mostly consisting of other than Panjabi knowing people, shall, I presume, be more interested to know the response to Buddhism in ideological terms. One of the main trend, prevailing during the modern period, has been to review Sikhism in the background of Buddhist heritage. This paper, therefore, is an attempt to identify this very trend and to decode its meanings, as well.

Sardar Kapur Singh I.C.S., a profound scholar of Sikh studies and a singular innovator of invigorating trend of reviewing Sikhism in the background of Buddhist heritage, in his book *Pundreek—A Collection of Cultural Essays*, written in Panjabi language and published in 1952, has devoted one full essay

*Paper presented in the Department of Buddhist Studies, University of Delhi on 11 February, 1986 under Extension Lectures Series.

entitled *Dhammapada*[2], covering about one hundred pages, to the study of the Buddhist classic. The essay begins with brief introduction to the development of Buddhism into various sects and schools, occasionally, referring to the related Buddhist texts. The author is of the view that the introductory remarks would help in "appreciating the substance and the background of the *slokas* [*gāthas*] of *Dhammapada*".[3] An introduction is followed by the translation of 101 *gāthas* of *Dhammapada* into Panjabi language. The transcription of these Pāḷi *gāthaṣ* into *Gurmukhi* script is not only faulty at many places, at times, it is highly offending to the Pāli knowing reader. An alluring factor of this essay is making references to the Gurūs of the Sikhs. A reference made to Gurū Gobind Singh, the tenth and the last Gurū of the Sikhs, is revealing. Sardar Kapur Singh, here, reffers to an autobiographical note of Gurū Gobind Singh', interprets the same, and, thus, identifies the latter's mission of life akin to the fulfillment of Bodhisattva Ideal.[4] Again, after making reference to the worship of *Tipiṭaka* in Sri Lanka, the author, as if joyous at his discovery, writes, that:

> This idea in its primordial and pure form reappears with the birth of Sikhism. After two thousand years the missing link once again found its continuity.[5]

He is, infact, alluding to the daily practice of worshipping of *Ādi Granth* by the Sikhs, as 'a living Gurū'. Also, while translating *gāthas* of *Dhammapada* Sardar Kapur Singh hardly fails to draw parallels to the compositions of the Gurūs of the Sikhs, wherever possible.

The parallels drawn, as such, between Buddhism and Sikhism, may to some appear spurious. But, for Sardar Kapur Singh these parallels are not only far from being incidental, rather, are essential for proper understanding of Sikhism. He seems to establish (we shall see in the following pages) that Sikhism has its roots in Buddhist tradition and not in Hinduism as generally understood and propagated. Similarities existing between the Buddhist and Sikh traditions have also been pointed out by some other eminent Panjabi litterateurs. Professor Mohan Singh in his Introduction to the translation of Sir Edwin Arnold's *Light* of *Asia* into Panjabi language, under the title *Asia Dā Cānaṇ* (1944) also mentioned about certain similarities existing between two traditions. The parallel drawn between *pañcavaggiyā bhikkhūs* of the Buddhist tradition and *Panja Piarās* or 'Five Beloved Disciples' of Sikh tradition deserves special mention. Professor Mohan Singh writes that when the Buddha preached his doctrine to the five disciples, at Sārnath, converted them into his fold had served them meals (*praśād*) sharing from one and the same *lohe dā bāṭṭa* or iron vessel. Gurū Gobind Singh, he adds, and in tune with Sikh tradition, also did likewise.[6] Sardar Kapur Singh's observation on this point adds more to it. "When Gurū Gobind Singh manifested *khālsā mat* (doctrine)" writes Sardar Kapur Singh in his short biography of *Gotama Buddha*, in prose form, to "his 'Five Beloved Ones' and named *khālsā mat* as *khalsa panth* (Path). Gotama's first Sermon in the ancient Buddhist scriptures is highlighted as *Dharma Cakkara-parivarnttana* or 'Gifts of Nector' (amrit dān).[7] The derivations of Sardar Kapur Singh, here, are unparallel. "Offering nector and wearing *Cakkara* made of iron" opines the author, "are an integral part of the precepts of Sikh tradition."[8]

Attempts are also made to point to parallels existing between the life of the Buddha and Gurū Nānak, the founder of Sikhism. In this context specific mention is made to two events. Firstly, when, both the Buddha[9] and Gurū Nānak[10] were sent to their respective teachers for undergoing training in formal education, are stated to have disarmed their teachers with rare wisdom.

Secondly, it is recorded in Buddhaghosa's *Jātāka Aṭṭhakathā* that "on the day of the Ploughing Festival when (the Buddha) sat on the royal seat under the shade of a rose-apple tree, the shadow of the tree moved not."[11] Likewise, we find in the biographies of Gurū Nānak, revered as *Janam Sākhis* in Sikh tradition that reads:

> (Having gone to grove and stretched out under the tree Bābā (Nānak) slept through the day without stirring. Rai Bular had come out hunting and (while passing that way) he happened to observe some one sleeping under a tree. The shadow of that tree remained stationary.[12]

Whatever may be the nature of affinity between these parallels, one thing clearly emerges that Panjabi litteratuers have always cherished the memory of the Buddha while writing about Sikh tradition. This fact is also highlighted by Professor M. Singh (Lahore), "When at last the time came for writing a life of Nānak" states Prof. M Singh "his biographers did not forget Buddha and Buddhism."[13]

The relation between the Buddhist and Sikh tradition acquires new dimension when Sardar Kapur Singh, that too based on scriptural evidences, puts forth an altogether new definitions of the terms Sikh and Singh. Sardar Kapur Singh in one of his short note on *A Sikh and Singh*, included in his book, *Prasharprasna* (1959) in English, repudiating the Sanskrit word *Shishya* as the root of the word Sikh, comments that:

> ....Nor, indeed is the word 'Sikh' a corrupted form of the Sanskrit *Shishya* as is generally supposed for the word Sikh is a technical term which occurs in the Pāli *Dhammapada*, with an unimbiguous definition of its dennotation. Indeed, the Sanskrit *Shishya* appears to be an artificial extraction made by Pānini or his predecessors—purists from the original older and richer Pāli Sikh.[14]

In support of his argument the author quotes *gāthas* number 44 and 45 from Pāli *Dhammapada* and the relevant part is as follows:

Verse 44 : *ko imaṁ paṭhaviṁ vijessati*

... ... ---

ko dhammapadaṁ sudesītaṁ

... ...

Verse 45 : *sekho paṭhaviṁ vijessati*

... ...

sekho dhammapadaṁ sudesītaṁ

... ..."[15]

Sardar Kapur Singh's translation of these two *gāthās* into English are quite revealing and which is as under:

Verse 45 : who shall be the victor

... ...

who shall achieve the life everlasting

... ...

Verse 45 : The Sikh shall be the victor

... ...

The Sikh shall achieve the life everlasting[16]

... ...

Obviously, the word "Sekho" has been translated as 'Sikh'. Dr. L.M. Joshi,[17] a well-known Buddhist scholar, it may be mentioned, here, also, in a way concurred with Sardar Kapur Singh, while describing 'Sekho' as equivalent to the word 'Sikh.'

Thereafter, Sardar Kapur Singh switches over to an appellation 'Singh'. Here, quoting from *Aṅguttara Nikāya*, the author decoding the meaning of the term *tathagata*, concludes that:

"What is truth finder? *tathāgatha*, the generic name for which is a lion, a Singh."[18] Further, dilating on the precise relation between the term "Sikh" and "Singh", Sardar Kapur Singh states, that:

> The term Sikh implies a person who is a learner, who is set on the Path of spiritual perfection and self-realization, who has not yet found the truth in entirety, and who therefore, cannot be designated as a *tathagatha*, or a Singh. When a Sikh has ceased acting with the fulcrum of his little ego, he becomes a Singh, the perfected one.[19]

Nārad Mahāthera's explanation of the term "Sekha", may be useful and we quote:

> The term "*Sekha*", literally one who undergoes training, is applied to a disciple who has attained the first stage of Sainthood (*Sotāpattl*), until he attains the Arahatta Magga (Path) Stage. When he totally eradicates passions and attains this final fruit stage of an *Arahant*, he is called an "Asekha" as he has perfected his training.[30]

When we compare the two explanations of the term "Sekha", we are left with no option than to accept the broad agreement that exists between the two scholars on the subject.

There is one more dimension of pointing to parallels with altogether different motive. Dr. L.M. Joshi in collaboration with Dr. Sharda Gandhi has translated the entire Pāli *Dhammapada* into Panjabi language alongwith critical and explanatory notes and published under Guru Nānak Quincentenary Series by Panjabi University, Patiala. The transcription is preceeded by Introduction. It is for the first time that Panjabi knowing reader is introduced to Buddhism in an authentic Buddhist idiom. The transcription of Pāli *gāthās* into Gurmuki script at places, is not correct. Also, there are quite good number of *gāthas* whose text does not tally with the Scriptures. The author, while adding explanatory notes to certain *gāthās* occasionally refer to the composition of Farid,[21] Kabir,[32] Guru Nānak,[23] Gurū Arjan,[24] besides, at times comparing the substance of these *gāthās* with Upanisads and also with verses from Mahābharta. The motive of comparison, especially to the composition of *Ādi Granth,* is no other than to lay in a way, a sound base for a comparative study of Buddhism and Sikkhism, a welcome attempt, indeed, for any comparativist. Dr. L.M. Joshi had already moved in this direction and also published few papers[25] on *Buddhism and Sikkhism.* In one of his paper Dr. Joshi hopefully concluded that :

> There are many points on which Buddhism and Sikkhism make common bridge of understanding. It is hoped that some will take up the task in future and make further study of the subject,[26]

So, there are two main trends prevalent : (i) comparing Sikkhism and Buddhism with all the sobriety of a scholar, a comparativist and (ii) Finding roots of Sikkhim in Buddhism. And, the second one is quite alarming. To some Sardar Kapur Singh's interpretation of the terms 'Sikh' and 'Singh' may seem to be far-fetched and also motivated. In case we agree to that, then, I am afraid, we should be too willing to submit to the notion that such an interpretation within the framework of Buddhism, only, reflects that psyche of the Sikhs which is *aware of* the 'fraternal embrace' of Hinduism.

References and Notes

1. The number of creative writings in Panjabi language based on Buddhist themes may be much more. In a short span of about two months I could search out only a few and which are enlisted below:
   i. Singh, Puran, *Buddhaji Da Dhyāni Butt*, poem included in *Puran Singh Jiwani Te Kavita*, pp. 340-341.
   ii. Safeer, Pritam Singh, *Kapalvastu Di Yashodhara Da Swāmi*, a poem included in *Agam Agochar*, pp. 23-24.
   iii. Kour, Prabhjot, *Aman Da Paighambara*, a long poem consisting of 30 pages.
   iv. Hasrat, Sukhpal Veer Singh, *Sūraj Hinduttan Da* a poem included in *Hasrat Kavya* pp. 246-246.
   v. Sukhinder, *Gotam Di Wāpsi* a poem included in *Lakaḍ Diān Macchiyān*, pp. 24-26.
   vi. Shehr yaar, *Siddhartha Di Wāpsi* a poem included in *Siddharatha Di Wāpsi* pp. 1-3.
   vii. Prectlari, Gurbaksh Singh, *Gori Te Bhagwan Buddha* a short story included in *Preet Kahāniayan*, pp. 35-49.
   viii. Khanna, Guran Ditta, *Amar Jyoti* a biography of the Bundha in verse consisting of 66 pages.
   ix. ————————, *Buddha Jataka Kathāvāna*, consisting of 231 pages.
   x. Duggal, Kartar Singh, *Buddhaṁ Sarnaṁ Gacchaṁi* a radio play.
2. Singh, Kapur, *Pundreek*, pp. 228-320.
3. Ibid., p. 233.
4. Ibid., p. 237.
5. Ibid., p. 262-263.
6. Singh, Mohan, *Asia Dā Cānaṇ*, p. 6.
7-8. Singh, Kapur, *Sapat Shring*, p. 141.
9. For details see :
   Bays, Gwendolyn (Trs.) *The Voice of the Buddha : The Beauty of Compassion* (translation of *Lalitavistara*) vol. I, pp. 191-194.

10. For details see :
    i. Singh, Bhāi Vir, (ed.) *Purātān Janam Sākhi* (biographies of Gurū Nanak) pp. 1-5.
    ii. Mcleod, W.H. (ed. and Trs.) *The B* 40 *Janam Sākhi* (biography of Gurū Nānak) pp. 5-9.
    iii. Singh, Mohan, op. cit. p. 5.
11. Cowell, E.B. (ed. and Trs.) *Jātakas* Vol. VI. pp. 247. Jātaka No. 547 (Vessantara Jātaka).
12. Mcleod, op. cit. pp. 11-12.
13. Singh, M. Prof. (Lahore) later on Dr. Mohan Singh Oberoi 'Diwāna'). *Buddhism and Sikhism*, p. 283.
14. Singh, Kapur, *Parashar prasna*, p. 274.
15-16. Ibid., p. 275.
17. Joshi, L.M. and Gandhi, Sharda, (Trs.) *Dhammapada*, p. 279.
18. Singh, Kapur, *Parasharpraśna* p. 279.
    cf. A. v. 32-33.
19. Ibid., p. 282.
20. Nārad, Mahāthera (Trs.) *Dhammapada*, p. 326.
21-24. Joshi op. cit., pp. 64, 67, 69, 73, 75, 81, 93, 94, 114, 134.
25. Joshi, L.M. (i) *Buddhism and Early Sikhism*, pp. 126-143.
    i. *Buddhist tradition and Gurū Nānak*, pp. 146-145.
    ii. *Buddhism and Sikhism*, pp. 24-26.
26. Ibid., p. 26.

14

MĀRA AND MĀYĀ*

Anyone, while studying the concept of *Māyā* as enhsrined in *Nānakbāṇi* (of Mahallā),[1] and familiar with *Pālitipiṭaka* and and its commentaries, is sure to recall the concept of *Māra*. Since, both *Māra* and *Māyā* are counterparts to each other, when viewed in the background of the Buddhist and Gurū tradition, respectively. The only difference and a striking difference, indeed, being that *Māra* is a villain[1], whereas, *Māyā* is defied as villainess. In what way *Māra* and *Māyā* attempt to whisk the beings away from the Path of Truth, to perceive this and find way out of it, we propose to analyse their mode of functioning.

Pāḷitipiṭaka, as if an epitome of cosmic play, very vividly presents before us Siddhārtha Gotama and *Māra*, playing the role of a hero and a villain, respectively. Right from the moment, Siddhārtha resolved to relieve himself of Power, *Māra* started chasing him. A little while before he attained to *Sambodbi*;[2] and long after that *Māra*, relentlessly, kept on chasing Siddhārtha.

Theravādin Buddhist tradition holds the view that Siddhārtha Gotama (624—544 B.C.) in the twenty-ninth years of his life i.e., in the year 595 B.C.; went forth on *abhinisakaramaṇa* or

*Paper presented and published in the proceedings of the International Seminar on *Ādi Granth*, organised by *Vismādnād*, Ludhiana during 4-6 November, 1993.

Great Renunciation. When Siddhārtha left Kapilavatthu, his home-town, for Magadha, *Māra* confronted him, first time, on that very way. In the *Maḍhuraṭṭhavilāsinī*, we find a reference to this first encounter between Gotama and *Māra*, when the latter made a very liberal offer, requesting :

> *Mā nikhama mahāvira, ite te Sattame dine*
> *Dibbaṁ tu cakkaratanaṁ addhapātu bhavissati.*[3]
> Do not depart, great hero, in seven days from now the devalike treasure of the wheel will certainly appear to you.

Gotama, resolutely, turned down this offer of *Māra* and continued with his pilgrimage. After Gotama had arrived at Magadha, he selected a secluded spot, in the forest of Ururelā, in the vicinity of Gayā (now, Bodha Gayā) and close to the village *Senānigāma*, as his *tapobhūmi* or place of austersity. Here, on the bank of river *Nerañjarā*, where Gotama was absorbed in meditation, a fierce battle took place between him and *Māra*. Besides, at several places, else where, in both the Pāḷi canonical and non-canonical works, the detailed account of this battle is available in *Padhāna Sutta*[4] of *Sutta Nipāta* and in the section of *Nidānakathā*[5] of *Jātakaṭṭhakathavaṇṇaṇā*. Before we look into any aspect of this battle, we ought to know about the area of influence of *Māra*, besides, his capacity and the extent to which he can harm 'ignorant worldling' folk. Better to seek guidance from the Buddha on this point. In the *Saṁyutta Nikāya*, the Buddha answering the question of Rādhā as to the existential status of *Māra*, replies, thus : '.........corporeality is *Māra*.........consciousness is *Māra* ....' In brief, all the five *khandhās* are stated to be under the dictatorial rule of *Māra* that symbolizes evil[6]. Five *khhandhās* consist of i. *rūpa*; ii. *vedanā*, iii. *Saññā*, iv. *Viññāṇa* and v. *Saṅkhāra*. The sum total of these constitute corporeal organism we call personality. These five in association with *taṇhā* or thirsting-will as a result of craving for things, beings and ideas, take the form of *pañcaupādānakkhandha*. This is defied as a nefarious design of *Māra*. The Buddha, while summing up *dukkhabodha*, repeatedly stated that :

> *Saṁkhittena pañca-upādāna-kkhandha pi dukkha*[7].
> In short, five *khandhas* constitute suffering.

Not only the Buddha, but, *Māra* too, is quite aware of his evil genius. In *Kassaka Sutta of Saṁyutta Nikāya*, *Māra* claims sovereignty over the entire domgin of human personality addressing the recluse, thus :

> Mine recluse, is the eye, mine are the material shapes, mine is the field of visual consciousness, where can you go. recluse, to escape from me ? Precisely, mine, recluse are the ear; sounds, the field of auditory consciousness; the tongue, tastes, the field of gustatory consciousness; precisely mine, recluse, is the mind, mine are the mental states, mine is the field of mental consciousness.[8]

Māra's claims are not at all disputed, rather these are willingly conceded to. This means that the entire *Saṁsāric* existence forms the domain over which *Māra* rules as an unchallenged despot. One thing is abundantly clear that the life of *puthujjana* (one who has not commenced his piligrimage on the Middle Path) is governed by the will of *Māra*.

After undergoing rigorous practices of austerities for about six years, Gotama realized that these austerities were no more conducive to gain *sambodhi* (enlightenment). He, therefore, abandoned the path of *attakilamathānuyoga* (self-mortification) and took to the normal life of a recluse. Gotama, one day, took his bath at the spot known as *Suppatiṭṭhita*, on the bank of river *Nerañjarā*, and ate milk-rice offered by Sujātā, committing himself to *adhiṭṭhānāsana*, sat on the mat made of grass, offered by Sotthiya, the grass-cutter, under a *Pīpal* tree and solemnly declared that :

> Let my skin, and sinews, and bones become dry, and welcome! and let all the flesh and blood in my body dry up! but never from this seat will I stir, until I have attained the supreme and absolute wisdom.[9]

This mighty resolution of Gotama was a sufficient cause of alaram for *Māra*, that prompted the latter to plan a attack. Thousand-armed *Māra* while riding over his elephant, *Girimekhala*, led the army of his followers armed with dreadful weapons, assuming fearsome shapes. *Māra* made use of whirlwind, rain-storm, showering of rocks, weapons, live coals, hot ashes, sand, mud and causing darkness as weapons inorder to dislodge Gotama from his *adhiṭṭhānāsana*. On seeing *Māra*, thus attacking Gotama, all the gods who were a little while before surrounding him and, in a way, flattering him, out of fear, suddenly disappeared. Now, *Bodhisatta* was all alone! Later on, Gotama the Buddha, giving the vivid description of the battle enumerated that the army of *Māra* was ten-fold, consisting of—

> i. Lust (*Kāma*); ii. Aversion (*dosa*); iii. Hunger and thirst; iv. Craving (*taṇhā*) v. Sloth and torpor (*thīna-middha*) vi. Cowardice; vii. Doubt (*vicikicchā*); viii. Hypocrisy and Stupidity; ix. Gains, Fame, Honour and Glory manipulated and x. Self-admiration and con demnation of others.[10]

Bodhisatta, at this crucial juncture availed himself of *Dasapāramīs* (Ten Perfections) he had acquired during the course of his ten previous lives. The *dasapāramīs* with which *Bodhisatta* counter attacked the *Māra* are identified as :

> i. Alms giving (*dāna*); ii. Morality (*Sīla*); iii. Renunciation (*nekkhamma*); iv. wisdom (*paññā*); v. Energy (*Viriya*); vi. Patience (*Khanti*); vii. Truth; viii. Thinking (*Saṅkappa*); ix. Loving kindness (*mettā*) and x. equanimity(*upekkhā*).[11]

This battle faught between the *Bodhisatta* and the *Māra* is, therefore, interpreted to have symbolic overtones. While decoding the symbolic meanings of the said battle, T.W. Rhys Davids has stated that all the Buddha's,

> Old temptations came back upon him with renewed force. For years he had looked at all earthly good through the medium of a philosophy which had taught him that it, without exception, carried within itself the seeds of bitterness and was altogether worthless and impermanent, but now, to his wavering faith, the sweet delights of home and love, the charms of wealth and power, began to show themselves in a different light and glow again with attractive colours. He doubted and agonized in his doubt, but as the sun set, the religious side of his nature had won the victory and seems to have come out even purified from the struggle.[12]

Bodhisatta, ultimately, emerged victorious, no doubt, but, *Māra* refused to accept his defeat. *Māra* and his followers still claimed that the seat which Gotama was occupying belonged to *Māra*. The Buddha claimed, No! it belonged to him and produced earth as a witness to that effect. The earth in its peculiar way, while roaring, testified the claim of the Buddha. At least, that part of the earth was no more a part of the regime of *Māra*. This evidence itself, was sufficient to show the victory of the Buddha over *Māra*. This event, in the Buddhist tradition, is marked as a *bhūmi sparśa mudrā* of the Buddha. Now, *Māra* alongwith the band of his devotees, took to heels. And, the gods, who, at the very sight of *Māra* and his army, had run away, were attending to the (victorious) Buddha. Look at the demeanour of the gods!

The *Māra*, like vanquished enemy, had left before the sunset. After the sun had set, obviously, it was night and it was during the first watch of the night *Bodhisatta* gained the knowledge of previous lives (*pubbenivāsānussati ñāṇa*); in the second watch he acquired the divine eye (*dibba-cakkhu*); and in the third watch of the night he witnessed the Law of Dependent Origination (*paticcasamuppāda*) in order of both arising (*anuloma*) and cessation (*patiloma*). Thereafter, when the dawn had commenced the *Bodhisatta* comprehended Four Noble Truths (*Arya cattāri saccānī*). It was, precisely, after having gained the above stated four kinds of knowledge, that Gotama the *Bodhisatta* had become Gotama the Buddha. After becoming the Buddha his first utterance, known as *udāna vatthu,* was, that :

Anekajātisaṁsariṁ
Sandhāvissaṁ anibbisaṁ
gahakānaṁ gavesanto
dukkhā jāti punappunaṁ
Gahakānaka diṭṭhosi
puna gehaṁ na kāhasi
Sabbā te phāsukā bhggā
gahakuṭaṁ visaṅkhataṁ
visankhāragataṁ cittaṁ
taṇhānaṁ khayamajjhagā.[13]

Thro' many a birth in *Saṁsāra*
Wandered I,
Seeking out but not finding, the
builder of the house.
Sorrowful is repeated birth

O house-builder! you are seen
you shall build no house again,
All your rafters are broken
your ridge-pole is shattered
To dissolution (*Nibbāna*) goes my mind
Achieved is the end of craving.

Who is, after all, this *gahakāraka* (house-builder)? We can certainly satisfy our query with reference to craving (*taṇhā*). It is the bundle of *tanhā* that the *Māra*, successfully, goes on placing on the head/shoulder of a *puthujjana*. It is on account of this malady of *taṇhā* that one is born again and again (*anekjātisaṁsāriṁ*). *Taṇhā* is like a 'well of ego' destined never to be filled up. We need to wash it up and, thus, gain the purification of mind (*citta visuddhi*). This result is achieved, when metaphorically conceived, by conquering *Māra*. Since, undergoing the process of repeated births only means to add into the life-span of the sovereignty of *Māra*. The Buddha could gain the knowledge as regard to *anekajātisaṁsāriṁ*, only after he had conquered *Māra* and in no case before that.

The Buddha in a fight against *Māra* emerged victorious. But *Māra* was not prepared to accept his defeat; and he was, as if, determined to dislodge the Buddha from his Buddhahood. The *Māra* continued to carry out his nefarious design against the Buddha. Now, *Māra* commissioned his three beautiful daughters, namely, *taṇhā*, *Arti* and *Ragā* (*athakho Taṇhā ca Arti ca Ragā ca Māra dhitro*) to entice the Buddha. All the three, several times, made several attempts, but, failed in their mission. One thing certainly goes into their favour that they proved themselves wiser than their father, *Māra*, as they, gracefully, accepted their defeat.

As we have pointed out earlier, quite substantially, that the *Māra* was not prepared to give in, so, he kept up chasing the Buddha, even after, the latter had gained *Sambohi*. The Buddha, in the beginning, was reluctant to preach the *Dhamma*, as he had drawn his conclusion, that, the Path he had discovered was difficult to traverse. More so, as the eyes of the folk were filled up with the dust of *taṇhā* and it was of no avail to preach it, at all. This again, as interpreted, was an attempt on the part of *Māra* to dissuade the Buddha from preaching the *Dhamma*,

'Good in the beginning, good in the middle and good in the end'. It was at the intervention of *Brahmā Sahampaṭi* that the Buddha agreed, and conceded to his request to preach.

We also find a detailed description of the mischiefs, played by *Māra*, against one person or the other, in the *Māra Saṁyutta* of *Saṁyutta Nikāya.* The Buddha must be dislodged from his hard earned Buddhahood, to achieve this end, *Māra* did not spare any means available to him. Sometimes, he would assume himself to be an elephant or snake in order to frighten the Buddha. Has he really become the Buddha or it is just an illusion, *Marā* would inject ideas like that, creeping like snakes in his being. At times, *Māra* would disturb the assembly in one way or the other, at the time of delivering discourses. We learn from *Māhaparinibbāna Sutta* of the *Dīgha Nikāya* that when the Buddha was enjoying the bliss of *Sambodhi*, sitting under Ajapala Banyantree, at Uruvelā, *Māra* came over there with a request to enter into *Mahāparinibbāna.* The Buddha refused to oblige him and told him, instead, that he must established *buddhasāsana* before he bids farewell to the world.[14]

Māra not only kept chasing Gotama the *Bodhisatta* and Gotama the Buddha; he also continued with his design as regard to *Bhikkhunis*, like, Kissā Gotami and Khema; *upāsikā* like Dhaniyā and *upāsikā*, such as, Dhaniya's wife. He did not spare even *arahatas*, namely, Vakkali and Channa. One can understand wnen *Māra* attempts to whisk the *Bhikkhus*, *Bhkkhunis*, *upasaka* and *upasikas* away from the Path shown by the Buddha. But, one certainly fails to understand as to how *Māra* keeps up his morale so as to cause a great anxiety to several *arahatas* and the Buddha. Here, it needs to draw a distinction between the Buddha and *arahat*. Apart from several distinctions between the two one significant distinction is that Buddha helps others to attain to *Nibbāna*, where as, *arahat* is one who has realized the state of *Nibbāna*, but is not competent to guide others to become *arahat*. In order to unravel the mystery of *Māras* chasing Buddha and *arahat* we should look into two kinds of *Nibbāna* : i. *Sāupādisesa-nibbāna* and ii. *Anupādisesa-nibbāna.* The detailed distinction between the two has already been worked out, elsewhere[15]. Here, it is sufficient to underline that in the case of *Saupādisessa-nibbāna*, both Buddha and *arahat*, being alive, continue to have 'ground relations'. It is on the ground of this kind of 'relation' that *Māra* feels confident, musters his courage and hopes to tresspass into the lives of Buddhas and *arahatas*.

To conquer *Māra* is not every body's job. Only a few, called Buddhas and *arahats*, can accomplish this Herculean task. The Buddha, in the *Dhammapada*, has made us known the nature of task and vigilence required, in these words :

Taṁ vo vadāmi bhaddaṁ vo
yāvante'ttha Samāgatā
taṇhāya mūlaṁ Khaṇatha
Usīratthora bīraṇaṁ
mā vo naḷaṁva Sotova
māro bhañji punappunaṁ[16].

This I say unto you.
Good luck to you all who assembled here !
Dig up the root of craving as
One in quest of Birana's sweet root.
Let *Māra* not crush you again and again
as the flood, a reed.

Māra's attack is likened to that of a flood and one is advised to remain ever mindful, lest, it washes out one victim of *pamāda* (unmindful) like a reed. One is completely out of reach for *Māra* after entering into *Nibbānapurama*[17] or the city of *Nibbāna*, the only territory where *Māra* dares not to tresspass. Entrance to *Nibbānapurama* means the realization of the *State* of *Nibbāna*. This *State* of *Nibbāna* is realized, only, after the fire of *taṇhā* is extinguished. In fact, it is the state of extinction of fire of *taṇhā* that is *characterized* as *Nibbāna*. How to extinguish this fire ? Not by blowing it out. The only 'reasonable' device is to stop the supply of its fuel and the fuel is no other than *taṇhā* itself. It was precisely to extinguish the fire of *taṇhā* that the Buddha had shown the Noble Eightfold Path (*ariyo aṭṭhiṅgako maggo*). In other words, successful escape from the deadly attacks of *Māra* would be possible, only, when the Buddha has been accepted as *mārgadātā*, deified as *Mārabhibu Muni*.[18]

Māyā in *Nānakbāṇi is* a villainess depicted not in the form of a character, like *Māra*, but, primarily, in the guise of a concept, with multiple connotations. We are advised to fully comprehend the role of *Māya*, in our day to day living, thus, emancipating overselves from the maladies attending to it. The villainous character of *Māyā* is highlighted by calling it '*mohaṇi*'[19], (enchantress), '*ceri*',[20] (maid servant), '*kalavālī*'[21] (seller of spirits), '*Sāira kiputtri*'[22] (*Lakśmī*, daughter of ocean), '*makkhi*'[23] (fly), and 'māī'[24] (*Lakśmī/māyā*). Those who are attached to *Māyā* are looked down upon and called '*Sākatu*'[25] (worshipper of *Śakti*; worldly person) and '*manamukhu*'[26] (self-willed person). At one place *Māyā* is also called '*kaūā*'[27] (crow). After knowing about the personification of *Māyā* and its devotees it is necessary to fully acquaint oneself with its range of influence. The range of *Māya*, in *Nānakbāṇi*, is gauged with the use of expressions, such as, '*sagala bhavanu terī māyā*':[28] whole world consist of your *māyā*', '*sahhujagu dekhiū māya chāiā*':[29] whole world appears to be *māyā* and its shadow', '*māyā moha bhavajalu hai*':[30] 'infatuation of *māyā* is likened to water of existence, '*tribhavaṇu sāji mekhulī māyā*':[31] after creating three words (you) roped these in with *māyā* etc. One can easily imagine the limitless range of influence of *māya* while contemplating upon the quoted word-formations, such as, '*sagala, bhavanu*', '*Sabbhu Jagu*', '*bhavajalu*' and '*tribhavaṇu*'. At the same time, pointing it out as '*terī māyā*' (your Māyā) also suggests drawing distinction between *Māyā* and its Creator. How does the little details operate within the vast range of *Māyā*? Without fully comprehending this phenomenon, it would not be possible to appreciate the role of *Māyā*, in our day to day living. We find a very large variety of these details in *Nānakbaṇi*. Some of the foremost important details we quote as under :

Trisanā māyā mohani suta bandhapu ghara nāri. (*Ā. G., p. 61*)

Craving is Māyā that attacheth one to one's sons, kins, house hold and wife.

Mātapā suta nehu ghanerā māyā moha sabāī (*Ā. G., p. 75*)

Deep attachment to mother father, and sons All's but Māyā.

Nārī purakha sirjiai bikhu māyā moha piāro. (*Ā. G., p. 580*)

Man and woman create venom of attachment that is Māyā.

Dekhi kuṭambu māyā grihu mandaru sākatajaṁjāla prāli piā.
(*Ā. G., pp. 906-907*)

Sākata while looking at his family ties,
Māyā and home entangles (him self), unnecessarily.

Māyā suta dāra jagata piārā coga cugāi nita phāse
(*Ā. G., p. 1110*)

(He) attaches oneself to *māyā*, son, wife and the world, and thus picks up grain and is invariably trapped.

Māta pitā māyā deha 'Si' rogi rogi kuṭambu saṁjogi (*Ā. G., p. 1153*)

(Those) who are in union with mother, father, māyā, body family ties suffer from ego.

Jārau āisī prīti kuṭambu sanabandhi māya moha pasārī
(*Ā. G., p. 1198*)

I ought to burn the attachment of my family. members which is nothing but extension of attachment to *māyā*.

Not only the domestic relations, too, have the characteristics of *Māyā* they are also the result of a coincidence and, therefore, deserve to be discarded. The domestic relations, it appears, are devalued. What kind of relations we have with one and other? In substance, they are cast in the pattern of delusion of *Māyā* one suffers, precisely, because of one's delusion like that. Because *Māyā* is characterized as :

Māya mohu saraba Jaṁjālā (*Ā. G,. p. 222*)

Attachment to māyā yields nothing but entarglement.

Māyā mohi Jagu bādhā Jamakāli (*Ā. G., p. 412*)

As a result of attachment to *māyā*. Death has trapped the entire world.

Jama rāje ke herū āe māya kai saṅgali baṅdhi laiā. (*Ā. G., p. 432*)

The spy of Death come and take away those tied up with the chains of māyā trying up with those very chains.

At the same time, *Māyā* is described akin to venom :

Māyā maganu ahinisi magu Johai
nāmu nā levai marai bikhu khāi. (*Ā. G., p. 596*)

(He) remains sunk in *māyā* day and night and awaits
Does not repeat the Name (Thus) dies (as if) having consumed venom.

Bikkhu māya cittu mohiā bhāi caturāi pati khoi (*Ā. G., p. 637*)
The venom of *māyā* has deluded one's mind.
And, one is, hence, destroying his honour due to cunningness.

Manu māyā bandhio sara jāli
ghaṭi ghaṭi biāpi rahio bikhu nāli (*Ā. G., p. 831*)
Māyā has trapped the mind with the attachment of the ocean of existence.
God is dwelling in every heart but alongwith the venom of *māyā*.

Amriti choḍi mahā bikhu pīvai
māyā kā daiwānā. (*Ā. G., p. 1013*)
Forsakes nectar and drinks great venom of *Māyā*.
(The poor) ! mad after *Māyā*.

Māyā bikhu bhuigṅgamu nāle
ini dubidha ghara bahote gāle. (*Ā. G., p. 1029*)
The serpent of venom of Māyā also keeps company.
This dualism has destroyed number of families.

Māyā is also compared with liquor. Some of the references we quote :

Kalikalavāli māyā madu mīṭhā
manu matavālā pīvatu rahai. (*Ā. G., p. 350*)
Kaliyuga is akin to seller of Spirits.
The sweet is like a liquor.
The intoxicated mind is perpetually drinking.

Māyā madi māte tripti na āvai
tripti mukati mani sācā bhaivai (*Ā. G., p. 832*)
There is no satiety while drunk in the liquor of Māyā.
Satiety and liberations are available only when one relishes Truth inherent, within.

Nāma Visari māyā madu piā. (*Ā. G., p. 832*)
You drink liquor of Māyā only
When you forget (Divine) Name.

The consumption of liquor, decidedly, makes one unconscious. No doubt, it is also intoxicating, but, just for a while. The people consume liquor because of its intoxicating nature. This act, in the final analysis, puts one on the wrong track. Since, the 'intoxication of *Māyā*' does ensure the origination of *haumaiṁ* (ego). Infact, *haumaiṁ* is nothing but the microcosmic form of *Māyā* scattered all over. In spite of being in the grip of 'intoxication of *Māyā*' the anxiety of ensuing wrath of *yama rāia* or *yama* the king—the king of Dead, continues to haunt, unceasingly, such as :

Māyā mamtā pavahi khāilim
Jomapuri phasahiga Jamajāli (*Ā. G., p. 993*)

When you fall into thoughts of attachment to *Maya.*
You are sure to be trapped by the net of *Jama* in the city of death.

Sākata jama ki kāṇi nā cūke
Jama ka ḍaṇḍā nā kabahuin mūke. (*Ā. G., p. 1030*)

Sakata is never free from the fear of *Jama.*
The stick of *Jama* always haunts him.

Sākata phasī paṛai ikelā
Jama vasi kiā andhu duhelā. (*Ā. G., p. 1031*)

Sakata is trapped, all alone.
The ignorant one is put under the authority of *Jama* and, thus, suffers.

There are some other dimensions of *Māyā*, too, as :

Nihacalu mahalu nahīm chāiāa Māyā. (*Ā. G., p. 228*)

Immoveable is mansion (of God)
Remains unaffected by the shade of *Māyā.*

Māyā is not immovable in its nature. This is why it breeds suffering and its impact is short lived. While describing this kind of characteristics of *Māyā*, Bābā Nānak has described it synonymous with pelf—

Pāpām bājhho hovai nāhim
muiam sāthi na jāī. (*Ā. G., p. 417*)

You can not amass it without committing sin.
And it does not accompany you when you die.

Haumaim mamta Māyā
Sangi na jāi Rāma. (*Ā. G., p. 437*)

Ego, attachment and *Māyā.*
Do not go well with Being, Oh Rāma !

Bābā Māyā sāthi na hoi. (*Ā. G., p. 595*)

Oh Bābā ! Māyā is not going to give you lasting company.

Māyā sañci rāje ahaṁkāri
Māyā sathi na cale piārī. (*Ā. G., p. 1342*)
The self-centred ruler amassed Māyā.
When this dear one is not going to accompany for a long.

When a person in order to capture *Māyā* develops infatuation (*moha*) with her one begets nothing but transmigration :

Sākat kūṛe bandhī bhavāiahi
mari Janamhi āi jāī he. (*Ā. G. p. 1026*)
Sakata is caused to wander in false relationships.
He moves in the cycle of birth and death.

Man dies, because of his *moha* for *Māyā*, several times, since, he takes birth several times. Here, both *Māra* and *Māyā* are in accord with each other.

In the context of Buddhism we have discussed as to how to equip ourselves with ways and means to conquer *Māra*. In *Nānakbaṇi*, too, the Path is delineated leading to the emancipation from *Māyā*. This Path is named as 'Path of *Nāma Simrana*' (Meditating upon Divine Name). Which means that *Māyā* can be conquered with the use of *Nāma* as a weapon. To substantiate our view we quote from *Nānakbaṇi* :

Hari kā nāmu na cete prāṇī
bikalu bhaiā saṅgi māyā. (*Ā.G.*, p. 75)
O man ! you have not remember the Name of God.
You have been rendered helples being in the comping of Māyā.

Nāmu visāri māyā moda piā
binu guru bhagati nāhī sukha thīā
You drink liquor of Māyā and forget the (Divine) Name
You can not be satisfied without devotion to Gurū.

Sākata māyā kau batu dhāvhi
nāmu visārī kaha sukha pāvhi.
Sākata hankers after Māyā much.
How can you be satisfied when you forget (Divine) Name ?

Now, a new problem crops up that how and where from *Nāmu* (the Divine Name) can be made available ? This problem is properly looked into. *Nāmu* shall be available at the instance of the Grace of *Satigurū*. *Satigurū* out of Compassion shall pass on *Śabada* (the Divine Word). Other related factors falling in the purview of *Nāmu*, in *Nānakbāṇī*, are described as under :

Gurū prasādī pāiā, titthai māyā mohu cukāiā (*Ā.G.*, p. 73)

You realize (Truth) by the Grace of Gurū
Therefore, the attachment to Māyā withers away.

Sablu jagu dekhiā chāiā māyā
Nānak guramati nāmu dhiāiā. (*Ā.G.*, p 345)

The entire world is under the spell of *Māyā*.
One can meditate upon (Divine) Name only under the wise counsel of Gurū.

Māyā mohu gura sabadi jalāi (*Ā.G.*, p. 412)
nirmala nāmu sada hirde dhiāi.

The attachment to Māyā is burnt by the word of Guru.
And always remembers holy Name in his heart.

Māyā mohi jagu bādhā Jamakāli (*Ā.G.*, p. 412)
baṁdha chutai namu samhāli.

As a result of attachment to *Māyā* the Death has entrapped the entire world
The entrapped one shall liberate themselves through the remembering of (Divine) Name.

Māyā mohu bivaraji samāe (*Ā.G.*, p. 904)
Satigura bheṭai mela milāe.

That Being shuns the attachment of Māyā and merges in God who comes across *Satigurū* that bring him together (in union with God).

Mava mohu bhavajala hai aüdhū, (*Ā.G.*, p. 908)
Sabadi tarai kula tārī.

Oh Yogi ! the attachment to *Māyā* is akin to water of Existence.
One can cross over it through Divine Word.
And, thus, also saves his whole assembly.

Ehu mana māyā mohia aüdhu
nikasai sabadī vicārī.

Oh Yogi ! This mind of mine is captivated by *Māyā*.
Can liberate itself only through contemplating upon Divine Word.

Satigurū sabadā rahahi raṅga rātā
taji māyā haumaiṁ bharātā he.

Satigurū always remains immersed in the Divine Word.
He shuns ego and Māyā, Oh Brother !

Sākata nāri sabadi surati kiu pāīai,
Sabada surati binn āīai Jāiai.

How can *sākata* be mindful of Divine word,
Without that he comes and goes. (*Ā.G.*, p. 1042)

Notwithstanding, suggesting the way leading to the emancipation from *Māyā*, Gurū Nānak still upholds the view that :

Kiā bharama kiā māyā kahīai
Jo tisa bhāvai sai bhalā. (*Ā.G.*, p. 433)

What to talk of illusion and *Māyā*
All is well that pleases Him.

To Sum up, entire thrust is on *bhāṇā* (God's Will). What is this *bhāṇā*, after all ? In fact, some explanation is called for to explain the undergoing change, perpetually. In *Svetāsavatara Upaniśada* this change is explained away propounding number of theories, such as, *svabhāvāda* (Naturalism), *Niyativāda* or *Niyati* (Destiny), *Iśvaravāda* (God's Will), *Yadṛcchāvāda* (chance) *Kālavāda* (Time) and *Karma* etc. Gurū Nānak's *bhāṇā* falls in the purview of *Iśvarāvāda.* Whatever is happening it is in accordance with the Will of God. One has to susrender one's personal Will to the Will of God. This surrendering amounts to the *bhāṇā mannṇā* or accepting God's Will. Precisely, this is the message conveyed through the following dictum ;

Jo tisa bhāvai saī bhalā.

All is well that pleases Him. (*Ā.G.*, p. 433)

This must also be kept in mind that *Māyā* is no more a taboo for *Guramukha.* We find a reference, upholding this position in *Sāraṅga kī Vāra Mahalla IV* as :

Gurumukhi sabha pavitu hai
Dhanu sampai māyā,
Hari arthi jo kharacadc daimde sukhapāiā. (*Ā.G.*, p. 1246)

The amassing of wealth by *Guramukhi* is a sacred act
As he spends it for giving comforts to others.

Māra and *Māyā* when viewed in the perspective of Buddhist and Gurū traditions, respectively, though, counterparts to each other, yet, the Paths delineated to do away with the both, are altogether different from each other. In the *Theravādnī* Buddhist tradition it all depends upon one's own efforts. *Tathāgata* is there to suggest the Path only :

Tumhehi kiccaṁ ātappaṁ akkātāro tathāgatā.[32]
You yourselves should make an effort;
The *Tathāgatas* (Buddhas) only can show the way.

Whereas, according to the Gurū tradition, it is not at all possible to emancipate oneself from *Māyā*, without initially, with the Grace of Gurū and finally in the absence of Grace of God. The marked distinction between an ancient Indian religious traditions, such as, *brahamaṇic* and *śramiṇc*,[33] as noted by Orientalists is that the former advocates the view of God's Grace and the latter one that of one's own Grace. Attainment of *Nibbāna* in Buddhism and *Kevalaya* in Jainism, are the results of one's own efforts. These two religions, obviously, belong to *Śramaṇic* traditions. Whereas, the Gurū tradition *has* its roots in *brahmaṇic* tradition.

The depiction of *pāpa* (Evil), both in the Buddhist and Gurū traditions, fairly reflects the extent of Suffering that mankind undergoes, as a result of ignorance of Truth.

References and Notes

1. In *Vibhaṅga*, the Second book of *Abhidhamma Piṭaka* the possibility of woman becoming *Māra* is ruled out. See ; Rhys Davids, Mrs. (Ed.) *Vibhañga*, p. 336.
2. *Sambodhi*, has been characterised as *Svabodhanama* signifying the fact that one can accomplish it only through

one's own efforts and without an extraneous aid from any agency, human or divine.

3. Horner, I.B. (Ed.) *Mhdhuraṭṭhavilāsinī*, p. 282.
   Horner, I.B. (Tr.) *The Clarifier of the Sweet Meaning* (translation of *Madhuraṭṭhavilāsinī*), p. 405.
4. Fausbol, V., (Tr.) *Sutta Nipāta*, pp. 68-71 (*Padhāna Sutta*, verses : 424-448).
5. Kausalayan, Anand (Tr.) *Nidāna Katha* (Hindi) *Māra-vijaya*, pp. 143-147.
6. Feer, L. (Ed.) *Saṁyutta Nikāya*, Vol. III, pp. 188-89.
7. *Ibid.*, Vol. V, p. 421.
8. *Ibid.*, Vol. I, p. 115.
   Horner, I.B., *Buddhist Text*, p. 155.
9. Warren, Henry, C., *The Life of the Buddha*, p. 76.
10. *Padhāna Sutta*, op. cit.
11. *Nidāna Katha*, op. cit.
    Cf. *Vaṭṭaka Jātaka* (No. 35)
12. Malalasekhera, G.P., *Dictionary of Pāli Paper Names*, Vol. II, pp. 614-15.
13. *Dhp.*, verses : 153-154.
    Narada, Mahīthera (Tr.) *Dhammapada*, p. iii.
    Also See : *Bodhikathā* in Mv. (*Vinaya Piṭaka*).
14. Rhys Davids, T.W. and Carpenter, J.E. (Eds.) *Dīgha Nikāya* (Sutta No. 16).
15. See, pp. 45ff of this book.
16. *Dhp.* verse : 337.
    Dhammapada, op. cit., p. 255.
17. Horner, I.B. (Tr.) *Milinda Question*, Vol. II, pp. 98, 175, 214.
18. *Sutta Nipāta, op. cit.*, verse : 545.
19. *Mohiṇī* : *Triśnā māyā mohiṇī sutta bandhapa ghara nāri.*
    Ā.G., p. 61
    Due to his attachment for son,
    relatives, home and wife
    the Being is suffering from desire of Māyā the enchanrtess
    Also see Ā.G., pp. 243, 752, 937, 1344.
20. *Cerī* : *Cerī dī sevā karahi ṭhākuru nahi dīse.* *Ā.G.*, p. 229
    (He) Serves the maid servant
    and fails to see the Lord.

21. *Kalavālī* : *Kala kalavālī māyā madu mīṭhā*
mana matavālā pīvatu rahaı. *Ā.G.*, p. 350
Kaliyug is akin to seller of spirits.
The sweet is like a liquor
The intoxicated mind is perpetually drinking.

22. *Śāira kī puitrī* : (*Lakśmī*)
Sāira kī puttrī parahari tiāgī carṇa tale vīcāre. *Ā.G.*, p. 437
I have abandoned (Lakṣmi) the daughter of Ocean
And have crushed her under my feet
aided by the word of Gurū.

23. Mākhī : *Karama dharama nahī māyā mākhī.* *Ā.G.*, p. 1035
At that time neither there was performance of rituals
nor honey-bee the *Māyā*.

24. *Māī* : *Rāma ravantā jāṇāīai ika māī bhogu karei.*
Ā.G., p. 1172
Only he is the meditator of God
who swallows M*āyā*

25. *Sākata* : *dekhi kuṭāmbu māyā grihu mandaru sākata*
jaṁjali parali pāiā. *Ā.G.*, p. 906-907
Sākata while looking at his family ties,
Māyā and home entangles (himself) unnecessarily.

26. Manamukhu : *Bina nāve sabha dūkkha nivāsa*
Manamukhu mūṛhu māyā citta vāsu. *Ā.G.*, p. 222
Dwelling devoid of (Divine) Name.
Self-willed one is stupid whose mind is always in M*āyā*.

27. *Kaūā* : *Jagū kaūā nāmu na cīti.*
Nāmu bisāri gire dekhe bhīta. *Ā.G.*, p. 1187
The world is like a crow,
Abandons (Divine) Name and comes down to eat grain
Sprinkled on ground (to snare the bird).

28. *Sagala bhavanu teri māyā moha* *Ā.G.*, p. 1169
The whole world appears to be your
Māyā and her allurements.

29. *Sabhu jagu dekhiā māyā chāiā*
Nanak Guramati nāmu dhiāiā. *Ā.G.*, p. 354
The whole world appears to be your
Māyā and her shadow.

30. *Māyā mohu bhavjalu hai aūdhu sabadi tare kula tārī.*
Ā.G., p. 908

Oh Yogi ! the attachment to *Māyā*
is akin to water of Existence
One can cross over it through (Divine) world
And (thus) also save his whole assembly.

31. *Tribhavanu sāji mekhuli māyā āpi upāi khapāidā*
(God) himself created *Māyā* the rope.
Produces and causes to perish.

32. *Dhp.*, verse : 276
Tin, Daw Mya (Tr.) *Dhammapada*, p. 407.

33. For details see, Pande, G.C., *Śramanic Tradition.*
Also, see chapter 3, *Nibbāna*, p. 33.

15

ON TRIŚNĀ*

While reading *Mājha kī vāra* of Gurū Nānak as a (Buddhist) Vipassī, I had stuck up number of times, at one place and i.e., *Tana maṁhi trisnā aggi sabadi bujhāīai* : There is a fire of craving within (which can be) extinguished with the Word [communicated by the *Satigurū*].[1] The Buddha has also, in his discourses, worked out the process of extinction of the fire of *triśnā* (Pāli : *taṇhā*). Such like fire according to the Buddha, can be extinguished while evoking *Paññā* (Skt. : *Prajñā*) within. This state of 'total extinction', in Buddhism, is described as *Nibbāna* (Skt. : *Nirvāṇa*). In what way *Sabadi* of Gurū Nānak and *Paññā* of the Buddha, in their peculiar ordering of things and ideas, help in extinguishing the fire of *triśnā*, to realize this is the only aim, at the moment.

2

I have referred above to two traditions, namely, Buddhist and Gurū tradition. Chronology demands that the Buddhist tradition should be taken up, first. There are several Buddhist traditions, but, the present attempt is confined to a tradition, known under several names, I prefer to call *Theravādin* tradition.

*Paper presented at the Seminar on Gurū Nānak Dev held at Department of Gurū Nānak Studies, Guru Nanak Dev University Amritsar, in March 1992.

The Buddha in his first discurse, *Dhammacakkappavattana Sutta*, spelling out the third Noble Truth i.e., *dukkha samūdayaṁ ariyasaccaṁ* : Noble Truth of Origin of Suffering, stated that—

> Now, this, O Bhikkhu, is the Noble Truth concerning the Origin of Suffering.
> Verily, it is that thirst (or craving), causing the renewal of existence, accompanied by sensual delight, seeking satisfaction now here, now there—that is to say, the craving for the gratification of the passions, or the craving for a (future) life, or the craving for success (in this pressnt life).[2]

The above translation of the term *vibhava taṇhā*, rendered by T.W. Rhys Davids, seems to be faulty. There is no dispute over three kinds of *taṇhā*. The problem lies in the interpretation of the terms used in original. Nārada Mahāthera, in some other context, rightly interprets the terms under reference, as :

> Craving is threefold, *viz.*, craving for sensual pleasures (*Kāma-taṇhā*), craving for connected with the view of Eternalism (*bhava-taṇhā*), and craving connected with the view of Nihilism (*vibhava-taṇhā*).[3]

The above reference to *bhava* and *vibhava* in the context of *taṇhā* are very significant, as, infact, these are the philosophical positions that the Buddha disapproves of with his peculiar gesture of Noble Silence (*ariyomona*).[4]

We are enjoined to extinguish the fire of craving (or clinging) which is threefold, and as identified above.

Apart from reference to *taṇhā* as a root-cause of suffering, in the First Discourse, and having, in a way, sway over the entire Pāḷi Canon, a full chapter entitled *Taṇhāvagga* of *Dhammapada* consisting of twentysix verses (334-359) is devoted to point out its various dimensions. We quote some of the verses, in order to have a fair idea of how *taṇhā* prevails upon the minds of the people, that reads :

> *The craving of the man addicted to careless living grows like a creeper.
> He jumps from life to life like a fruit-loving monkey in the forest.[5]

*Just as a tree, with roots unharmed and firm,
Tho' cut down springs up again; even so while latent craving is n-
rooted out.
This sorrow springs up again and again.[6]

*Everywhere flow the floods (craving),
The creeper sprouts and stands,
Seeing the creeper that has sprung up,
With wisdom, cut off the root.[7]

What we learn from the above quoted verses is that craving (*taṇhā*) is like a flood that sways over the hearts and the minds of the people. This is a descriptive metaphor. The characteristics of craving resemble to a creeper and/or roots of the tree that needs to be cut off with *Paññā* (wisdom). The most significant thing is that metaphors and similies used to describe craving belong to order of Nature. According to the Buddhist tradition Sidhāratha Gotama was born at Lumbini under a tree; Gotama attained *Sambodhi* and became the Buddha, under a tree; the Buddha delivered his First Discourse at Isipatana, under a tree and entered into *Mahāparinibbāna* at Kusinagar, under a tree. This is history or legend, in any case, it signifies one thing that it is the Law of Nature that needs not only to be known, but, it requires to cast one's life-patterns, accordingly.

Taṇhā is like a creeper or the roots of a tree and which is to be cut off with *Paññā*. We should not equate *Paññā* with the knowledge acquired through reading of the books or instructions received from the teachers—ignorant worldling. *Paññā*, in fact, is a wisdom that is evoked, within. The process of evoking *Paññā*, within, is necessarily conceived, in the background of Order of Nature. As regard to the characteristic features of Order of Nature, the Buddha tells us, that—

Sabbe Saṅkhārā aniccā', ti

Transient are all conditioned things.[8]

Again, at the time of *Mahāparinibbāna* while consoling distressed Ānanda, the Buddha addressed him, saying :

Handa dāni bhikkhave āmantayāmi vo :
vyadhamma saṅkhārā, appamādena sampadetha' ti.

> Verily, I say unto you now, O monks :
> All things are perishable; work your deliverence with earnestness.[9]

Transient (*aniccā'ti*) are *Saṅkhārā;*[10] perishable (*vyadhammā*) are *Saṅkhārā*, this is the Truth about the nature of things. But, this Truth is not be grasped and appreciated merely as an intellectual exercise. Rather, the realization of the said Truth must result in the transformation of one's vision. This is why that after stating, *Sabbe Saṅkhārā aniccā,'ti* it is aidded that, '*yadā paññāya passati* : When this with wisdom one discerns'.[11] So, it is through *Paññā* the Truth of transient nature of things needs to be grasped. In the same manner the nature of *Saṅkhārā* as *vyadhammā* is to be comprehended with *appamādena* (head fulness)[12]. *Paññā* and *appamādena* is evoked through practising *Vipassanā*.

The way *taṇhā* operates is made known using different expressions. After delineating the wide range of Suffering and diagnosing its cause, the Buddha stated :

> *Saṅkeitena pañca upādānakkhanda pi dukkhā.*
> Five groups of grasping, inshort, constitute suffering.[13]

The term *upādāna* is a key-word that needs to be comprehended unimbiguosly. *Upādana* means clinging. One's heart and mind does not cling to that idea or thought alone which one likes; these also cling to that idea or though which one does not like. The first kind of clinging is called *rāga* and the second one is known as *dosa* (*skt. dveśa*). Both these reactions generate impurities and cause pollution of heart and mind. Increasing impurities (of *rāga* and *dosa*) result in enhancing the quantum of Suffering. The Suffering, in other words, lies in mental disposition of *upādāna* (clinging). *Upādāna* is nothing but the manifestation of *taṇhā*, in practice. The only way to free oneself from the clutches of *taṇhā* or *upādāna* is, knowing the existential nature of things and ideas. I have not used the word knowledge, deliberately, because it does not connote the process, rather, it suggests something fixed or static and which is contrary to the nature of existential reality. The 'nature of existential realiy' is the substance of *Mahāsatipaṭṭhāna Sutta*[14] the

Buddha delivered at Kammas dhamma, modern Kaithal, in Haryānā. In this *Sutta,* the Buddha has explained fourfold foundations (*Pali* : *Kammṭṭhāna*) of Mindfulness (*Sati*). Such as, i. *Kāyānupassanā,* ii. *Vadanānupassanā,* iii. *Cittānupassnā,* and iv. *Dhammānupassānā.* Practising of these four kinds of *vipassanā* was advised according to the temperament of the *vipassi* concerned.[15] The Buddha, himself, used to give training of *vipassanā* in *Buddhavihārās.* It used to be course of fortydays—first ten days for *ānāpāna* (inbreathing and outbreathing) and rest of the thirty days for practicing *vippassanā. Anāpāna* only means to be mindful about the ongoing process of inbreathing and outbreathing. Connected with this kind of *Dhyāna* (Pāli : *Jhāna*) are quite a good number of factors which provide it a universal character. In-breathing and out-breathing is a process which is natural and, hence, not an exclusive privilege of particular individual, caste or community. Rather, it is a privilege bestowed by Nature upon every living being. Moreover, making in-breathing and out-breathing as an *ālambana* in the course of mediation is also to discard those *ālambana* which generate *rāga* and *dosa.* The process of in-breathing and out-breathing is not only universal but it also falls outside the purview of any possibility of originating *rāga* and *dosa.* There is yet another a very significant role that in-breathing and out-breathing plays in this process of meditation. The main objective of *vipassanā* is to wash away *vikārā* (impurities) of one's mind. In-breathing and out-breathing is directly connected with *vikāras. Vipassi* (one who practices *Vipassanā*) knows it at experiential level that whenever *Vikāra* arises in the mind the process of breathing gets disturbed. This kind of abnormalcy in breathing-process is, in a way, a signal indicating, arise of *vikāras* in the deepest layers of mind that otherwise remain hidden. In this way practice of in-breathing and out-breathing helps in observing the changes that take place in corporeal organism, besides, sharpening the mind. The sharpening of mind, and which is a continuous process, infact, is a prerequisite condition for fruitful performance of above stated fourkinds of *vipassanā. Vipassi* observes that every particle of his corporal organism is under constant flux. He also arrives at a stage when he *sees* that his whole organism, is a sum total of bubbles. This picture of proper perspective is beautifully drawn in the *Saṁyutta Nikāya*, thus :

> Like to a ball of foam this body is :
> Like to a bubble blown the feelings are.[16]

Sabbe Saṅkhārā aniccā'ti' and '*vyadhammā Saṅkhārā*, these expressions already referred to, only hold testimony to bubble-like flux. When one, comes to know the existential reality of things and ideas, as a natural consequence, he learns as to the futility of reactions to things and ideas, the mind starts avoiding to craving for things and ideas. This realization of transitoriness of things and ideas puts mind on the path of purification. New tendencies (*Saṅskāra*) that pollute the mind may not originate as quite appropriately referred to in *Ratna Sutta*, as :

> *Khīṇaṁ pūranaṁ navaṁ natthi sabhvaṁ.*
>
> The old is destroyed, the new has not arisen.[17]

But, the tendencies stored up in the deepest layers of mind, when required, are bound to appear on the surface-layer of mind. An origination of new tendencies, destruction of old ones, and cessation of origination of new tendencies, these are some of the stages, the mind has to pass through before it is finally emancipated. I shall discuss this process with reference to *Vedanānupassanā*, alone.[18] The *Vipassī* stores up the tendencies through the working of five sense-organs, such as, nose, ears, eyes, tongue and body. The eyes work through the consciousness (*Viññāṇa*). The eyes aided by consciousness look at thing/ things. At once, eyes recognize (*Saññā*) thing/things. Then there is a reaction which can be both pleasant or unpleasant (*Vedanā*). An origination of pleasant feeling impels one to possess the thing. This attitude of mind is termed as *rāga*. Similarly, an unpleasant feeling causes revulson (*dosa*). Under both the set of circumstances, such as. *rāga* and *dosa* one is giving birth to new tendencies. When pleasant feeling originates, it is at this point of time, that two options of adopting either the path of *paññā* or that of *avijjā* are available. One, who with aid of *ānāpāna*, has become a perfect *vipassī*, and fully aware of transitoriness of things/ideas/feelings, no more clings to these being mere processess. As *vipassanā* means to see things as they really are.[19] When one undergoes such experience testifying transitory character of phenomenal world, one learns to dispense with one's craving directed towards both the pleasant and unpleasant feelings. Consequent upon that, now, one no more originates new tendencies. The old tendencies, stored up in mind, come to operate. The body needs food, say, twice or thrice in a day. But *citta* must have it every moment. Now, *citta* does not get its *āhāra* from outside, in the form of tendencies. The old tendencies, stord up, come up to feed *citta*, as per requirement. Suppose, *citta* is in dire need of *kāma* or *karodha*, then, only the tendencies relating to these alone would come up. In this process, the tendencies of various kinds, stored up in mind, gradually decrease leading to their exile from the store-house. This is why the Buddha while characterizing his Path has categorically stated :

> *essa maggo visuddhiyā.*[20]
>
> This is the Path of Purity.

Purity from what ? Purity from tendencies called *vikāra* that generate impurities of mind and cause Suffering. During the course of practising *vipassanā*, *ānāpāna* helps in more than one way. In the beginning, it appears that one is breathing in breathing out. But, gradually *vipassī* comes to learn, oh ! no ! the process of in breathing and out breathing is going on on its own. This realization also helps in arriving at the point of *anattā* (not I). Next to *aniccā* it is *anattā* that needs to be realized while moving on the Path leading to *Nibbāna*. As regard to *anattā* there is a statement, comprehensive in nature, in *Dhammapada* that reads :

> *Sabbe dhammā anattā'ti.*
>
> Soulless is everything that is.[21]

The realization of *aniccā* and *anattā*, both are prerequisites for cessation of Suffering (*dukkha nirodha*). One of the fundamental causes of Suffering lies in the impermanent nature of things or transitoriness of their character. "Whatever is transitory is painful"[22] is the dictum quite often pronounced in the Buddhist scriptures.

The existing state of Suffering can also be explained in terms of doctrine of *Anattā*. The doctrine, in its essence, refers to a state, combining both physical and mental, *that one is not.*[23]

The state of complete elimination of *vikāra* (dark passions), that generate impurities of mind is identified in Buddhism, as *Nirvāṇa* (Pāli : *Nibbāna*). The word *Nivārṇa* is derived from 'nir' meaning absence and *vāta* that stands for wind; and the suffix '*ta*' is changed into '*na*'. The expression to 'blow out' instantly suggests blowing out of the fire. This phenomenon takes the form of the simile of the wind and the flame. The frequent use of this simile, underlying an idea of *annihilation* of activities, has caused a grave concern in certain quarters.[24] Whereas, such an explanation leading to nihilism, can hardly explain the fact of an active life of Gotama the Buddha, covering a span of nearly half a century. The problem, however, is to be able to explain the meaning of the expression, 'putting out of fire'. The Buddha, as a matter of rule, preferred to communicate to his audience by means of similes and metaphors. Fire as a simile find special favour with the Buddha. The Sermon on Fire[25] is just one instance. In this Sermon, we come across expression, such as, "every thing is on fire...on fire with the flames of desire, hate and illusion". *Nibbāna* means extinction of this flame. The extinction of flame of desire, hate and illusion is not possible by blowing; we have to search for special means. In the *Therigāthā*[26], we read: "by winning the highest purity you must be extinguished like a fire by water. Again, "Kassapa meditates without fuel (*taṇhā*), extinguished among the burning."[27] So, the putting out of this flame is not as simple a phenomenon as blowing it out. An act (or process) of blowing sometimes, results in inciting the fire, too, than to extinguish it. What is required, ultimately, in order to extinguish the flame, is depriving it of further supply of fuel (of *taṇhā*). Thus, one attains the 'highest purity' and happens to be extinguished like a fire by water'. Alternatively put, *Nibbāna* is attained as a result of doing away with *taṇhā* which is like uprooting or cutting of creeper or roots of a tree.

3.

Before we move on to identity the process of extinction of the fire of thirsting-will with an aid of *sabadu* in the background of *Gurbāni*, we must look into the relevent references enshrined in *Mājha kī vāra.*[28] The term *sabadu* in this *vāra* of Gurū Nānak, is used variously, and we quote :

**Nā hauṁ nā meṁ nā hāuṁ hoā*
Nānak Sabadu vīcāri
I wish, sayeth Nānak, as a result of contemplating upon Word my ego ceases to exist.

**Saccā sabadu saccu mani*
Ghara hī māhi udāsā.
As a result of dwelling on True Word and Truth in one's heart, one lives in household as if detached.

**Tabalabāju bicāra sabadu suṇāiā.*
Guru the drummer has communicated this idea through Word to the world.

**Satigura khotiahu khare kare*
Sabadu saṁvāranahāru.
True Guru turns base in to pure one through Word and thus sets in order one's living.

**Saccā terā darbāra sabadu nisāniā.*
True is your court and True Word leads to it.

**Saccā sabadu vicāri saci samāniā.*
Those who contemplate upon Trueword remain absorbed in Truth.

**Saccā sabadu sālāhi sacci samāiai.*
Those who magnify True Word remain absorbed in Truth.

Onhaṁ khasamai kai dari mukha
Ujale saccai sabadu suhāia.
They are honoured in the Master's court, and by the (grace of) True Word look bright.

Saccai sabadu nīsāṇi thāka na pāīai.
One blessed with the stamp of approval of True Word shall not be checked up.

Tana maṁhi triśnā aggī sabadi bujhāiai.

The fire of craving within shall be extinguished with the Word.

Mahalā mañjhi nivāsu sabadi saṁvāriā.

Adorned with the Word they dwell in the abode of (God).

Sabadu saṁvārīāsu amritu pīviā.

Adorned with the Word they drink nectar.

Saccā sabadu bīcāri kālu vidhaūsiā.

Contemplation upon True Word results in the cessation of cycle of transmigration.

Ḍhāḍhi kathe akathu sabadu saṁvāriā.

(Guru) the Bard adorned with the Word describes the undescribable.

Saccai sabadi salāhi sukhīe sacca vāliā.

Aided by True Word one praises (God)
(Thus) attains happiness and becomes Truthful.

Saccu terā phuramāṇu sabade sohiā.

True is your command that radiates through Word.

Ḍhāḍhi kare pasāu sabadu vijāiā.

(Guru) the Bard celebrates the Word.

We have quoted above the verses which refer to the term *sabadu*, fully aware of the dangers attending to the method of over simplification, while analysing the verses out of perspective. The foremost significant thing about the *Sābadu* is that it concerns *Sccā Sabadu* (True Word), followed by identifying its *amala* (practice) and its results. Gurū Nānak claims that while 'meditating upon Sabadu' results in liberating from *hauṁ* (ego); while in household one is detached; the Word of *Satigurū* turns base in to pure; with an aid of *Saccā Sabadu* one gets absorbed in Truth and tastes nectar and on hearing *Saccā Sabadu Kāiu* or the cycle of transmigration comes to an end. These are some of the dimensions ensuing from *Saccā Sabadu*. But, at present, we are concerned, only with the manner in which the fire of thirsting-will (*Pāli-taṇha*) is extinguished invoking an aid of *Saccā Sabadu.* There is, also, one more dimension of the fire of thirsting-will that deserves our notice that reads:

Tisnā andari aggani hai na tipatai bhukhā tihāiā.[29]

In other words, on account of fire of thirsting-will that is burning within one remains discontented. The thirsting-will, therefore, manifesting variously, keeps one on toes.

The basic postulate under discussion is *Sabadu* rather, *Saccā Sabadu.* This suggests that there is, also, *Kūṛā Sabadu* (untrue word). Obviously, we can not talk of *Saccā Sabadu* without reference to *Kūṛā Sabadu.* As *Kūṛā Sabadu* has innumerable aspects, better we begin with *Saccā Sabadu.* The 'True Word' is that which originates right with the creation of the universe and which is discussed with reference to God and Existence. In other words, it is *anahadu nādu*[30] (unstruck melody), a perpetual resonance resounding on its own, without human agency. When Zen Masters suggest to their disciples to strike sound with one hand, a technique called *koan,* they are, infact, refering to this *anahadu nādu.* When one does hear; *sacaā sabadu* or *anahadu nādu*? Obviously, when *kūṛā sabadu* ceases to operate. What is, after all, *kūṛā sabadu*? *Kūṛā sabadu* is that which originates in *kūṛā* (untruth). In the terminology of *Gurabāṇi* all that *manamukhu* (self-willed person) speaks, writes, thinks etc. amounts to *kūṛa.* All the words that he uses to accomplish his ends of life, can, without any reservation be identified as *kūṛā.* On the contrary, the words of the *Gurūs* of the Sikhs, which is deified as *Gurabāṇi*, are True Words for the simple reason that these have their roots in Truth. This way the True Word is of two kinds—*anahadu nādu* and the Words of *Satigurū.* The latter are nothing but the spontaneous expressions of *anahadu nādu* manifested for the benefit of All.

One can hear *anahadu nādu*, only, when one's mind enters in to the Zone of Silence. This state is called *unamani* (state of No-mind) which is, of course, qualitatively different from absence of mind. In a way, the state of *anahadu nādu* is akin to a state devoid of words. When the words originating from phenomenal existence cease to exist then and only then one hears *anadha nādu* which is perpetually resounding at its sweet will. When Gurū Nānak, claims the extinction of fire of thirsting-will with an aid of words, he means this state, devoid of words or *anahadu nādu.* In short, the purpose of *Sabadu*-

Sādhanā (meditation on Word) is to arrive at the destination of No-Word. The words that *manamukhu* utters or put to writing either refer to some person or thing. Or reference is made to some mode of living. Such words are invariably accompanied by the army of *trisnā* (thirsting-will). One can not conquer this *Sabadu* without an aid of *nisabadu* (state of no-word). And, one can safely conclude that only with an aid of True Word, the fire of *trisnā* can be extinguished.

How *paññā* (Skt. : prajñā) and *Sabadu* can be instrumental in the extinction of fire of *trisnā*, this alone was my purpose to explore. One can choose the way that suits one. The foremost significant thing is not the Way but the result.

References and Notes

1. *Ā.G.p.* 147.
2. S.V. 42 (*Dhamma cakkappavattana sutta*):
   Idaṁ kho pana, bhikkhave, dukkha samūdaāaṁ ariya saccaṁ—yāyaṁ taṇhā ponobbhavikā, nani—darāga sahagatā tatra tatrābhi nanidanī, seyyathīdaṁ—kāma taṇhā, bhava taṇhā, vibhavataṇha.
   Rhys Davids, T.W. *Buddhist Suttas.*
   This Sutta is also found in *Mahāvagga Vp.*
3. Nārada, Mahāthera (Tr.) *Dhammapada*, p. 341.
4. For details, See: Holmes, Edmond, *The Creed of the Buddha*, Chapter VI, 'The Silence of Buddha'.
   Also refer to chapter 1, *Dukkha* p. 6.
5. *Dhp*. verse: 334:
   Manjuassa pamatta—cārino
   taṇhā vaḍḍhati māluvā viya,
   so plavati hurāhuraṁ
   phalaṁ iechaṁ'va vanasamiṁ vānaro.
   Nārada *op. cit*, p. 253.
6. *Dhp* verse: 338:
   Yathāpi mūle anupaddave dalhe

chinno' pi rukkho punareva rūhati
evam, pi taṇhānusaye anūhate nibbattati
dukkhaṁ idaṁ punappunaṁ.
Nārada, *op. cit.* p. 255.

7. *Dhp.* verse: 340:
Savanti Sabbadhī Sotā,
latā ubbhijja tiṭṭhati,
tañ ca disvā lataṁ Jātaṁ
mūlaṁ paññāya chindatha.
Nārada, *op. cit.* p. 257.
8. *Ibid.* verse: 277.
Nārada, *op. cit.* p. 207.
9. Rhys Davids, T.W., Carpenter, J.E., (Eds.) *Dīgha Nikāya* Vol. II p. 156.
10. *Saṅkhārā* is derived from the verb *Saṅkharoti* that means to make or put together. It refers to anything produced hence synonymous with production. The term *Saṅkhārā* or production can be used, therefore, for anything existing in the phenomenal world, since, everything is produced.
11. *Dhp.* verse: 277.
Nārada, *op. cit.* p. 207.
12. There is a full chapter in *Dhammapada* devoted to *Appamāda* (verses: 21—32).
13. S.V. 421.
The expression *Pañcaupādanakkandhā* consists of three components: *pañca+upādāna+khandha*. *Pañca* means five *upādāna* stands for craving (or clinging) and *khandha* refers to aggregates which are five in number, *viz.*, *rūpa*, *vedanā*, *saññā*, *viññāṇa* and *Saṅkhāra* that constitute the corporeal organism of man/woman. The aggregates, when associated with *upādāna* cause Suffering. When *upadāna* is eliminated these *pañca khandha* remain intact, but now free from Suffering.
14. Rhys Davids, T.W. Carpenter, J.E. (Ed.) *Dīgha Nikāya*, Vol. II, pp. 291-315.
Rhys Davids, T.W. and C.A.F. (Trs.) *Dialogues of the Buddha* (Translation of *Digha Nikāya*), Vol. III, Part II, pp. 327-346.
15. Tiwary, Mahesh, (Ed.) *Sumaṅgalavilāsinī* (commentary on

Digha Nikāya) Vol. III.

16. S. iii. 141-142:
Pheṇapiṇḍūpamaṁ rūpaṁ, vedanā bubbulapamā
Woodward, F.L., (Trs.) *The Book of Kindered Sayings* (Translation of *Saṁyutta Nikāya*) Vol. III, pp. 120-121.
When Gurū Tegh Bahādur, (Ninth Gurū of the Sikhs), says that:
Jaise jala te budabudā upajai binse nīta
Jaga racanā taise raci kaho Nānak suna mīta.
As the water-bubbles arise and vanish perpetually,
The creation of the world Oh Friend ! sayeth Nānak is likened to that. —*Saloka Mahalā IX Ā.G. 1427.*
he is not at all using the word 'bubble' as a poetic metaphor, rather, he is pointing out the transitory nature of existential reality he has known at the experiential level.

17. *Ratna Sutta*: 14
Fausboll, V. (Tr.) *Sutta Nipāta*, Vol. X, Part II, p. 39.

18. I have attended *vedanānupassanā* courses under the personal guidance of *kalyānamitta*, Shri S.N. Goenkaji, the Great Ācārīyā of *vipassanā*. My observations, therefore, are based upon my personal experiences.

19. For comprehensive understanding of *vipassanā* See, Sobti, Harcharan Singh, *Vipassanā: The Buddhist Way.*

20. *Dhp.* verses: 277-279.

21. *Ibid.* verse: 279.

22. S. IV. 1, *yaṁ aniccaṁ taṁ dukkhaṁ.*

23. S. iii. 186.

24. i. Jayatilleke, K.N., *Early Buddhist Theory of Knowledge*, p. 3.
ii. Maxmuller, F. and Others, *Studies in Buddhism*, pp. 51-52.

25. S. iv. 19f: (Fire Sermon)—
Sabbaṁ...ādittaṁ...rāgagginā
dosagginā mohagginā ādittaṁ.

26. *Ta. 415*: *pappuyya anuttaraṁ visuddhiṁ parinibbāhisi vārina va Joti.*

27. *Ta.* 1060: *Kassapo jhāyati anupādāno ḍayhamānesu nibbuto.*

28. *Ā.G.*, pp. 137-150.

29. *Ibid.*, p. 138 (*Mājha kī Vāra*).

30. All the following references to *anahadu nādu* are from *Nānakbāṇi* (Mahalā I).

i. *Anahadu bāṇi pāīai taha haumaṁ hoi bināsu*
Ego is destroyed only after
hearing unstruck melody *Ā.G. p. 21.*

ii. *Anahadu Suṇi māniā Sabadu vīcāri.*
(The mind) contemplates upon
Sabadu and hears unstruck melody. *Ā.G. p. 415.*

iii. *Pañca sabada dhuni anahāda vāje*
hama ghari sājana āi
There is a spontaneous
Resonance of Five Words within
As my beloved has visited my inner-self. *Ā.G. p. 764.*

iv. *Anahada Sabadu nirālā vāje.*
Unstruck melody that
Strikes within is cut off (from the world). *Ā.G. p. 839.*

v. *Dhuni vāje anahada ghorā*
manu māniā hari rasa morā.
The musical sound of unstruck melody like that of thunder strikes within.
And my mind is enjoying the bliss of *Harināma.*
Ā.G. p. 879.

16

ŚABADA : THE BUDDHIST PERSPECTIVE*

The *Sukhāvatīvyūha* or the Pureland Sect of Mahāyana Buddhism, promotes the practice of repeating the *mantra*, *Namo'mitābha-Buddhāya* (Glory be to Amita Buddha) believing it to be an unfailing device to evoke the Grace of Amitābha Buddha. The *mantra*, obviously, consists of *Śabadas*. So, it is a set of certain *Śabadas* that paves the way for a devotee, leading to the Pureland, a heavenly residence of Amitābha Buddha. *Śabadas*, in the instant case, therefore, have potentials to evoke Grace.

Few words about the canonical sources of *Sukhāvatīvyūha* Sect. The canon comprises three texts: i. *Sukhāvatīvyūha Sūtra* (Long Discourse); ii. *Sukhāvatīvyūha Sūtra* (Short Discourse) and iii. *Amitāyur-Dhyāna Sūtra*. These *Sūtras* are believed to have been collected, as available in their present form, sometimes, during the third or second century B.C. An orator of these discourses is, decidely, none else but Gautama the Buddha. The opening words of these discourses, identical to the practice followed in *Pāḷi Tipiṭaka*, are *evam maya Srutama*: Thus I have heard. The original language of these canonical texts, as generally believed, is Sanskrit.

At what stage of development (or distoration) of the

*Paper presented and published in the proceedings of the Seminar on *Śabada* organised by *Vismāda Nāda*, Ludhiana, during 3-4 December, 1992 at FICCI, New Delhi.

Buddhist tradition the cult of '*Śabada*' came into practice is a query, if satisfied, is very likely to unravel the nature of development of the Buddhist tradition, mysterious in character. The cult of *Śabada*, as envisaged in *Sukhāvativyūha* Sect, is unknown to *Theravādni* Buddhist tradition, and there is no dispute on its being original. The original Buddhism (of *Pāḷitipiṭaka*) is based on *Jhāna* (Skt. *Dhyāna*). Right from Mahākashyap (close contemporary of the Buddha) to Bodhidharma (5-6th AD) we have twenty eight Great Buddhist Masters, who adhened to *Theravāda* Buddhism. None of them either practised or promoted the cult of *Śabada*. All of them, without exception, adhered to the technique of *Jhāna* as discovered, prasticed and delineated by the *Tathāgata* himself.[1] *Śabada* and *Jhāna* both promise in assisting a wayfarer to arrive at one and the same Goal. But, one thing is certain that it is, comparatively, much easier to tread on the Path of *Śabada* than that of *Jhāna*. At the moment, we are not interested in the Goal. We aim at identifying the Path with all its characteristic features, if possible, and that too the Path of the *Śabada*.[2]

Sukhāvativyūha Sūtra[3] (Long Discourse), the basic scriptural text of *Sukhāvativyūha* Seet, the Buddha delivered at *Girdharkuṭa* hill, in Rajagiri. It commences with dialogue between the Buddha and Ānanda. Later on, the discourse is addressed to Ajita. Similarly, *Sukhāvativyūha Sūtra*[4] (Short Discourse), the Buddha while addressing Sāriputta, delivered it in Anathapinḍaka's *Gītā Udhāna*, at Śrāvasti. Both these *Sūtras* only give detailed description of *Sukhāvati Loka*, the Abode of Amitābha Buddha. The detailed descriptions with regard to the repetition of the Name of Amitābha Buddha i.e., *Nāma-Sādhnā* and the allied subjects, are available only in *Amitāyur-Dhyāna Sūtra*. It would not be possible to ascertain the spirit of the *Nāma-Sādhnā* without looking into the set of circumstances under which the said discourse was delivered. What happened[5] that the Prince Ajātaśatrū as instigated by Devadutta put his father Bimbasāra in prison and proclaimed that none was allowed to meet Bimbasāra the king. The queen-consort Videhi loved the king as a devoted wife. She would regularly visit the king in prison and served him there. Day succeeded day. One day the king right from the prison-house turned his face towards the Girdharakūta hill, where the Buddha was staying, and prayed, "Oh Bhagvāna ! kindly send Mahā Muggalāna, who is both my relative and friend, to shower his Compassion on me and give me instructions on *Aṭṭha Sīla*. Right at the moment when the prayer ended Mahā Muggalāna appeared and soon after gave instructions as desired by the king. The Buddha also sent his great disciple Pūraṇa to the prison to teach the king *Dharma*. Consequent upon learning about *Aṭṭhasīla* and *Dharma*, the king experienced the bliss and his face became bright and radiant. One day, Ajātasātrū enquired from the guard that if anybody had come to meet the king in the prison ? The guard told the queen-consort was regularly coming. Besides, Mahā-Muggalāna and Pūraṇa also frequently visited the king. It was not possible to check both of them. On hearing about the visits of his mother Videhi, Ajātaśatrū got furious and lost his balance. He put his mother into the prison as she had helped the rebel. Now, Videhi is in the prison cell in the palace. Videhi prays to the Buddha, "Oh Bhagavāna ! I am helpless, miserable. Kindly send Mahā Moggalāna and Ānanda to console me." Thereafter, she wept bitterly. The Buddha, who was staying at Girdharakūṭa hill, sent both of them to Videhi. The Buddha, soon after, also, arrived there. Videhi prayed to Buddha that may she be made familiar with all those places which are absolutely devoid of Suffering so that she may be reborn there. The Buddha made her to visualize number of worlds so that she could choose her abode according to her choice. She expressed her desire to be reborn in *Sukhāvatiloka*, the Abode of Amitābha Buddha. Videhi requested the Buddha to guide her so as to arrive at the desired abode. It was in this perspective that the Buddha delivered the discoure *Amitāyur-Dhyāna Sūtra*, propounding the Path of *Nāma Jāpa*. According to Japanese Buddhist tradition the Buddha delivered this discourse during the fifth part of his life *i.e.*, from seventy-one to seventy-nine years of life-span. The Buddha categorically stated that anyone repeating the mantra *Namo' mitābha Buddhāya* would be liberated from one's sins. At the end, Ānanda asked the Buddha as to what should be the name of the *Sūtra* ? The Buddha suggested several names and one of the names of the Sūtra was *Karamanāśu-Viśuddhi*, which means destruction of one's *karama* and consequently leading to *Sukhāvatiloka*. In other words, this *sūtra* propounding the Path of *Nāma Japa* help the devotees to liberate themselves from Suffering. Recalling of Theravādānī Buddhist tradition may suggest some one to doubt as to this original contribution of Mahāyāna. There are, atleast two references in the *Dīgha Nikāya* that need to be looked into. One such reference is available in the *Mahāparinibbāna Sutta* of the *Dīgha Nikāya* (No. 16). The Buddha while addressing Ānanda states that,

> It may be, Ānanda, that in some of you the thought may arise, the word of the Master is ended, we have no teacher more ! But it is not, thus, Ānanda, that you should regard it. Truth and the Rules of the Order which I have set forth and laid down for you all, let them, after I am gone, be the teacher to you.[6]

The commandment in Sikh tradition 'to adore Granth as Gurū', I believe, has certainly some thing to do with the *Theravādni* Buddhist tradition. Any how, inspite of all that the Buddha did not, in the *Theravādanī* perspective, refer to *Nāma Japa*, at all. The *pandita* of *Theravāda* tradition may also refer to the following adoration which is repeated very much like *mantra*, to prove that, no ! *Nāma Japa* has its roots in that very tradition—

> *Namo tassa bhagavato arahato sammā-samuddhassa.*
>
> Reverence be to the Blessed One, *Arahat*, the *sammā-sambuddha*.[7]

The above reference is from the *Sakkapañha Sutta* (No. 21) of the *Dīgha Nikāya*. Here, the Buddha had satisfactorily answered some of the questions of Devendra Śakka (Pāli : Sakka) and at the end of this meeting Devendra while paying his tribute to the Buddha, had uttered these words. These words, in no circumstances, can be upheld to serve a base for *Nama Simarana*. Therefore, the cult of *Nama Simarana*, when viewed in the Buddhist perspective, must have originated with *Amitayurdhyāna Sūtra*. *The Buddhanuūtti* enshrined in Pāli *Tipiṭaka* might be accepted as its seed. Moreover, in some quarters Mahāyāna too is considered to be the developing stage of *Theravāda* Buddhism.

In fact, *Nāma Simrana* as contemplated in *Sukhāvati vyūha*, is nothing but devotion accorded to Amitābha Buddha, who is very much like *Sukhāvatiloka*, inherently, present within. One devoted to Amitābha while repeating '*Namo'mitabha Buddhaya*' evokes his Compassion. In this way, the practice of devotion begins from the *Nama Simrana* of Amitābha Buddha, which in itself operates as a result of his *paraṇidhana* or Vow. Through *Nāma* the devotee desires to remain intune with Amitābha Buddha, which is present within. This means that the complete surrender of oneself to Amitābha Buddha is foundation stone of Amitābha *bhakti*. Since, the entire structure of *bhakti* lies upon the Compassion of the others', in the present case, upon Amitābha Buddha. In short the door of *Nibbāna-nagar* for Amitābha *bhakata* opens through his intuning with Amitābha while repeating his *Nāma*. When everything depends upon the 'Others' the dependence needs to be authentic in nature. This means that the devotee has to whole heartedly accept himself/herself helpless, ensuing full faith in the object of worship. One cannot cross the Ocean of Existence (*bhavasagara*) without it. *Arahat*, as conceived in *Theravāda* Buddhism, sits in one-man boat to cross the Ocean of Existence. Whereas, in Mahāyāna this one-man boat takes the forms of *beṛā*. 'To meditate one-self and help other likewise', the *beṛā* stands to put this ideal into practice. The *beṛā* has to cross the Ocean of Existence through the force derived from the *paraṇidhana* or the Vow of Amitābha Buddha. This ideal of *Nāma marga* may be easy to put into practice, but, it is handicaped by limitations of serious nature. The *mantra* chosen for repetition must consist of certaiu words and the words must belong to certain traditions, which in itself cannot be all inclusive. *Vipassanā*, on the contrary, is al-together free from any such limitations.

Lest one gathers an impression that *Nāma* and *Dhyāna*, a resultant of *vipassanā*, have hardly anything to do with each other, the relation between the two heeds a clarification. We learn from the experiences of Vibrant Beings that *Dhyāna* is natural outcome of *Nāma*,[8] but not the *vice a versa*. *Jini nāma dhyaiā* : those who meditate upon *Nāma*. This expression, I believe, holds testimony to this very truth. With reference to *Amitayurdhyāna* Sūtra we have already talked about *Karamanaśa*

Visuddhi which poses a very acute problem. We know that the defining factors of religion are neither God, nor Soul, or rebirth or transmigration etc. but Doctrine of *karma.* It is only Doctrine of *karma* that testifies Buddhism as religion. Whereas, *Karamavaraṇa Visuddhi* as conceived in the *nāma marga* of *Sukhavativyūha*, hardly allows the Doctrine of *karma* to subsist. Yes ! One has to reap the fruits of one's *karma* in case, one is not aware of its washing away. There is a way out for liberating oneself from *karma,* when practising *vipassanā.* May be that the element of *dhāyana* in *nāma* helps in the destruction of effects or fruits of *karma.* Still, one question remains unanswered. How to explain the Crucifixion of Jesus Christ or the torture that Gurū Arjan Dev (1563-1606 A.D.), the fifth Gurū of the Sikhs, had to undergo ? The Christians, however, found out the way to explain the Crucifixion of Jesus Christ through propounding the concept of vicarious atonement. Whereas, the Sikh tradition eulogises the concept of *Bhāṇā manaṇā* or surrender to the Will of God' and it is not the result of *Nāma Siṁraṇa,* rather it is prerequisite condition for adopting the Path of *Nāma.* In *Sukhāvatiyūha* the devotee as a result of Compassion showered on him/her by Amitābha Buddh, is blessed with enormous tolerance to face hardships ensuing from the effects of *karma.* There are those who believe that the effects of *karma* must be exhausted in one way or the other. There is no dearth of those also who hold the view that no ! there are ways worked out in *Gurabāṇi*, to completely undo the effects of *karma.* I place, both these views, before the learned scholars for deliberations.

I would like to conclude my paper giving a suggestion. I have made certain observations with regard to the Path of *Śabada-Nāma* as delineated in the *Sukhāvativyūha.* It has been a practice to deliberate upon the Path of *Nāma* worked out in *Gurabāṇi,* in the context of Bhakati Movement. I am of the view that this study of *Nāma,* if made in the background of *Sukhāvativyūha,* can be more fruitful, for the simple reason, that we talk of Bhakti Movement in relation to Alwāra Saints who flourished during the fourth to ninth century A.D., at a much later times than *Sukhāvativyūha.*

References

1. Upadhyaya, Bharat Singh, *Dhyāna Aur Nāma*, p. 8.
2. For the Path of *Jhāna*, see chapter on *Triśnā*.
3. Maxmullar, F., (Tr.) *Buddhist Mahāyāna Texts*, Vol. 49, Part II, pp. 1-72.
4. *Ibid.*, pp. 89-103.
5. *Ibid.*, pp. 161-201.
6. Rhys Davids, T.W. and Davids, Mrs., *Dialogues of Buddha* Vol. II, p. 171.
7. *Ibid.*, p. 289.
8. *Dhyāna Aur Nāma, op. cit.*, p. 1.

17

PANJĀB IN PĀḶI LITERATURE*

Pāḷi and Panjāb, these are two keywords of our proposed subject of the paper. Obviously, first word refers to the language and the latter one to the geographical region. Both these names of the language and the region are of later times. The language of *Tipiṭaka* the canon of *Theravāda* Buddhism, is Māgadhī, only later on known as Pāli. We propose to study the image/picture of that region as depicted in *Pāḷi ṭipiṭaka* and its commentaries, which came to be known as Panjāb in later times and prior to the Partition of India in the year 1947.

Our first task is to determine the period during which the text of *Pāḷi tipiṭaka* was either delivered or collected. According to *Theravādini* tradition the Buddha entered into *Mahāprinibbāna* in 544 B.C. The Buddha himself, as recorded *Mahāparinibbāna Sutta* (No. 16) of the *Dīgha Nikāya*, during his conversation with his disciple Subhadda, tells that fiftyone years ago, at the age of twentynine, he renounced the world (*abhinisakramaṇia)*[1] This means that the Buddha entered into *Mahāparinibbāna* at the ripe age of eighty. Accordingly the Buddha was born in 624. B.C. The Buddhist tradition holds the view that after undergoing austerities for about six years, Gotama attained *Sambodhi* and, thus, became the Buddha, when he was thirtyfive years old. Naturally, the Buddha delivered his discourses,

*Paper presented at the Seminar organised by Panjabi Academy, Delhi and published in its January—March and April—June, 1993, issue of *Samadarshi*.

thereafter. The first discourse the Buddha delivered, under the title of *Dhammacakkappavattana Sutta*[2] at Isipatana, Sāranātha, in 589 B.C. and this practice continued for the rest of fortyfive years, till he entered into *Mahāparinibbāna* in Kusīnagar. Immediately after the *Mahāparinibbāna* of the Buddha the task of collecting *buddhavacanas* commenced. This, in the Buddhist tradition is called *Saṅgīti*, also refered to as the First Buddhist Council, was held in 544. B.C. under the supervision of Mahākashyap, during the reign of Ajātaśattū, at Rājagaha, the capital city of Magadha. The text of *Vniaya Piṭaka* and *Sutta Piṭaka*, was collected and compiled at this First Council. The Second Buddhist Council was held about one hundred years after the *Mahāparinibbāna* of the Buddha under the patronage of Bhikku Sabbakāsī at Vesāli. Similarly, the Third Council, under the patronage of Tissa Moggliputta, was held during the regime of Asoka (273-236 B.C.) at Pātiliputta, now known as Paṭnā Sāhib. Apart from other things the importance of this Council is that the *Abhidhamma Piṭaka*, the third *Piṭaka* was compiled in this Council. At the same time, immediately after the conclusion of this Council Asoka had sent his son Mahinda and daughter Saṅghamitta to Siṅghala-dipa (Sri Laṅka) in the company of several Bhikkhus, to preach the *dhamma*. The (*Pāḷi*) *Tipiṭka* through oral transmission, thus, reached Sri Laṅkā. It was here that during the reign of Vaṭṭagāmaṇi Abhay (101-77 B.C.) the (Pāḷi) *Tipiṭaka* was first time transcribed in Singhali letters. This historic task was entrusted to Mahāthera Rakkhita.

Besides Pāḷi Tipiṭaka, the commentaries written on different collections, also help to extract the image of Panjab as depicted in these writings. The authorship of these commentaries, called *aṭṭhakathās*, is ascribed to Buddhaghosa. According to *Mahāvaṁsa* the task of writing of commentaries was accomplished by Buddhaghosa (5th century A.D.) at the instance of Mahāthēra Revata who was head of the *Bhikkhū Saṅgha* at Bodhagaya. Buddhaghosa also obtained ordination (*upasampada*) from Mahāthēra Revata. It was Mahāthēra Revata who told Buddhaghosa that only "*Tipiṭaka* has been brought from Siṅghaladip. Neither commentaries nor the material concerning the developed Buddhist tradition was with them."[3] In order to get all this material Buddhaghosa went to Siṅghaladip during the reign of Mahānāma (5th century A.D.) while staying at the monestary of Anurādhapur, Buddhaghosa accomplished the historic task.

The period of delivery of discourses and its compilation runs from 589 B.C. to the reign of Asoka i.e. 3rd century B.C. In case we also include the commentaries then it will extend to 5th century A.D. The image of Panjāb that reflects in *Pāḷi Tipṭaka* and its commentaries, naturally, covers the said period.

Bharat, during the Buddhist period, in *Pāḷi Tipiṭaka* and its commentaries, is called *Jambūdip* (Skt. *Jambū-dvip*). *Jambū-dip* refered to in *Tipīṭaka* is different from that of *Purāṇic Jambū-dip*.[4] We are concerned about *Jambūdip* of *Tipiṭaka*. *Jambūdip* in *Tipiṭaka* is stated to have consisted of five units, e.g. 16 *Mahājanapadas*, 7. *Gaṇatantara*, 3. *Mandalas*, 4. States or 5. Provinces. At the moment we are interested in the first kind of unit. According to this division *Jambūdip* was divided into 16 *Mahājanapadas*[5], as under:

> i. Anga, ii. Magadha, iii. Kāsi, iv. Kosal, v. Vajji, vi. Malla, vii. Cheti, viii. Vamsa (Vatasa), ix. Kurū, x. Pañcāla. xi. Macha, xii. Surasena, xiii. Assaka, vix. Avanti, xv. Ghandhāra, xvi. Kambaja.

Firstly, we must find out that which of the *Mahājanapadas* were situated in the Panjab we are concerned with.

As we have already stated that we are only concerned about the Panjāb that existed prior to the Partition of India in 1947. In other words that area which was called Panjāb during British regime. The borders of Panjāb were demarcated by the British crown and we shall depend upon the documents prepared by the British government. There can not be more authentic document than *Imperial Gazetteer of India* (1908). While damarcating the borders of Panjāb it is stated in the said document, thus:

> (Panjāb) is the country enclosed and watered by the Jhelum, Chenāb, Rāvi, Beās and Sutlej; but the province as now constituted includes also the table-land of Sirhind between the Sutlej and the Jumna to the south of the former rivers, the Sindsāgar Doaba or wedge of country between the Jhelum and the Indus and west of

the either river, the two tracts which form Derā Ghāzikhān and part of Mianwāli District.[6]

Some area of the kūrū *Mahājanapada* was a part of Panjab during British period. While demarcating the borders of kūrū *Mahājanapada* Bharat Singh Upadhyaya in his book *Buddha-kālina Bhartiyā Bhugola* (1961) writes that, "we can include modern Meerut, Muzafar Nagar, Bulandshara, Saharanpur, Delhi, Kurukshetra and Thanesra in kūrū *Mahājanapada*."[7] In this way the area of Delhi, Kurukshetra, and Thenesra that formed part of Kūrū were included in Panjāb of British period.

Apart from the area called Kūrū, major part of the (modern) Panjāb was included in *Uttarapath*. *Uttarapath* infact, was the name given to the trade routc between Sāvathi and Ghandhāra *mahājanapada*, later on, the areas that this route crossed, were named after it. In addition to Ghandhāra and Kamboja, Siri, Mada and Kaikay *Janapada* also formed the part of *Uttarapath*. The area between Swat and Jhelum river was called Ghandhāra. Modern West Panjab and eastern Afghanistan formed the part of Ghandhāra *mahājanapada* Takhśila was the capital city of Ghandhāra now known as *Shāh di Dḥeri* which is about fifteen kilometre from Rawalpindi in Pakistan.

Better if we begin our story from our (now) homeland i.e. Delhi. In about 400. B.C. Rāja Dilū laid the foundation of Delhi. Infact, it was Indraprastha (Pāḷi: Indapatha) which was, at one time raised by Pāṇḍavas over which, later on, Delhi came up. It is the same Indraprasatha which is refered to in Mahābharat and it should be some where near the old fort. Indraprasatha was the capital of Kūrū *mahājanapada*. It is stated that, at one time, it was ruled by Kūrū and therefore, this area was named after him. According to Mahāsuta-Soma-Jātaka (No. 537) Kurū *mahājanapada* and Indraprasatha covered the area of about three hundred and seven *yojanas*, respectively.

The Buddha delivered number of discourses at Kammasa-dhamma (or kammāsdamma) located in Kūru. According to *Raṭṭhapala Sutta* of *Majjhima Nikāya* (No. 82) Kauravya ruled over Kurū during the life-period of the Buddha. Attempts are made to identify the geographical location of Kammāsa dhamma. D.C. Ahir in his book, *Buddhism in North India* (1989)[8] has identified modern Kaithal, (which is in Haryana and thirty eight miles away to the west of Karnal) as ancient Kammāsa-dhamma. And, Bharat Singh Upadhyaya[9] is of the view that Kammāspur (or Kamāsapur) which is at the distance of seven or eight miles from the town Bagpat (Dist. Merrut) and on the other side of the river Jamuna, in Panjāb, could be Kammāsa dhamma, Anyhow, in both the cases, this town formed the part of Panjāb, as defined by us. The Buddha delivered the following discourses at Kammāsa dhamma :

a. *Dīgha Nikāya*
 i. *Mahānidāna Sutta* (No. 15)
 ii. *Mahāsatipaṭṭhāna Sutta* (No. 22)

b. *Majjhima Nikāya*
 i. *Satipatthāna Sutta* (No. 10)
 ii. *Māgindaya Sutta* (No. 75)
 iii. *Ānavñjasappāya Sutta* (No. 106)

c. *Saṁyutta Nikāya*
 i. *Nidāna Samyutta*
 ii. *Sammasanna Saṁyutta.*

Besides delivering discourses at Kammāsadhamma the Buddha also delivered the *Raṭṭhapal Sutta* at Thulakaṭhita. It is believed that Thulakoṭhita was none other than Thānesara, a town in district Karnal.[10]

One thing is certain that on the basis of Pāḷi Tipiṭaka we can say that the Buddha did not deliver any discourse in any part of modern Panjāb except in Kurū *mahājanapada*. Infact, the "Buddha commenced his *Cārikavāna* in *Madhadesa* or *madhamanḍala* and in the region of Kosī-Kurukshetra that too in the midland between Himalaya and Vindhiyacala."[11] The discourses which the Buddha delivered at Kurū have one and the same subject that of '*essa maggo visudhiyā*' or to delincate the Path of Purification. These discourses were delivered in Kurū, alright, but we hardly get any information more than that. In other words, these discourses are silent about revealing any information about (modern) Panjāb. But one thing is there that why such profound discourses the Buddha delivered in Kurū. Buddhaghosa in *Sumaṅgala vilāsinī*—a commentary on the *Dīgha Nikāya*—tells us something revealing about the style of life of the people of Kurū, while, writing his commentary on the *Mahāsatipaṭṭhāna Sutta.* Buddhaghosa tells us that people of Kurū that include *Bhikkhus, Bhikkhunis, Upāsakas, Upāsikās* and the common folk, infact, all practice *Satipaṭṭhāna*, because of congenial climate all of them are blessed with physical and mental purity. While practising *Satipaṭṭhāna* one has to adhere to number of precautionary measures but the uppermost importance is accorded to avoiding frivolous talks. And, the people of Kurū while drawing water from the wells and spinning yarn always refrain from such abuse of tongue. This is why the Buddha chose to deliver such a profound discourse for the benefit of the people of Kurū and through them to One and All. Buddhaghosa further reveals that not only the people of Kurū were blessed with *Sati* or awareness the birds too shared the some blessings. In this context Buddhaghosa has narrated an episode subline in nature. Once upon a time, a certain *therī* undertook an obligation to train a *Suggā* (parrot) in the art of practising *Vipassanā. Vipassanā*, in short, means to emancipitate oneself from the *Vikāras* (dark passions) of mind. *Therī* instructed the parrot to repeat the words: '*asathi, asathi*'. Day succeeded day. One day the parrot was enjoying the sunshine in open. Another bird saw the parrot, picked him up and flew away. Those who saw threw stones on the bird taking away the parrot. As a result of hitting of stones the parrot got out of the clutches of the bird and fell on the ground. The *Bhikkhūs* brought the parrot to *therī. Therī* asked the parrot as to "how was he feeling when he was in the tight clutches of the bird?" The parrot replied and that too in very few words that, "I felt as if one skelton of bones was carrying another skelton of bones".[12] The parrot neither got frightend nor he experience any pain. This only means that the parrot had reached the state of *tathtā* (Suchness). One of the epithet, therefore, used for the Buddha is *Tathāgata.* The above narrated episode may not be literally true but it does reveal the pattern of life of people of Kurū and which was of higher order leading to *paññā* (wisdom).

Takhśilā was the capital city of Gandhāra. Besides being the capital of Gandhāra, Takhśila was the centre of higher studies both in Pre-Buddhist and Buddhist eras and was considered an institution of repute through out Jambūdipa. The instructions in three Vedas and eighteen kinds of disciplines were imparted at this centre of higher learning. Rājā Pasendi of Kosala, Maḥāla Licchvi, Bandhulamala and Aṅgulimala, during the Buddhist era, all these had their education at Takhśilā. Jivaka, a great vaid of Buddhist era, also had studied at Takhśilā. Kaṇakina, Yamadatta and Dhammapāla etc. before taking refuge in Buddhist Saṅgha, had been the students at Takhśilā.

Prior to the Buddhist era, also, Takhśila had been the centre of higher studies and the referrences to this fact are available in plenty in Jātaka tales that the Buddha, when he was *Bodhisatta*, had received instructions in different disciplines while a student at Takhśilā. There is hardly any difficulty in accepting the fact that the *Bodhisatta*, before he became the Buddha, was born number of times. But, Takhśilā existed all these times, this seems to be a legend not a fact, at all. Anyhow, Yes, the *Bodhisatta* did join Takhśila. Sometimes the *Bodhisatta* was born as a Rajakumara to Raja Brahmadatta of Benares; (*Dumedha Jātāka* No. 50; *Pañcavuddha Jātaka* No. 55) and studied at Takhśilā. Another time born to a certain Brahamaṇa (*Asātamanta Jātaka* No. 61; *Tittara Jātaka* No. 117) had joined Takhśilā. One time the *Bodhisatta* also served as *acarīyā* at Takhśilā (*Varaṇa Jātaka* No. 71; (Nāma Siddhi Jātaka No. 97). In one of his previous birth the *Bodhisatta* also took birth as a Bull named Nandi Visāla at Takhśilā. (Nandi Visāla Jātaka No. 28).

Gandhāra is also referred to in Pāli text in other contexts also. There was a famous Pokharavati town in Gandhāra *Mahā-Janapada*. In the commentary on the *Theragāthā*[14] this town is stated to be a birth place of Tapussa and Bhallika. Both of them were brothers doing business. These were the two brothers who were first to serve the first food to the Buddha just after attaining to *sambodhi*. The rice-milk served by Sujata, prior to the attainment of *sambodhi* and the food served by Tapussa and Bhallika, these two foods, in the Buddhist tradition are rerved most as foods. At the same time, Tapussa and Bhallika were first to have taken refuge in the Buddha and *Dhamma*. They took refuge in only two *i.e.*, *Buddhaṁ Saraṇaṁ Gacchāmi* and

Dhammaṁ Saraṇaṁ Gacchāmi as the third refuge of *Saṅgaṁ Sarṇaṁ Gacchāni*, came to being in later times.

Kamboja *Mahajanapada* that formed the part of *Uttarapatha* is also referred to in Pāli text, although casually. During the Buddhist era Kamboj was famous for horses and mules.[15] Buddhaghosa in *Sumagṇala Vilāsini* has described Kamboja as '*asavaṁa āyatanaṁ*'[16] or the 'house of horses'. Also, Buddhaghosa in his *Bhūridatta Jātaka*[17] (No. 543) has mentioned certain peculiar traits prevalent in the people inhabiting Kamboja. They are violent in nature. They kill snakes, frogs and flies and think that these violent acts promote purity of mind. They also indulge in looting.

Besides reference to Gandhāra and Kamboja that formed the path of *Uttarapath*, the rivers flowing in these areas are also referred to in Pāli text. There is a special reference made to the rivers Sind, Jhelum and Chenāb (Jhanan) (now in Pakistan) in Pāli texts. Modern Sind is referred to as Sind but Jhelum is referred to as *Vitamma* (or Vitamata) and Chenāb as *Chandabhēga* (or Chandrabhāga). We find atleast one reference to the Buddha in the context of Chenāba. It is mentioned in the commentary of the *Anguttara Nikāya* i.e., *Manortha pūrṇi*,[18] that when Mahakapina, the resident of Kukavatti, in the frontier area, was going to meet the Buddha in Madhadesa, then the Buddha met him on the bank of river Chenāb. The Buddha, it is stated, had flown through the air route and arrived there to bless Mahākapina.

There was a town named Sāgala in the Uttarapatha, now known as Sialkot. A *Janapada* named Raṭṭha existed in between the river Rāvi and Chenāb and Sāgala was the capital city of this *Janapada*. This Sagāl town later on was made the capital city by Greek king 'Milinda' whose Greek name was Menendar, during first century A.D. King Milinda was deeply interested in the religions of his time. King Milinda was in the search of someone well versed in religions, when he met Buddhist Bhikkhu Nāgasena. Milinda asked number of questions on Buddhism and Nāgasena answered these queries, which we find, today, in *Milindapañño*, in Pāli language. This book consists of seven parts and 304 questions in the form of dilemmas are posed and solved. The dilemmas posed are those which every serious student of Buddhism is interested to get them resolved. The relation of *Milindapañño* with Panjāb is only this much that this book was written in Sialkoṭ.

We do not find a wholesome picture of Panjāb in Pāli text. One of the reason is that besides Kurū the Buddha did not visit modern Panjāb and hence, could not deliver his discourses. And, where he delivered his discourses the picture of those areas is also missing because the Bikkhus who collected and compiled these discourses were only interested in *Buddhavacanas* and certainly not in the historical set-up. Buddhaghosa has provided some such details in his commentaries. But, at the same time we should not overlook this fact that Pāli text is a literary text and not a historical record. To the exent the literary text can provide historical informations the Pāli text does furnish that.

References

1. Rhys Davids, T.W. and Carpenter J.E. (Ed.) *Dīgha Nikāya* Vol. II.
2. S.V., pp. 420-421.
3. Jinnanand, B., 'Four Buddhist Councils' in Bapat, P.V. (Ed.) *Twenty Five Hundred Years of Buddhism*, pp. 41-42.
4. Upadhaya, Bharat Singh, *Buddhakālīna Bhartiya Bhugol*, pp. 53-56, n.1.
5. A.i. 213; IV, 252, 256, 260.
6. *The Imperial Gazetteer of India*, Vol. 20, p. 245.
7. Upadhyaya, Bharat Singh, *op. cit.*, p. 406.
8. Ahir, D.C., *Buddhism in North India*, p. 6.
9. Upadhyaya, Bharat Singh, *op. cit.*, p. 410.
10. Ahir, D.C., *op. cit.*, p. 6.
11. Sankaratyana, Rahul, (Tr.) *Majjhima Nikāya* (Hindi), p. 6, (Introduction).
12. Tiwary, Mahesh, (Ed.) *Sumaṅgala Vilāsinī*, Vol. III, pp. 40-41.

13. See Chapter 9. *An Image of Woman As Reflected in Jātakas* pp. 97-98.
14. Woodward, F.L. (Ed.) *Paramatthadīpanī* (*Commentary on Theragāthā*) Vol. IV.
15. Fausbol, V. (Ed.) *Jātakas*, Vol. IV, p. 645.
16. Tiwary, Mahesh, *op. cit.*, Vol. I, p. 124.
17. Fausboll, V., *op. cit.*, Vol. VI, p. 110.
18. Walleser, M., (Ed.) *Manorthapūrṇi*, Vol. I, p. 175.

BIBLIOGRAPHY

Ahir, D.C., *Buddhism in North India,* Classic India Publications, Delhi, 1989.

Ali, Abdullah Yusuf (Translator and Commentator) *The Holy Qurān.* Shaikh Muhammad Ashraf, Lahore, third edition, 1938.

Ambedkar, B.R., *The Buddha and His Dhamma,* Siddhartha Publication, Bombay, 1957.

Arnold Matthew, *The Poems of Matthew Arnold* (edited by Miriam Allott) Longman, London, Second edition, 1979, (First edition 1965).

Aung, Shwe Zan and Rhys Davids Mrs. (trs.) *Compendium of Philosophy* (translation of Abhidhammattha-Saṅgaha) P.T.S., 1910.

Ādi Grantha, Srī Damdami Biṛ Various editions. Standard pagination, 1430 pp.

Bahm, A.J., *Philosophy of the Buddha,* Vikas Publishing House Pvt. Ltd., Delhi, First Indian Edition, 1982.

Bapat, P.V., *Twenty Five Hundred Years of Buddhism,* Publication Division, Govt. of India, 1956.

Barua, Benimadhab, *A History of Pre-Buddhistic Indian Philosophy,* Motilal Banarsidas, Delhi : Reprint, Delhi, 1981, (First edition, London, 1951).

Basham, A.L., *History and Doctrines of the Ājivikās.* Motilal Banarsidas, Delhi : Reprint, Delhi, 1981. (First Edition, London, 1951).

Bays, Gwendolyn, (trs.) *The Voice of the Buddha : The Beauty of Compassion* (translation of Lalitavistara Sūtra) translation into English from French, 2 Vols. Dharma Publishing, California, 1983.

Bedi, Sohinder Singh, *Panjabi Lakadhāra Viśavakośa*, Loka Sahity Sahitya Prakashan, Delhi, Vol. 2, 1978.

Bible, The Holi, The British and Foreign Bible Society, London.

Bose, M.M. (ed.) *Itivuttaka Commentary Paramatthadīpanī* II) 2 Vols. P.T.S., Vol. I 1934; II, 1936.

Brecht, Bertolt, *Plays* (*The Life of Galileo*) Vol. I, Methuen and Co. Ltd., London, 1961, (First published 1960).

Bronowski, J. and Mazlish, Bruce, *The Western Intellectual Tradition*, Penguin Books, 1963.

Burlingame, Eugene Watson (translator), *Buddhist Legends*, (Commentory on Dhammapada by Buddhaghosa, Harvad Oriental Series, Part-I, 1921.

Burt, Edwin Arthur, *The Metaphysical Foundation of Modern Physical Science*, Routledge Kegan Paul, London, 1949.

Butcher, S.H., *Aristotles Theory of Poetry and Fine Art*, Lyall Book Depot, Ludhiana, Second edition, 1968.

Camus, Albert, *The Plague*, Hamish Hamilton, London, Eighth impression October, 1964, (La-Peste' : First published in France by Gallimard, Paris, 1947.

Carus, Poul, *The Gospel of Buddha*, National Book Trust, India, Delhi, 1981 (Reprinted).

Chalmers, Lord (translator), *Further Dialogue of the Buddha* (translation of Majjhima Nikāya) Humphery Millford London, 2 Volumes, Vol. I, 1926; II, 1927.

Chalmers, R. (ed.) *Majjhima Nikāya*, Vol. II, 1896-98, II 1899-1902, P.T.S.

Chatterjee, Heramba, *The Buddhist Concept of Nirvāṇa*, article published in Mahabodhi, Vol. 63, No. 5, May 1985.

Childers, Robert Caesar, *A Dictionary of Pāli Language*, Rinse Book Company, Kyoto. First edition, London, 1985. Reprint, 1976.

Commaraswamy, Anand, K. and Horner, I.B., *The Living Thoughts of the Gotama the Buddha*, Munshi Ram Manohar Lal, Delhi, 1982.

Copernicus, Nicholas, *On the Revolutions of the Heavenly Spheres* (translation of *De Revolutionibus Orbium Coelestium*, translated by : C.G. Wallis) Great Books of the Western World Series, Vol. 16 (Book I), The University of Chicago, 1952.

Copleston, Frederick, *Arthur Schopenhauer : Philosopher of Pessimism*, Burms oates and Wash bourne Ltd., London, 1946.

Copleston, R.S., *Buddhism—Primitire and Present*, Longman, London, 1946.

Cowell, E. B., (Gen. editor), *The Jātakas*, 6 Vols., P.T.S. Cambridge, 1895-1913.

Dalal, C.D. and Shastry, R.A. (Eds.) *Kāvyamīmāṅsā of Rājasekhara.*

Darwin, Charles, *The Origion of Species*, Oxford University Press, London, Reprint of the Sixth edition, 1985.

Diwana, Mohan Singh Oberoi, *Buddhism and Sikkhism* a paper presented at International Congress of Orintalists, Vol. I, 1936 held at Itly, Rome.

Duggal. Kartar Singh, *Buddhaṁ Saranaṁ Gachāmi*, Navyug Publishers, Delhi, 1987.

Feer, L., (ed.) *Saṁyutta Nikāya*, 5 Vols., Vol. I, 1884; II, 1888, III, 1890; IV, 1890; V, 1899. P.T.S.

Fousboll, V. (ed.), *Jātakas*, P.T.S. 6 Vols.; Vol. I, 1877; II, 1879; III, 1883; IV, 1887; V, 1891; VI, 1896.

———*Sutta Nıpāta,* S.B.E., Vol. X, Part II, First Published : Oxford, 1881.

Galileo Galilei, *Dialogue on the Great World Systems* (translation of *Dialogo Dei Massimi Sistemi*) A Salisbury translation. Revised annotated and with an introduction by Giorgio de Santillana, University of Chicago Press, Chicago, 1953.

Grimm, George, *The Doctrine of the Buddha*, Motilal Banarsi Dass, Delhi, Reprint, 1973 (First Edition ; Berlin ; 1958).

Hall, G. Stanley (ed.) *The American Journal of Psychology*, Clark University, Woreester, Mass, Vol. xxi 1910.

Hardy, E. (ed.) *Aṅguttara Nikāya*, 3 Vols. P.T.S., Vol. III, 1895: IV, 1899; V, 1900.

Hardy, R., Spence, *A Manual of Buddhism*, William and Norgate London, 2nd Edition 1880 (First published, 1866).

Hare, E.M., *Woven Candences of Early Buddhists* (translation of *Sutta Nipāta*) Oxford 1947, (Reprinted) First published, 1945.

————*The Book of the Gradual Sayings* (translation of *Aṅguttara Nikāya*) P.T.S., Vol. III, 1934; IV, 1935.

Hasrat, Sukhpal Veer Singh, *Suraj Hindustan Da*, (a poem included in *Hasarat Kavya*, New Age Book Centre, Amritsar, 1975.

Heraculitus, *The Cosmic Fragments* (edited by Kirk, G.S.) Cambridge University Press, 1954.

Holmes, Edmond, *The Creed of the Buddha*, The Bodley Head, London, Reprinted 1949 (First published, 1908).

Horner, I.B., (Translator) *The Collection of the Middle Length Sayings* (translation of *Majjhima Nikāya*) 3 Vols. Vol I, 1954; II, 1957; III, 1959, P.T.S.

————*The Book of the Discipline* (Translation of *Vinaya Piṭhaka*) P.T.S., 6 Vols. I, 1948; II, 1940; III, 1919; IV, 1951; V, 1952; VI, 1966.

————(Translator), *Milinda's Question*, P.T.S., 2 Vols. Vol. I, 1963; II, 1964.

————(Ed.) *Madhuraṭṭhavilāsinī* (Commentary on *Buddhavaṁsa*) P.T.S., 1946.

————(Tr.) *The Clarification of the Sweet Meaning* (translation of *Madhuraṭṭhavilāsinī*) P.T.S., 1978.

Imperial Gazetteer of India, Claredon Press, London, Vol. 20, 1908.

Indu, Inderjit, *Science of Symbols—Deeper View of Indian Deities*, Geetanjli Publication, New Delhi, January, 1948.

Jayatilleke, K.N., *Early Buddhist Theory of Knowledge*, George Allen and Unwin, London, 1963.

———*The Message of the Buddha*, (edited by Ninian Smart) George Allen and Unwin, London, 1975.

Johanson, Rune, E.A., *The Psychology of Nirvāṇa*, George Allen and Unwin Ltd., London, 1969.

Jones, Ernest, *Hamlet and Oedipus*, W.W. Norton and Company New York, 1949.

Josni, L.M. and Gandhi, Sharda (trs.) *Dhammapada*, Panjabi University, Patiala, 1969.

Kalupahana, David, J., *Buddhist Philosophy*, The University Press of Hawaii, Honolulu, 1976.

Kausalayan, Anand (Tr.) *Nidānakathā*, Hindi Sahita Sammelan, Prag, 1941.

Kepler, Jonannes, *The Harmonies of the World*, Great Books of the Western World, Vol. 16: Editor in Chief: Robert Maynard Hutchins. The University of Chicago, 1952.

Khanna, Guran Ditta, *Amar Jyoti*, a biography of the Buddha in verse. Panjabi Sahitya Akademi, Ludhiana, 1958.

———*Buddha Jātaka Kathāvāna*, Panjabi Sahitya Akademi, Ludhiana, 1963.

Kour Prabhjot, *Aman Dā Paigambara*, Language Department, Patiala, 1974.

Laplace, Pierre Simon, *Celestial Mechanics* (translated with Commentary by Northanicl Bowditch) Chelsa Publishing Co. Inc. Bonx, New York, 1966 (4 Vols.).

Law, B.C., *The Buddhist Conception of Spirit*, Bhartya Publishing House, Varanasi, 1974.

———*A Designation of Human Types*, (translation of *Puggala-paññatti*) P.T.S., 1922.

———*Historical Geography of Ancient India*, Societe Asiatique Deparis, Paris, France, 1954.

Lawerence, Jerome and Lee, Robert, E., *Inherit the Wind*, Bantam Books Inc, New York, 1967.

Leon, E. Arnold, *Secularization*: *Science Without God*, SCM Press Ltd., London, 1967.

Macauliffe, Max Arthur, *The Sikh Religion*, 6 Vol., S. Chand and Co., Delhi. Reprint 1963. (First Published : Oxford University Press, 1909.

Malalasekera, G.P., *Dictionary of Pali Proper Names*, J. Murray, London, 2 Vols. 1930.

Maxmuller, F., (trs.) *The Dhammapada*, S.B.E., Vol. X, Part I, 1965. (First Published 1881).

———(trs.) *Buddhist Mahāyāna Texts*, S.B.E., Vol. 49, Part II.

Mcleod, W.H., (editor and translator) *The B 40 Janamsākhi*, Guru Nanak Dev University. First edition 1980.

Mehta, Rati Lal, N., *Pre-Buddhist India*, Anmol Publications, Delhi 1985, (Reprint).

Mitra, Rajendra (trs.) *Lalitavistara*, Asiatic Society of Bengal, Calcutta, 1881.

Morris, R. (ed.) *Aṅguttra Nikāya*, 2 Vol, P.T.S., Vol. I, 1885; II 1888.

Muller, Max Arthur and others, *Studies in Buddhism*, Indological Book House, Delhi, 1978.

Narad Mahāthera (trs.) *Dhammapada*, Mahābodhi Society of India, Calcutta 1976.

Narasu, P. Lakshmi, *The Essence of Buddhism*, Thacker and Co. Ltd., Bombay, 1948. (First published 1907).

Narla, V.R., *Traditional Indian Culture and other Essays*, Vijaya Books, Vijayavada, 1969.

Naz, Nanak Chand (ed. and trs.) *Zafar Nāma*, Bhai Jawhar Singh Kripal Sing,h Amritsar, 1959.

Newton, Sir Isaac, *Philisophiae Naturalis Principia Mathematical* (translated by Andrew Motte. Revised by Florian Cajori). University of California : Fifth Printing 1975. (First Printed 1934).

Oldenberg, Hermann (ed.) *Vinayapiṭaka*, 5 Vols., P.T.S., Vol. I, 1872; II, 1880; III, 1881; IV, 1882; V, 1883.

Pandey, G.C., *Śramaṇa Tradition*, L.D. Institute of Indology, Ahmedabad, 1978.

Preetlari, Gurbaksh Singh, *Gori Te Bhagwan Buddha* a short story included in *Preet Kohaniyan*, Lahore Book Shop, Ludhiana. Fourth edition 1950 (First edition 1938).

Rajneesh, Bhagwan, *The Hidden Harmony : Discourses on the Fragments of Heraclitus.* Rajneesh Foundation, Poona, First edition, April 1976.

———*Essa Dhammo Sanantano*, Rajneesh Foundation, Pune, 1976.

Rao, Gopinath, T.A., *Elements of Hindu Iconography*, Indological Book House, Delhi, Vol. II, Pt. I, 1971 (2nd edition).

Ray, Ginger, *Six Days or Forever ? Tennessee* vs. *John Thomas Scopes.* Beacon, Boston, 1958.

Rhys, Davids, C.A.F., *Psalms of the Early Buddhists*, Brethren (translation of Theragātha) P.T.S., 1913.

Rhys, Davids Mrs., (ed.) *Vibhaṅga*, P.T.S., 1902.

———*Dialogues of the Buddha* (translation of *Dīgha Nikāya*) Humphrey Milford, London, S.B.B., Vol. III, 1921.

———*The Book of Kindered Sayings* (translation of *Saṁyutta Nikāya*) P.T.S., Vol. I, 1917; II, 1922.

———and Rhys Davids, T.W., *The Dialogues of the Buddha*, Humphrey, Milford, London, S.B.B., Vol. II, 1910.

Rhys Davids, T.W., *Dialogues of the Buddha*, S.B.B., Vol. I, 1899.

———*Buddhist Suttas*, S.B.E., Vol. XI, Reprint 1980. First Published, Oxford, 1881.

———The Questions of King Milinda (translation of *Milindapañha*) 2 Vols. S.B.E., Vols. XXXV, XXXVI, Reprint 1975. (First Published, Oxford, 1894-1895).

———and Stede William, *Pāli-English Dictionary*, P.T.S., (First published 1921-1925).

———and Carpenter, J.E., (ed.) *Sumaṅgalavilisnī* (Commentary on Dīgha Nikāya) P.T.S., Vol. I, 1886.

———and Carpenter, J.E., (ed.) *Dīgha Nikāya*, 3 Vols. P.T.S., Vol. I, 1889; II, 1903; III, 1910.

———and Oldenberg, H., *Vinaya Texts*, Vol. XVII, Motilal Banarsidass, Delhi, 1965.

Ross, Sir David, *Plato's Theory of Idea*, Claredon Press, Oxford, 1951.

Safeer, Pritam Singh, *Kapalvastū Di Yashodra Dā Swami*, a poem included in *Agam Agochar*, Navyug Publishers, Delhi. 1981.

Saṅkaratyan, Rahul, (trs.) *Majjhima Nikāya*, Mahabodhi-Sabha, Sarnath, 1933.

Santillana, Giorgio de *The Crime of Galileo*. Time Inc., New York, 1962. (First published by University of Chicago 1955).

Schopenhauer, Arthur, *The World as Will And Idea* (translated by Haldane, R.B. and Kem 1.) Routledge and Kegan Paul Ltd., London, 3 Vols. 9th impression, 1948 (First published 1883).

———*The World As Will and Representation* (translated by Payne, E.F.J.) Dover Publication Inc., New York, 2 Vols. 1958.

———*Parerga and Paralipomena*, Clarendon Press, Oxford, 2 Vols., 1974.

Shackle, C., *A Gurū Nānak Glossary*, Heritage Publishers, Delhi 1981.

Shakespeare, William, *Complete Works of William Shakespeare*, Abbey Library, London.

Sharma, R.S., *Material Culture and Social Formations in Ancient India*, Macmillan Ltd., Delhi, 1983.

Shastry, J.L., (ed.) *Ancient Indian Tradition and Mythology*, Motilal Banarsidass, Delhi.

Shehryaar, *Siddhartha Dī Wāpsi* a poem included in *Siddhartha Dī Wāpsi*. Harnakasha Publications, Amritsar, 1975.

Silacara Bhikkhu (Trs.) *Buddhist Essays* (of Paul Dalke, from

German) Indological Book House, Delhi, 1978 (First published : Macmillan, 1908).

———*The First Fifty Discourses from the Collection of the Medium Length Discourses of Gotama the Buddha* (Translation of Majjhima Nikāya). Probsthan and Co., London.

Silva Lynn A de, *The Problem of Self in Buddhism and Christianity*, Macmillan, 1979.

Singh, Bhai Vir, (ed.) *Puratan Janam Sakhi*, Khalsa Samachar, Amritsar, 1952.

Singh, Gopal, (tr.) *Śrī Gurū Granth Sāhib*, World Sikh University Press, Chandigarh (India) 1978.

Singh, Kapur, *Sapat Shring* (Life Sketches of Seven Great Men) Lahore Book Shop, Ludhiana, First edition, 1952.

———*Parasharprasna*, Hind Publishers Ltd., Jullundur. First edition 1959.

———*Pundreek*, Attarchand Kapur and Sons, Delhi, Second edition 1958, First edition 1952.

Singh, Kirpal (ed.) *Jaram Sakhi Prampra*, Panjabi University, Patiala, 1969.

Singh, Mohan, *Asia Dā Cānan*, (translation of Sir Edwin Arnold's *Light of Asia*), Hind Publishers Ltd., Amritsar, Third edition 1952 (First edition 1944).

Singh, Puran, *Buddha Ji Dā Dhyāni Butt*, a poem included in *Purān Singh Jiwani Te Kavita* (edited by Mohinder Singh Randhawa) Sahit Akademi, Delhi, 1965.

Smith, Helmer (ed.) *Khuddakapāṭha with Commentary—Paramatha Jotikā*, P.T.S., 1975.

Sobti, Harcharan Singh, *Nibbāna in Early Buddhism*, Eastern Book Linkers, Delhi, 1985.

———(ed.) *Vipassanā—The Buddhist Way*, Eastern Book Linkers, Delhi, 1992.

Stace, W.T., *Religion and the Modern Mind*, J.B. Lipponcott, New York, 1960.

Strachey, James (Gen. ed.) *The Complete Works of Sigmund Freud*, The Hogarth Press, London, 1965. (First edition 1953.

Tylor, A.C., (ed.) *Kathāvattū*, P.T.S., Vol. I, 1894; II, 1897.

Tin, Daw Mya (trs.), *Dhammapada*, Central Institute of Higher Tibetan Studies, Sarnath, Varanasi, 1990.

Tiwary, Mahesh, (ed.) *Sumaṅgala Vilāsinī*, Nalanda Mahāvihāra, Nalanda, 1976, Vol. III.

———(ed.) *Bodhi-raśmī*, Indian Council for Philosophical Research, Delhi, 1984.

Trenckner, V. (ed.) *Majjhima Nikāya*, Vol. I, P.T.S., 1888.

Upadhyaya, Bharat Singh, *Dhyāna Aur Nāma*, Kamladevi Upadhaya Publisher, Gzahiabad, 1986.

———*Buddhakālīn Bhartiya Bhugol*, Hindi Sahita Sammelan, Prag, 2018 Bikrami.

Vaidya, P.L. (ed.) *Lalitavistara*, The Mithila Institute, Darbhanga 1958.

Walleser, M., (ed.) *Manorathapūrnī* (commentary on *Aṅguttara Nikāya*) P.T.S., Vol. I, 1924.

Warren, Henry, C., *The Life of the Buddha*, Eastern Book Linkers, Delhi, 1986.

———*Buddhism in Translation*, Asian Publication Services, New Delhi, 1980. First published in Harvard Oriental Series; 1890.

Windisch, E., (ed.) *Itivuttaka*, P.T.S., 1890.

Winternitz, Maurice, *History of Indian Literature*, Oriental Books Reprint Corporation, New Delhi, Vol. II, 1972. (First published by University of Calcutta, 1927).

Woods, J.H. and Kosambi, D., (eds.) *Papañcasūdanī* (Commentary on *Majjhima Nikāya*) P.T.S., Vol. II, 1978.

Woodward, F.L., (trs.) *The Book of the Kindered Sayings*, (translation of *Saṁyutta Nikāya*) P.T.S., Vol. III, 1924; IV, 1927; V, 1930.

———*The Book of Gradual Sayings*, (translation of *Aṅguttara ttikāya*) P.T.S., Vol. I, 1932; II, 1933; V, 1936.

———(trs.) *Minor Anthologies of the Pāli Canon* : Verses of Uplift (*Udāna*) and As it was said (*Itivuttaka*) P.T.S., Vol. II, 1935.

———*Some Sayings of the Buddha*, Humphrey Milford, London, 1925.

NAME INDEX

(A) PERSONS

(b) PLACES

(c) WRITINGS

SUBJECT INDEX